A New Agenda?
The European Union and Cultural Policy

Hans Erik Næss

This book is published in
collaboration with Fritt Ord, Oslo,
and European Cultural Foundation
(ECF), Amsterdam.

ALLIANCE
PUBLISHING
TRUST

Contents

Foreword

A large number of books, articles and reports have been published about the European Union (EU). Despite this, as a British diplomat dryly pointed out, 'not many books about the European Union are fun to read.'[1] With a few exceptions, this literature, mostly in the sphere of academic political science, is written in a parched style, has a specialized thematic scope, and is usually intended for professionals working with these matters. Graver than this, however, is that even less is written for a larger public about the EU and its expanding relationship with culture.[2] With this book, I've done my best to narrow down some of this discrepancy and write in a more informal style than is often the case.

My primary aim is to look into the EU's new efforts on culture 'in the making', as it were. Centre of attention is the 2007 European Commission Communication 'A European agenda for culture in a globalising world' – allegedly, in their own words, 'the first-ever European strategy for culture'. Rather than merely concentrating on the complex constitutional set-up of the EU, this book considers the EU's new agenda for culture against the corollaries of 'culture', the intricacies of 'cultural policy', and the challenges and opportunities today's diverse Europe bring to the fore.

For the sake of clarity, and because it is not this book's intention to question in any profound way the ideological roots of the European Union, my viewpoint is framed by the concepts and definitions recurring in the EU's official documents. That does not mean a gullible adoption of the EU's worldview. In contrast to the Union's and Member States' dominant self-image of Europe as a mosaic of nation-states, there is a clear transnational drift in my text, even if not a systematic one. This implies a set of discussions throughout the book where my and the EU's opinions on how the world is put together differ quite thoroughly.

Moreover, because I come from a country where 99 per cent of all discussions about Europe and the European Union involve an ecstatic YES or an angry NO to membership, I have tried to choose a different point of departure. As I hope to show in the upcoming chapters, to vote yes or no in a discussion of European culture is like standing in the doorway and being forced to decide if you're indoors or outdoors. My exploratory premise has as a result been less concerned about how the EU's cultural policy innovations relate to tiresome membership debates than with potentially enabling some creative opportunities.

Finally, I must point out that writing this book has been something of an experiment. I set out as the 'adventurous sociologist', not being an authority on either the EU or policy-making, entering the field as an outsider. As a result, this book is not primarily intended for experts on EU or culture, although of course I hope it has something for everybody. Mainly, by providing an informative entry to some links between culture, the EU, Europe, and the complexities of cultural globalization, I hope to engender debate. That's what Europe is built upon.

Hans Erik Næss, Oslo, March 2009

[1] Cooper, 2005.

[2] One seminal exception is Shore, 2000.

Acknowledgements

Writing a book like this cannot be done alone. To all of you involved I want to say that your contributions have been most encouraging, and I apologize for not being able to take advantage of all your wisdom. My deepest gratitude goes to Fritt Ord (the Freedom of Expression Foundation, Oslo), which initiated this book and supported me all the way. Particular thanks to Xavier Troussard at the European Commission for sharing his time and knowledge. Most appreciated has also been the generous support from Erik Rudeng, the Director of Fritt Ord, and from Gottfried Wagner and Isabelle Schwarz of the European Cultural Foundation (ECF). Furthermore, I am indebted to Caroline Hartnell and Andrew Milner at Alliance Publishing Trust (APT), this book's publisher, for how well they have taken care of this project.

Strong appreciation for their consultations is expressed to (in alphabetical order): Professor Helmut Anheier at the University of California, Los Angeles (UCLA); Astrid Bjerke at the Arts Council Norway; Associate Professor Hans Hauge at the University of Aarhus; Brit Holtebekk at the Norwegian Archive, Library and Museum Authority; Tommi Laitio of the StrangerFestival; Ragnar Lie, Administrative Director at the Centre for European Studies, University of Oslo (ARENA); and the publicist Arne Ruth.

Additional thanks go to Tamas Baranyay; Maria-Anna Butera at the Education, Audiovisual and Culture Executive Agency

(EACEA); Professor John Erik Fossum at ARENA; Nils Klevjer Aas at the Norwegian Film Institute; and David Watkiss at Phoenix Ink Communications. Finally, thanks to Vibeke, for all your love and patience.

1 Meeting point Brussels

Given that the European Union has launched a new agenda for culture, it is important to identify the bigger context in order to see the relevance and necessity of such an initiative. Broadly speaking, besides statistics showing that Europeans are progressively positive towards a cultural policy at EU level,[1] there are certain aspects of globalization which seem to be closely related to policy reorientations. These are combined with the increasing ability of people to realize what the major changes of our time are all about and how they affect their lives. I therefore discuss in this chapter how culture has become part of global politics and review, in connection with this, some arguments about why the EU should develop a more comprehensive cultural policy.

On my walk through Brussels, I found it to be a rather odd place. While Paris or New York has a distinct urban ambience of shifting faces, sounds and smells, Brussels was to me characterized by the impression that 'there was no there, there', to borrow a saying from the American author Gertrude Stein.

Except when it comes to everything connected to the European Union. This is no surprise, I guess, when you think of the fact that the European Commission, the European Parliament and the European

Council are all located there. Together with 159 embassies and a bunch of international institutions such as the NATO headquarters, it makes Brussels the largest centre for diplomatic activity in the world next to New York City. Almost 250,000 foreigners are employed in these activities, making up approximately a quarter of the city's total population.

I came to the city only a couple of days after the Irish rejected the Lisbon Treaty, a decision which produced shock waves all the way through Europe and made *The Economist* pronounce 'Just Bury It' on the much-maligned document.[2] Graveyard metaphors are nothing new to the magazine though. In 1982, on the occasion of the 25th anniversary of the Treaty of Rome, it led with a cartoon of a tombstone dedicated to the EEC. The inscription included the dates 'born 25 March 1957, moribund 25 March 1982' and an epitaph borrowed from Tacitus – *Capax imperii nisi imperasset* ('It seemed capable of being a power, until it tried to be one'). Backed by growing dissatisfaction from the British Thatcher government, *The Economist* confidently declared the EEC to be 'in a near-death coma, at risk of collapsing into prolonged crisis or total stagnation'.[3]

Their diagnosis was, well, wrong. Only three years later, the Euro-visionary Jacques Delors became Commission President and launched the Single Market programme which breathed new life into the EEC and paved the way for the Single European Act (SEA) and Maastricht Treaty on the EU. In the ensuing years, the EEC (later the European Community and then the EU) both widened – adding a substantial number of Member States – and deepened, extending majority voting, enhancing the powers of the Parliament and the European Court of Justice (ECJ), gaining new powers in existing areas of economic policy-making and extending its authority to a host of new areas outside the purely economic realm. Eventually, the progress even led Mark Leonard, the politically savvy 'Cool Britannia' guru, and Jeremy Rifkin, President of the Foundation on Economic Trends, to come up with two widely read books called *The European Dream: How Europe's Vision of the Future is Quietly Eclipsing the American Dream* and *Why Europe Will Run the 21st Century* in 2004 and 2005, respectively.[4]

Obviously, the road ahead is no empty *Autobahn*. Besides the Treaty quarrels, the 2008 report *Global Trends 2025: A World Transformed* portrays the European Union by 2025 as a 'hobbled giant' crippled by internal bickering, conflicting national agendas and a euro-sceptic citizenry.[5] Question is: what to do to avoid this? Associate Professor of Political Science, R Daniel Kelemen, points out that if the EU is facing any crisis, 'it is an existential crisis, driven more by anxiety and a panicked search for meaning than by any objective failings of the system.' Having in mind the indifference Europeans sometimes demonstrate towards the EU, the recent clash caused by the Lisbon Treaty could be a good thing since 'the collective dialogue concerning the objectives of the EU that this crisis has sparked is surely good for a Union that has long failed to inspire much interest or passion on the part of its citizens.'[6] Thoughts like these are attention-grabbing considering the fact that the EU has begun to cover new ground in an area they have avoided for a very long time: *culture*.

To anyone familiar with the history of the European Union, including culture in this way is groundbreaking news. Economic agreements, peace-building, international politics – this is essentially how the story of European integration goes. Monica Mokre, researcher at the Institute for European Integration Research in Vienna, wrote in 2003 that 'EU cultural policy seems to be a field nobody is especially interested in. Not the artists who tend to look with distrust at the European integration process, not national politicians who feel that culture and the arts are a prerogative of the Member States, and even not the EU institutions themselves who fear conflicts with national interests.'[7] Be that as it may, the status of culture has changed in the EU and in the world in general. The amount of money spent on cultural activities among European governments, markets and business sectors as well as 'third sphere actors' (like foundations) has increased steadily in the last two decades.[8] Ján Figel, European Commissioner for Education, Training and Culture, therefore put it well at a conference in Budapest in 2005: 'culture is moving higher up the ladder of priorities. Conceptually, and operationally.'[9]

It wasn't just empty words. Two years later, the Communication
on a 'European Agenda for Culture in a Globalising World' emerged,
founded on three common sets of objectives: cultural diversity
and intercultural dialogue; culture as a catalyst for creativity; and
culture as a key component in international relations.[10] Dubbed
their 'first-ever European strategy for culture', it was published by
the European Commission on 10 May, after having been approved by
the College of Commissioners on the same day. Later, during their
November 2007 meeting, the European Ministers of Culture adopted the
Communication.[11] Seeing the Communication together with the EU's
Culture Programme 2007–2013 and MEDIA 2007 (the latter supporting the
audiovisual industry in Europe, with a total budget of more than €1 billion),
and being aware that 2008 was the European Year of Intercultural
Dialogue (EYID), there are several reasons to ask what renewed
European self-reflection this fresh centre of attention could bring.

Nuts and bolts of the EU
During the writing of this book I soon discovered that the European
Union is something that virtually all Europeans have heard of. Rare are
the ones – and I'm not one of them – who actually know how it works.
Professor of Political Science John McCormick even writes in his
brilliant 2008 book *Understanding the European Union* that the answer to
what the European Union is depends on who you ask.[12] Let me therefore
refer to McCormick himself, who describes the EU as a functional
agreement between states, 'incrementally bridging the gaps between
states by building functionally specific organizations'.[13] Cooperation is
thought to be better promoted by technical experts than by government
representatives, with the aim of transferring loyalty away from the
state into transnational bodies, thus reducing chances for aggressive
nationalism and conflict.

The set-up of the specific organization in this case, the
EU, can be outlined like this: the European Commission (EC)[14] and
the Committee of Permanent Representation (Coreper)[15] develop
proposals for new laws and policies, on which final decisions are
taken by the Council of Ministers[16] and the European Parliament.[17]

Once a decision is made, the European Commission is responsible for overseeing implementation by the Member States. Meanwhile, the Court of Justice works to ensure that laws and policies meet the terms and spirit of the treaties, while the European Council[18] brings the leaders of the Member States together at periodic summit meetings to guide the overall direction of the European Union.[19]

Organizational chart of the European Union

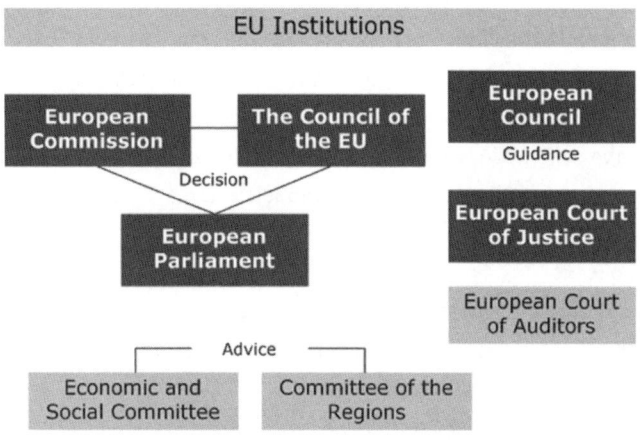

Source www.dadalos-europe.org/int/grundkurs4/eu-struktur_1.htm

For reasons of space and thematic choice, I will hereafter focus mainly on the Commission. It stands out as the 'all-round hub' of the EU, representing a multi-national bureaucracy using an extensive system of committees within which very close cooperation takes place both with the Member States and with national and European associations.

A another discovery of mine was that it was not at all a given that culture should be included in the EU's portfolio of actions. Priorities for the European Coal and Steel Community (ECSC), the new intra-European organization launched in 1950 consisting of a handful of countries that would eventually become the European Union, was a postwar economic construction, born of the desire to prevent European nationalism leading once again to conflict, and the need for security in the face of the threats posed by the Cold War.[20] Together with social development and political cooperation, these have roughly been the pillars of European integration up until today.

The new policy orientation of the EU begs the ubiquitous and notoriously difficult question: *What is Culture?* Unlike Lord Raglan (1788–1855), who once claimed that culture is roughly anything we do and monkeys don't, libraries are full of books trying to nail down a clear-cut meaning of the term. Here, however, I will, for the sake of clarity, in accordance with the EU's new agenda, regard culture as 'a set of distinctive spiritual and material traits that characterize a society and social group. It embraces literature and arts as well as ways of life, value systems, traditions and beliefs.'[21] More than the need for developing precise definitions of culture, also argued by the authors of works like *Creative Europe*,[22] the policy reorientation of the EU is due to transitions and transformations gathered in the term globalization.

The global context
Many are sceptical as to whether 'globalization' really is something new, or just an invented word for changes that have been around for centuries. Historian Nayan Chanda's extraordinary work *Bound Together: How Traders, Preachers, Adventurers and Warriors Shaped Globalization* documents no less than 10,000 years of globalization. Steamboats, railways and telegraphs did tie the world closer together in the 18th century, and French author Jules Verne could write about Phileas Fogg and his journey around the world in 80 days. And, yes, the British economic profile of the late 19th century included granaries in Chicago and Odessa, forests in Canada and the Baltic, sheep farms in Australia, gold and silver mines in California and Peru, and tea plants in China.[23] But the increased speed, intensity of exchange and mixing of people, goods, communication and information technologies, services and symbols we have witnessed in the last 20 years has forced a new kind of complexity to emerge.[24] Four interlinked developments, by no means exclusive, can be outlined as constitutive of the new era.

First, the end of the Cold War and the Yugoslav wars (proving the recurrent power of radical identity politics and nationalism) are two examples of the way that cultural perspectives have become deeply interwoven with global politics, including powerful political movements which insist that cultural differences should be constitutive of who we are, and central to social and political life.[25] In the United Nations Development Program's (UNDP) *Human Development Report 2004* we can read that 'cultural liberty is a vital part of human development because being able to choose one's identity – who one is – without losing the respect of others or being excluded from other choices is important in leading a full life.'[26] Nations that have adopted the 2005 United Nations Educational, Scientific and Cultural Organization (UNESCO) Convention on Protection and Promotion of the Diversity of Cultural Expression are obliged to be aware that 'cultural diversity creates a rich and varied world, which increases the range of choices and nurtures human capacities and values, and therefore is a mainspring for sustainable development for communities, peoples and nations.'[27]

Second, culture has become an economic keyword. The term *cultural economy* is indicative of a particular subsection of economic activity that is concerned with cultural products and activities, such as music, film, video games and fine art.[28] Because cultural amenities and conditions are seen as central to the degree of innovation and productivity in so-called creative industries, and those industries subsequently contribute significantly to cultural newness, technological development and economic growth on a variety of levels, mutual relationships between culture and economy have received a lot of attention in the form of political will and economic research. Finding successful links between cultural creativity and commercial activities is not difficult. In 2006, Europe accounted for more than half of world exports of cultural goods and services.[29] The very same year the EU's balance of external trade with the rest of the world in the main cultural goods (books, newspapers and periodicals, CDs and DVDs, works of art, collectors' pieces, antiques and musical instruments) showed a surplus of €3 billion.[30]

Third, culture is no longer a concept exclusively bound to national territories or ethnic groups. As Sociology Professor Charles Tilly writes, we have no 'a priori guarantee that current national-state boundaries, as the most important means of identifying societies in sociology, mark the limits of interpersonal networks, shared beliefs, mutual obligations, systems of production, or any of the presumed components of a "society"'.[31] Ontologically and practically, culture is perhaps the best example of what, in the age of globalization and transnational networks, Sociology Professor Manuel Castells calls 'the new social morphology of our societies', whereas 'the diffusion of networking logic substantially modifies the operation and outcomes in processes of production, experience, power, and culture'.[32] And, Castells adds, while networking logic has existed in other times, new information technology provides the material basis for its pervasive expansion throughout the entire social structure.

Fourth, the level of public awareness concerning cultural exchange on a global scale has entered a new phase. Sociologists such as Ulrich Beck and Anthony Giddens claim that people throughout the 1990s became increasingly aware ('reflexive' is an often-used term) of what globalization is about and what it does to their lives in terms of cultural matters.[33] Consequently, transnational media and the power of globalized phenomena like chop suey, the atrocities on 11 September 2001, and frequent disputes about multiculturalism and national identities have moved culture to the centre-stage of politics.[34] We all know what happened to Salman Rushdie and Theo Van Gogh. Comparatively, pop stars David Byrne and Brian Eno got off lightly when they turned Koranic recitation into groovy dance music in 1981.[35] On the positive side, as climate change or financial crises care nothing for national borders, globalization also unites people culturally and forces us to rethink the darker sides of nationalism.

The financial crisis
As I will elaborate further in chapter 3, the European Union and its Member States have jointly decided to make culture a vital element of the Union's activities for a variety of reasons. Besides the bigger circumstances sketched in the foregoing pages, it seems that the EU is signalling a relatively novel kind of political culture when the Communication says that 'Europe's cultural richness and diversity is closely linked to its role and influence in the world.'[36] A natural response

to this is that the Union includes in its work other aspects connected to Europe than the economic and political ones. The collapse of Wall Street giants during the autumn of 2008 and the following global financial turmoil, which had a deep impact on European national economies in 2008 and will continue to slow them down in 2009, makes it difficult to see why there should be such divisions at all.[37]

Although *Deutsche Welle* in October 2008 could report that cultural sponsoring in Germany was more or less untouched by financial crisis woes,[38] other forecasts were more pessimistic: from the North Korean state symphony orchestra postponing its UK tour after the withdrawal of its main sponsorship, to a venerable theatre venue in New York making 'pay what you can' offers to sell tickets for a night show.[39] According to a 2008 study by British network consultancy Arts & Business, 63.4 per cent of firms involved in sponsorship in the United Kingdom were planning to maintain spending levels in 2009. But the economic downturn is, according to spokespersons for several large culture institutions including the Tate Britain gallery in London, bound to hit budgets.[40] Some have already felt the current belt-tightening mood. Designer Allegra Hicks, for instance, had to pull out of London Fashion Week at the last minute after her sponsor withdrew.[41] The international art market is also cooling down according to Forbes, with an eye on Sotheby's whose stock in November 2008 was down 83 per cent from October 2007.[42] European Capital of Culture 2009 in Vilnius had its budget for the coming 12 months slashed from €12 million to €7 million, among other things due to the cancellation of the sponsorship deal with Lithuania's flagship airline FlyLAL as it went bankrupt.[43]

By contrast, the downturn also brings new opportunities in the global landscape of the cultural economy. At a time of crisis, writes Russian journalist Vladimir Kozlov, people tend to spend more on entertainment as a way to escape the harsh reality. And while currently most domestic movies released in Russian cinemas according to Kozlov 'show lacklustre performances', the crisis may push people to cinemas. Ironically, although there could, in Russia's case, be fewer movies released, attendance could be much higher.[44] Similar thoughts come from the Chinese. Several speakers at the 2009 China New Year

Forum of International Cultural Industries pointed out that people now turn away from the material world and seek satisfaction and fulfilment in culture-related products: designing, the arts, film-making and home entertainment such as PCs and online games. The ongoing world financial crisis is therefore said to be a perfect opportunity for China to develop its culture and innovation industry.[45]

For these reasons, and many more, the global financial crisis urges the EU to develop its already active cross-sectoral policy outlook in a more flexible and responsive way. 'Mastering the crisis,' writes Helmut Anheier, Director of the Center for Civil Society at UCLA's School of Public Affairs, 'demands a proactive stance on the part of Europe's cultural leadership – not by asking for old wine to be served in new bottles (as the American car giants or European banks and manufacturers have been doing), but by embracing what cultural policy stands for: making space for creativity and innovation and preserving past achievements for the benefit of all.'[46] By cutting back on schematic application procedures and giving more weight to 'fluid' interaction between citizens and culture programmes, in addition to aiming for fewer ad hoc ventures and more long-term partnerships when it comes to the EU's relations to corporate funding and philanthropy in arts, our time could be destined to be not only a phase of economic misery and employment loss but also a time for what economists call 'creative destruction' – making room for new ideas by retiring the old ones and speeding up the convalescence of European economies.[47]

A novel approach
In this context it is easy to see why the European Union is more concerned about its role in cultural affairs than before. But do we need a *European* cultural policy? Is Europe ready to make the shift, as Vladimir Sucha, Director-General of Culture, Multilingualism and Communication, puts it, from 'the integration of states to the integration of people'?[48] Even if the art and life of Europeans have been a part of the EU's overall vision for some years now, I was told by a number of people with much knowledge about the EU that the new strategy for culture is really new. I was having a cup of coffee in sunny Amsterdam with

Isabelle Schwarz, head of cultural policy development at the European Cultural Foundation (ECF), and she summed it up expressively: 'I believe this strategy can contribute to a mind shift, beyond funding and power, to a more strategic dimension at a European level of culture and art. It is a completely new idea demanding that EU countries work differently and use culture in their external relations.'

So I went to see one of those in charge. I must admit that I had mixed feelings of fear and curiosity when I walked towards Madou Tower in Brussels, home of the Directorate-General for Education and Culture at the European Commission. The fancy design by Robert Goffeaux towering up in front of me certainly confirmed the image of the EU I had received from TV.

Madou Tower

Source Wikipedia Commons

More precisely, I was on my way to see Xavier Troussard, acting Head of the Unit for Culture, Directorate-General for Education and Culture, European Commission. Welcomed into his relatively austere office, at

least compared with the Dubai-esque skyscraper façade, he explained
that the new agenda for culture has a threefold background:

'The first is political. I think the first negative referenda in Netherlands
and France raised some more acute questions about the relationship between
the EU and its citizens. An efficient EU for markets and jobs is not enough.

The second element is that the cultural sector, previously considered a small
size economic sector, has now been recognized as an important element
in economic terms per se and as a fundamental driver for fast-growing
industries, particularly in connection with the digital economy. The third
element is linked to the international dimension. The joint negotiation in
UNESCO on the 2005 Convention has resulted in a fresh look at the added
value to the community of having common values, and a stronger recognition
that we might work differently together even in this field where subsidiarity
is key.[49] So based on those three major evolutions, and also supported by the
personal convictions of President Barroso, probably the first Commission
President to speak so forcefully about culture, we decided that it was time for
the Commission to come up with a comprehensive vision of the role of culture
in the European Union.'

I will return to my conversation with Mr Troussard in later chapters, but
suffice to say that such an agenda has been for years the wish of many
Europeans, for instance Croatian author Dubravka Ugrešić. In the 2005
pamphlet *On the Road to a Cultural Policy for Europe* she writes that 'an
effective European cultural policy would promote shared values and
solidarity. It would demonstrate that Europe values the work of its most
creative citizens, the artistic community which is able to transcend
borders.' Ugrešić also argues that 'by encouraging creative solidarity
among its citizens, such a cultural policy would go a long way towards
ensuring the participation of an informed civil society'.[50]

In light of a 2006 study of European cultural policies, Ugrešić's
argument broadens. Here the authors show that the EU 27 evidenced a
wide array of policy priorities.[51] Supporting artists is a main objective
of cultural policy in the Nordic countries, Austria, the Netherlands and
Luxembourg. The importance of art education and social cohesion is
particularly emphasized in Sweden, Denmark, Finland, some Baltic

countries, the United Kingdom, France and the Netherlands. The protection and development of heritage remains highly important for Italy, Greece, Cyprus and Malta. Other than that, trends indicate that the economic effects of culture are becoming more of an objective in shaping cultural policies. This is strongly emphasized and implemented in the United Kingdom, Denmark, Austria, Germany and the Netherlands. Very recently this priority has gained policy attention in the Central and Eastern European countries, but it remains more of a target than a substantive policy change. Last but not least, the report shows considerable variation in cultural policy administration, not least when it comes to degrees of decentralization.

The way I read Ugrešić in light of this is that, rather than being 'trapped' in the overabundance of bureaucratically defined ideas of national culture and cultural policy, often steeped in politics, artists would be better off being enabled to explore their artistic talent with help from more open-ended amenities. Salman Rushdie, as an example, writes in his essay collection *Step Across this Line* that 'good writing assumes a frontierless nation'.[52] As an example, Ugrešić uses James Joyce, the Irish rebel writer who left his home, his church and his country, and even literary tradition, to finish 'the biggest literary monument of European modernism' with the novel *Ulysses*. Now, the question is, she asks rhetorically, 'would our cultural managers be able to recognize his genius?' The real need for a European cultural policy thus lies in the fact that many great artists are not representative of national mainstream culture. Even though European cultural life in general relies heavily on state funding (for example, 94 per cent of Germany's overall arts budget of over €8 billion in 2007),[53] transnational festivals of all sorts and shapes – from Rock am Ring to StrangerFestival or Prague International Poetry Festival – are first-class examples of the fact that, in the age of globalization, people and artists need more space to manoeuvre culturally than the nation-state can provide for them.

This is also mirrored by the fact that Europeans seem up for more involvement in culture from the European Union, too. According to a 2007 Eurobarometer survey a very large proportion of Europeans – a whopping 89 per cent – perceive a greater need for 'culture' to be promoted at EU level. Similarly, 88 per cent felt that cultural exchanges are important, and they called on the European Union to facilitate cultural exchanges for Europeans, and so promote intercultural dialogue. Seventy-six per cent agreed with the sentiment that it is the existence of European cultural diversity that gives European culture its unique flavour and enhances its value. The respondents were also asked which actors are best placed to launch initiatives that reinforce culture and cultural exchange in the EU. Looking at the average, national institutions scored 50 per cent, with the EU scoring 44 per cent. However, when we look only at the numbers relating to first place, we see a surprising reversal of this pattern: EU institutions are given as an answer by 28 per cent with national governments mentioned by 25 per cent.[54]

If not as passionate as fans at a football match between Liverpool and Manchester United, Europeans are ever more upbeat about taking advantage of what the EU has to offer. Culture 2000, the Union's predecessor to today's Culture Programme (see chapter 3), annually received about 700 applications. Of these, 85 per cent met basic application criteria, whereas 220 projects were granted support – a success rate of 30 per cent. Even Norway, which is not a formal member of the Union, benefited greatly from these funds: 75 projects with Norwegian participation on different levels received some €22 million in financial support.[55] All in all, therefore, it seems that the EU tangos much better with the European people when it comes to carefully implementing cultural policies than when enforcing remote treaty discussions upon them. By taking small steps towards a coherent cultural policy since the Treaty of Maastricht in 1992 formalized the EU's cultural responsibilities, the EU and its Member States have now moved cultural issues into the premier league of politics.

[1] Cultural policy can be defined as 'the promotion or prohibition of cultural practices and values by governments, corporations, other institutions and individuals.' See *International Journal of Cultural Policy*, www.tandf.co.uk/journals/titles/10286632.asp

[2] *The Economist*, 2008.

[3] Cited in Kelemen, 2007.

[4] Rifkin, 2004; Leonard, 2005.

[5] NIC, 2008.

[6] Kelemen, 2007.

[7] Mokre, 2003.

[8] Cf Klamer, Petrova and Mignosa, 2006.

[9] Figel, 2005.

[10] European Commission, 2007a.

[11] More info about the run-up to this Communication can be found at www.cultureactioneurope.org/advocate/eu-agenda-for-culture

[12] McCormick, 2008: 21.

[13] McCormick, 2008: 6.

[14] The EC is headed by a College of Commissioners with 27 members (one from each Member State), serving a five-year term and functioning as a European cabinet. Commissioners are appointed by their national governments, but must renounce any defence of national interests. Leading the Commission is the President, appointed by the European Commission, and endorsed by the European Parliament.

[15] The Committee of Permanent Representatives (Coreper) prepares Council agendas, decides which proposals go to which council, and makes many of the decisions about which proposals will be accepted or will be left for debate by ministers.

[16] The Council of Ministers is the key decision-making branch of the EU, comprising national government ministers and functioning as a place for voicing national interests and encouraging cooperation.

[17] The European Parliament is the only directly elected international legislature in the EU (and the world). It has a single chamber, and its 785 members are elected by universal suffrage by all eligible voters in the EU for fixed, renewable five-year terms. The number of seats is divided up among Member States roughly on the basis of population.

[18] The European Council consists of the heads of government of the EU Member States, their foreign ministers, and the president and the vice-president of the European Commission. This is *not* to be confused with the Council of Europe, which is an international organization based in Strasbourg which comprises the 47 democratic countries of Europe set up to promote democracy and protect human rights and the rule of law.

[19] McCormick, 2008: 69.

[20] McCormick, 2008: 45.

[21] European Commission, 2007a.

[22] Cliche et al, 2002: 15.

[23] Palmer, Colton and Kramer, 2002; Chanda, 2007.

[24] See Eriksen, 2007, for a comprehensive introduction.

[25] Neumann, 2006.

[26] UNDP, 2004: 1.

[27] UNESCO, 2005: 1.

[28] Pratt, 2008: 44. For a comprehensive introduction to the cultural economy, see Anheier and Isar, 2008.

[29] Anheier and Isar, 2007: 453.

[30] EuroStat, 2007: 103.

[31] Tilly, 1990: 23.

[32] Castells, 2000: 500.

[33] Giddens, 2002; Beck, 2006.

[34] For an extensive coverage of this subject, see Anheier and Isar, 2007.

[35] This point was made by American musician and anthropologist Steven Feld at a seminar arranged by the research programme CULCOM (Cultural Complexity in the New Norway) at the University of Oslo, 9 October 2008.

[36] European Commission, 2007a.

[37] www.euractiv.com/en/euro/gloomy-forecasts-eu-crisis-hits-real-economy/article-176889

[38] *Deutsche Welle*, 2008.

[39] *Los Angeles Times*, 2008.

[40] Arts & Business, 2008.

[41] *Vogue*, 2008.

[42] *Forbes*, 2008.

[43] www.theparliament.com/latestnews/news-article/newsarticle/credit-crunch-threatens-vilnius-eu-capital-of-culture-showcase/

[44] Kozlov, 2008.

[45] *Crienglish*, 2009.

[46] Anheier, 2009.

[47] For a cultural account of this concept, see Cowen, 2004.

[48] See http://eacea.ec.europa.eu/culture/infoday/downloads_2008_en.htm for the whole programme. For Sucha's presentation, see http://eacea.ec.europa.eu/culture/infoday/documents08/pres/1_sucha.pdf

[49] The principle of *subsidiarity* is a key word in the European Union. Culture Action Europe (CAE) offers an easy-to-read explanation: it was established in EU law by the 1992 Maastricht Treaty and covers areas which do not fall within the EU's exclusive competence. One of these policy areas is culture. Hence, the Member States and the EU have shared competences in the field of culture. The Community can only intervene if certain objectives cannot be reached by the Member States and if it can guarantee greater efficiency. The EU has no mandate to lead or control policies in the cultural sector, but – as laid out in Article 151 – is only required to encourage cultural cooperation and exchange, and to supplement the actions of Member States 'if necessary'. Apparently, in the global era, it has become necessary. Source: www.cultureactioneurope.org/advocate/glossary?p=subsidiarity-principle

[50] Ugrešić, 2005: 26–27.

[51] Klamer, Petrova and Mignosa, 2006: 7–9.

[52] Rushdie, 2003: 67.

[53] *Deutsche Welle*, 2008.

[54] Eurobarometer, 2007a: 55. Regarding the very idea of culture itself, the most common concept – mentioned by 39 per cent – is one that involves arts, exemplified in the survey by architecture, paintings and art galleries. Literature, poetry and playwrights and traditions/languages/custom are each mentioned by 24 per cent. 18 per cent say they associate culture with lifestyles and manners, while only 9 per cent associate culture with values and beliefs.

[55] Bjerke, 2007.

2 What Europe? Whose Europe?

Any cultural policy must in some way or another embed the history and social characteristics of the region the policy is intended to serve. Paradoxically, as pointed out by Gerard Delanty and Chris Rumford, the European Union today is caught in the situation of having to define a European commonness that is universal but nevertheless distinct from the global. At the same time, the EU is committed to protect and even to enhance its internal diversity of cultures and social milieus.[1] Heightened interest in European culture among Europeans, as documented in the previous chapter, therefore involves some intriguing questions which will be discussed in this chapter. As two social scientists put it: 'What is Europe and the uniquely European? What was it yesterday, and what will it be tomorrow?'[2]

Seeing identity as one's sense of self, European identity is a multifarious concept. No matter how you look at it, whether from the point of view of values, expressions or anthropological issues, the cultural divisions of Europe are substantial. While European countries have been a leading entity in the global development of human rights and freedom of speech, Europe is also home to the Holocaust, organized crime networks and terrorist groups that have propagated for decades, ranging from Irish and Basque separatists to the Red Brigades in Italy, and the Red Army

Fraction and Baader-Meinhof group in Germany.[3] At the website 'Europe of Cultures',[4] an online multimedia archive of 50 years of artistic creation and cultural life from the EU 27 (although with a distinctively French/ Western European slant), anyone can revisit all sorts of events, from the techno-pounding 1997 Love Parade in Berlin to Maria Callas singing Bellini's *Norma* at the Opera in Paris in 1958.

Internal differences and minority/majority relations within national borders are also important: the Flemings and the Walloons in Belgium, the Catalans in Spain, North and South in Italy, and the Sami in Norway. Controversial yet interesting postwar studies like the World Values Survey and the European Values Survey have shown that Europe encompasses many different views on the importance of religion, parent-child ties and deference to authority, abortion, national pride and nationalistic outlook.[5] Europeans speak more than 40 languages, 'which are often vigorously defended as symbols of national identity'.[6] Centuries of British, French, Dutch, Belgian and Portuguese colonialism have cemented ambivalent cultural links with colonized people all over the world; for some, it established a socio-psychological legacy which today supplies artists, writers and others with creative substance (in many ways), but it also robbed the victims of colonization of much of their self-confidence in the regeneration of cultural independence during the first post-colonial decades.[7]

Defining the European
One gathering trying to disentangle these issues was 'A Soul for Europe' in 2004. Arranged by Stiftung Zukunft Berlin, the first Berlin Conference with 600 participants took place in the Dresdner Bank on the Brandenburger Tor, on 26 and 27 November, and brought together the political, cultural and administrative leaders of Europe with a wish to initiate a process for placing sustainable cultural growth at the heart of the European project.[8] To them, 'the cultural soul of Europe is becoming increasingly more important as a means of bringing Europeans together while determining to an ever greater degree the ability of the EU to act in its dealings with neighbouring states and the rest of the world.'[9]

In his draft opening address, Commission President José Manuel Barroso gave his thoughts on this by saying that 'Europe's true cultural identity is made of its different heritages, of its multiplicity of histories and of languages, of its diverse literary, artistic and popular traditions.' Furthermore, Barroso made the point that 'if the Judeo-Christian, classical Greek and classical Roman traditions are at the beginning of our civilization, it is also true that the European identity received inspiration from the Arab world, and contributions from Celtic, German and Slavic origins.'[10] Central to these wise words from Mr Barroso is the acknowledgement of the traditional cultural pluralism of Europe in a way that is not always included in history books or even the biographies of outstanding Union personalities.[11]

It does not, however, change the fact that the one-million-euro question remains: what is Europe? Rather, it complicates it even more. Whether a country is European in EU terms is in 2008 'subject to political assessment' by the Commission and the Council. At its June 1993 meeting in Copenhagen, the European Council agreed on a formal set of requirements for membership of the EU. Known as the Copenhagen Conditions, they require that an applicant state must a) be democratic, with respect for human rights and the rule of law, b) have a functioning free market economy and the capacity to cope with the competitive pressures of capitalism, and c) be able to take on the obligations of the *acquis communautaire* (the body of laws and policies already adopted by the EU).[12] Directly, the Copenhagen Conditions make no particular mention of culture, even if capitalism and democracy are organizing units in a system based on certain cultural preconditions. Indirectly, the questions are less easy to answer.

Consequently, even if Europe can be given borders, they don't make any sense unless we discuss Europe as more than geography.[13] In the absence of clear geographical boundaries, first and foremost eastwards, the EU and European nations have turned to historical and cultural elements to delimit the idea of Europe. A quick peek into history reveals that this doesn't make things any easier. 'Europe has never been united,' writes John McCormick, and while many have dreamt of unification, 'it has only been since the Second World War that the idea of setting aside insular nationalism [or ideological equivalents] in the interests of regional cooperation has won wide public and political support.'[14] Nevertheless, consensus is far from a reality. One example is Ukraine. While Commission President Barroso in 2005 stated that 'the future of Ukraine is in Europe',[15] German author Richard Wagner strongly disagreed. He believes Ukraine's bid for a European identity is bogus, that the country is firmly anchored in the Eurasian region where oligarchic interests and a bizarrely ad hoc party landscape define the political climate, and that 'no end of bold Orange revolutionaries will be able to change this'.[16]

Most notable, though, is the Turkish case. Since October 2005, when the European Union started accession talks with Turkey, it has been a continuous controversy across Europe. Those in favour of membership emphasize that Turkey would enhance the EU's position as a global geostrategic player, given Turkey's geographic location with large natural resources that are at the immediate vicinity of the EU's sphere of influence. Those against Turkish membership point to the continuous dispute with Greece, unsatisfactory efforts to meet the Copenhagen criteria, and that a predominantly Muslim nation is incompatible with 'Western values'.[17] A 2006 Eurobarometer survey showed that 59 per cent of EU-27 citizens were against Turkey joining the EU, the highest negativity rank of all potential newcomers to the EU, while only about 28 per cent were in favour. Eighty-five per cent expressed concerns about human rights as the leading cause, while 61 per cent stated cultural differences between the EU and Turkey as too important to allow it to join the EU.[18]

Historically also, Europeanness is a fiddly concept. According to McCormick, who sets a fairly early date to the 'birth of Europe' in comparison with other sources,[19] it was the emergence of a common civilization with Christianity as its religion, Rome as its spiritual capital, and Latin as the language of education in the Early Middle Ages (500–1050) that first created a sense of Europeanness. Continental unity, however, was far from being a reality. Feuding kingdoms and various invasions in other parts of Europe by the Huns, the Vikings and the Magyars made sure that a stable idea of Europe as a united continent remained a dream.[20] Much of 16th and 17th century Europe was also destabilized by religious warfare, not only between Christians and Muslims; things were just as rowdy between Protestants and Catholics, even into the 18th century. For instance, in the Seven Years War (1756–63) France, allied with Catholic Austria, was decisively defeated by Protestant Prussia, allied with Protestant England. In fact, their mutual hostility attained such proportions that 'the idea of a united Christian Europe was abandoned'.[21]

During the 17th and 18th centuries the idea of state sovereignty emerged. Monarchical authority was broken, religious powers were challenged, national identities were forged and took the shape of fierce nationalisms, where leading politicians and philosophers came up with an ideological construct seeking to build a connection between a self-defined group and territorially defined state.[22] Alongside hampering initiatives for achieving peaceful continental unity – Abbé de Saint-Pierre's *Project for Settling an Everlasting Peace in Europe*, Immanuel Kant's *Thoughts on Perpetual Peace* and Comte de Saint-Simon's *The Reorganization of the European Community* – nationalism was extremely effective in offering a 'metaphorical kinship',[23] a romantic idea of belonging and a sense of security in an unruly world, shaken by the eruptive forces of modernization and industrialization.[24] Unfortunately, insular nationalism, in a variety of forms, gained popular support. Nationalist aggression, unresolved previous disputes, an intricate system of alliances, and colonial and economic rivalry were defining features of Europe until the end of the Second World War in 1945.[25]

Before the Second World War, Europe dominated trade, finance and cultural business, and by 1914 the continent held more than 85 per cent of the earth as colonies, protectorates, dependencies, dominions and commonwealths.[26] After the war, Europe was left with more than 40 million dead and widespread devastation. Cities lay in ruins, agricultural production was decimated, and communications were appalling due to extensive damage to roads, railways, harbours and bridges. An existential shame covered large parts of the continent due to the atrocities of fascism and Nazism. Against this troubled background,

John McCormick writes, a number of European leaders began to champion the idea of European states setting aside former grievances and building cooperative ideas to remove the causes of war.[27] To put it in dramatic terms, once used by fiction author Don DeLillo about the US, Europe could be saved only by what it had tried to destroy.

Although reportedly there have been more than 200 attempts to unite Europe at different times,[28] the new era seemed to provide unique opportunities. As the popular site 'Europe in 12 Lessons' puts it:

> 'People who had resisted totalitarianism during the war were determined to put an end to international hatred and rivalry in Europe and create the conditions for lasting peace. Between 1945 and 1950, a handful of courageous statesmen including Robert Schuman, Konrad Adenauer, Alcide de Gasperi and Winston Churchill set about persuading their peoples to enter a new era. New structures would be created in Western Europe, based on shared interests and founded upon treaties guaranteeing the rule of law and equality between all countries.'[29]

With the exception of some one-off initiatives and general agreements that have been made on audiovisual culture, copyright law and heritage issues, culture was dwarfed by the other pillars up until the 1990s. None the less, as historian Norman Davies writes in his unbelievably massive work on European history (on pages 1076–8, roughly two-thirds of the way through the book), the cultures of Europe flourished after the Second World War. 'Europeana', a digital library for Europe funded by the European Commission, exemplifies this by giving users access to some 2 million (and growing) digitized books, films, paintings and newspapers.[30] Conditioned by the climate of political liberalism, by great advances in technology and the mass media, and 'by a tidal wave of American imports',[31] the overall effect on European culture could be seen as a loosening of conventional restraints and a reduction of national particularities.

Growing respect for social sciences – psychology, sociology, economics and political science – was, according to Davies, influential in shaping socio-political programmes and paired with developments of liberal democracy and rising living standards. Post-war social life was more relaxed and egalitarian than previously. Feminist movements, inspired by thinkers like Simone de Beauvoir and manifestos like *The Second Sex*, together with the sexual revolution of the 1960s (including the contraceptive pill), challenged conventional gender mores. Homosexuality, extramarital sex and divorce were in the process of being eliminated from social embarrassment. A number of structural changes made a deep impression on social attitudes. Old hierarchies of class, profession and family origins did not entirely disappear; but in large part due to the development of European welfare states people became more mobile and independent, and many of the traditional anxieties about ill health, unemployment and old age were removed.

Religious life underwent extensive change. Church-going ceased to be a social convention, and was left to the private inclination of families of individuals – a development which has later been phrased 'believing without belonging'. The communications media proliferated. Rising literacy, a freer press and the growth of quality papers such as *The Times*, *Le Monde*, *Corriere della Sera* or *Frankfurter Allgemeine Zeitung* were supplemented by telephone communication becoming available to the masses and a booming television industry. General broadcasting began in France in 1944, in Britain in 1946 and in West Germany in 1952. American influences on cinema, music and popular dress were according to Davies 'felt in almost every sphere'. Youth and pop culture, 'where adolescents dressed in unisex jeans jived and minced in imitation of film idols or rock stars, became entirely transatlantic and cosmopolitan'.[32] Consumerism, including the ramifications of motorization, made wealth the main criterion of status in many social milieus.

The return of the East

Becoming aware of such cultural richness makes you wonder how it is even possible to include everything in European policy reflections. Although Davies makes a bold attempt, it shifts in my view from what stories are told to how they are told. An argument like this, I believe, is central to Geert Mak's *In Europe: Travels through the Twentieth Century* from 2007. Having voyaged around the continent throughout 1999 in a camper van, with bunk and cooking ring, commissioned by the Dutch newspaper *NRC Handelsblad* to report on the history of the century from below, Mak's scope is nothing but impressive; he speaks to hundreds of eyewitnesses, including prominent figures like the grandson of Kaiser Wilhelm II as well as everyday people such as Adrinana Warno in Poland, with her holiday job at the gates of the camp at Birkenau.

Taking the above rough draft of European history into account, the fundamental lesson from Mak's travelogue – spinning a European narrative from Verdun to Vichy, Amsterdam to Auschwitz, and Guernica to Gdansk – is the ways memory plays an important role in the construction of identity.[33] David Goldblatt wrote eloquently in the *Independent* that 'everywhere he goes, Mak is quietly ruthless in unmasking the acts of forgetting, selective amnesia, myth-making and historical obfuscation that persist. He notes the faked-up monuments, uncorrected stories, ersatz plaques and unholy silences: the British bombing of Dresden, the Dutch acquiescence to the final solution, the inhumanity of the Greeks and Turks and everybody else to each other.'[34] What's more, Mak's journey also unearths that in debates concerning the ideas of Europe, even after the end of the Cold War, the former Eastern Bloc countries are more often than not stuffed away or presented in an absurdly stereotypical fashion.

Books like *Dynamics of National Identity and Transnational Identities in the Process of European Integration*, edited by Elena Marushiakova, and *Cultural Transitions in Southeastern Europe*, edited by Nada Švob-Đokić and Jirina Šmejkalova, conversely, show the necessity for a wide-ranging redefinition of the European landscape as known to many Europeans.[35] After more than 15 years of transition from communism and various repressive regimes to capitalism and globalization, including the terrible Yugoslav wars and 'constant state of emergency' in the 1990s,[36] the South-eastern European region has changed radically. Especially notable, writes Švob-Đokić, 'is the gradual awakening and rationalization of the cultural situation. There is a strong tendency to fully identify with European cultural values. Redefinition of cultural identities and selection of true values is still under way.'[37] The search for new national identities, while striving to tackle the forces of globalization, is indeed a double-edged quest.

On a policy level, Eastern Europe experienced significant changes in the 1990s. Among organizations based on arm's-length principles are the national cultural funds: the Hungarian National Cultural Fund (founded in 1993), the Cultural Endowment of Estonia (1994), the State Culture Fund for Slovakia, the Latvian Culture Capital Foundation (1998), the Lithuanian Fund of Support for Culture and Sports (1998), the Romanian National Cultural Fund (1998) and the Bulgarian National Cultural Fund (2000).[38] The scope of their activities differs among the countries, and they are considerable efforts compared to earlier ventures, but it is just as important to understand that the independent examples of cultural reorientation are vast. In popular music, for instance, the music genre *chalga* has been revitalized to become the new folk cool of Bulgaria's younger generation. Under Communism, *chalga* held connotations of worthless kitsch. After the fall of the Iron Curtain in 1989, *chalga* became the most successful musical genre in Bulgaria.

As a result, chalga music has enveloped the whole of Bulgarian society. From the *nouveaux riches* to politicians, gymnasts and hotel workers, many Bulgarians enjoy the *chalga* experience. In May 2006, market research agency Alpha Research placed *chalga* radio station, Vesselina as the second most popular station in the Eastern European state. In addition, more than a quarter of Bulgarians are familiar with the specialist *chalga* broadcasters Diema and Planeta TV. The nature of the music itself is rather basic; producers often take memorable melodies from the Balkan area, incorporating a blend of Arabic, Turkish, Greek and Roma (Gypsy) influences, as well as motifs from even flamenco and klezmer music, to which clearly accentuated rhythms and repetitive beats are added together with short and simple lyrics. Add to the performance some 'half-naked barbies', as journalist Srebina Bognar described them, 'and you have all the ingredients for an extremely palatable folkpop stew.'[39]

A visual confirmation of transition changes in Eastern Europe on a more societal scale is provided by the BBC series *Michael Palin's new Europe*, aired by European broadcasters in 2007–08. The impressions it made on the globetrotter and former Monty Python humorist Palin, who reportedly said that he knew more about Vietnam than Eastern Europe before he began travelling there, can be read on his website (which also contains episodes and photos).[40] Based on the route shown in the map below, Palin writes that 'like all my journeys, New Europe was largely the product of an insatiable curiosity. I thought I knew my own continent, but I realised that almost half of it had been closed to me, by politics and ideology, for most of my life.'

Michael Palin's new Europe – route map

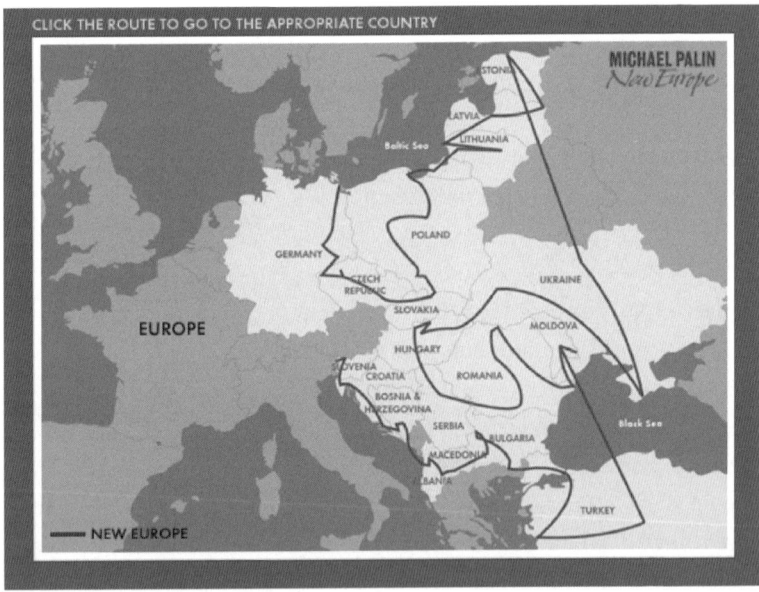

Source www.palinstravels.co.uk

After his travels, Palin was left with an entirely new impression of this formerly secluded part of Europe: 'Since the collapse of the Soviet Empire, a host of new independent states has emerged, all anxious to establish their own identity, parade their own culture and celebrate their own history. As I conclude on camera at the end of the series, there does seem a real hope that Europe could, for the first time in many centuries, be united by cooperation rather than conflict.' As the route shows, one country Palin visited is Poland, which is particularly well fitted by his description of large-scale alteration. As a well-populated country (38.5 million) with a communist history and an inconclusive relationship to other EU Member States (behold 'the Polish plumber') it is a large ship in European waters.

Far from being showered with money (public spending is among the lowest in Europe), the absence of a comprehensive cultural policy is, at least through Palin's lens, striking. But things are changing. On its official website, the Polish government writes in 2008 that 'entering the European Union imposed a lot of responsibilities on Poland, though it also created the possibility of benefitting not only from new financial sources, but also from European experiences in the area of culture support and protection. The Ministry of Culture and National Heritage is nowadays a department with the highest degree of absorption of the European funds.'[41] In 2004 the government launched the National Strategy for the Development of Culture 2004–2013. With a total budget of approximately €93 million it states, among other things, that 'Poland's accession to the European Union changes the view on the implementation of objectives in many aspects of public life for which – to a lesser or greater extent – the state and its governmental structures are held responsible.'[42]

Tools emphasized are greater financial resources for the implementation of the strategy in the coming years, changes in the system of organizing cultural activity, investments in human resources, and the use of available modern technologies in the popularization of culture. The Creativity Promotion Fund (Fundusz Promocji Twórczosci) is for example the state fund whose purpose is to support creators. There are also three schemes for individual artists provided by the Ministry: six-month and one-year stipends (salary supplements); the Fund to Support Artistic Creation (funding comes from income generated on sales of artworks with expired copyrights, so-called 'dead hand' funds) and the Stipend Exchange Programme in the framework of bilateral international agreements (these stipends are funded by the host country).[43]

According to Professor Dorota Ilczuk, since 1990, stress has usually been placed on the new 'patriotic' approach to national culture including the protection of national Polish values. Usage of EU funds, however, demands a more intercultural outlook, with positive effects.[44] Sites like www.culture.pl, moreover, reveal a vibrant cultural life which is less nationally bound.[45] One example is Mediations Biennale. The first international biannual contemporary art exhibition in the Polish city of Poznań, Mediations Biennale is intended to become one of the largest events of the kind in Central Europe. Poland's location on the borderland of European and Asian influences for centuries stimulated development of a unique cultural perspective, which differs from the post-colonial identity of Western Europe. Although it is difficult to talk about Central European art as a separate, consistent reality, each confrontation with it evokes a desire to name this phenomenon so deeply embedded in the region's reality.[46]

Transitions and transformations

Further substantiation that Palin's thoughts about Eastern Europe ring true can be found by looking at the literary development in the before-mentioned Ukraine. 'A wave of blogs, books and trendy bookshops is sweeping Ukraine, making writing the new playground of the country's twenty-somethings,' writes Prune Antoine, a journalist at *Café Babel*.[47] She think it's a literary revolution, sprung out of the post-Majdan era (after the Orange Revolution demonstrations in 2004 against Koutschma's pro-Russian government), with 'writers in short trousers leading what people here call the "1984 generation", a nod to George Orwell's eponymous novel.' Antoine makes a noteworthy point that this literary fever 'embraces and feeds the imagination of young readers, quick to identity with authors their own age who are accessible and unassuming'. Adults, on the other hand, 'are also delighted to dip into writing which is like an instruction manual for understanding the next generation, torn between East and West, hungry for easy money and celebrity, but also looking for a new political and democratic idea.'[48]

By opening the door to the emergence of modern Ukrainian literature, free of the stylistic straitjackets of National Socialism and traditional folklore clichés, authors like Oksana Zabuzhko (born 1960) have made the transition from the microcosm of intelligentsia to literary brand after the dismantling of the USSR. Despite substantial variance in quality, the literary development fulfils another function: describing and interpreting the cultural transition which is still under way. 'The silent trauma of the Soviet yoke still weighs on people,' Zabuzhko says, and for her the young generation's urgent need to write is symptomatic of this need to speak out.

It would be social scientific illiteracy not to accept that cultural transition of this scale demands a certain amount of time and creates a certain number of problems along the way. Zdzislaw Mach and Grzegorz Pozarlik, both researchers at the Institute for European Studies at Jagiellonian University in Krakow, lay emphasis on the importance of mental precautions:

'People in the West feel that Europe is changing, that new, less known and culturally different people joined the Union, that they bring not only sometimes unfair competition in the labour market, but also a different mentality, traditions, beliefs and prejudices. People in the East are afraid of opening up to the West, exposing themselves to new ideas, new ways of life, and new requirements of competence which they may lack. The EU, to which they now belong, is governed by principles, values and norms which they often do not understand.'[49]

Functionally speaking, one way to dampen this shared insecurity is to foster a stronger sense of European citizenship. Cultural progression is better catered for if mirrored by similar developments in cultural policies (but they are not the same). Consequently, a new feeling of citizenship – basically the rights and duties ascribed to members of a society in order to feel connected to a collective identity – must be allowed to emerge. Speaking about this very challenge, Violeta Simjanovska, director of Performing Arts Centre Multimedia in Skopje, back in 2002 confirmed that there were difficulties in defining the term 'cultural policy' in Macedonia:[50] 'We discussed this with experts in Macedonia, including those at the very top in the Ministry of Culture, and basically their attitude was that cultural policy did not exist in Macedonia and that we had to start to establish it.' Simjanovska continues: 'When we spoke to experts from Europe, however, we found that they had a completely different attitude. They maintained that a kind of cultural policy did exist in Macedonia, though it was unclear what its values were.'

An important part of citizenship is the freedom of speech and the availability of arenas where this right can be expressed. In Macedonia, the way has been long in this respect. The former Yugoslav republic, since 2005 a candidate for membership in the EU, is one of many Eastern European countries that had its cultural heritage and development suppressed by socialist malpractice. 'Macedonia does not have a tradition of public debate,' Simjanovska said, 'for the Bylaw Regulation concerning the National Programme, the Ministry of Culture gave people just two months to send their remarks or suggested amendments to the Ministry of Culture. This was a two-month period in which many people took their holidays.' Ministers and self-proclaimed experts who act as if they were the sole decision-makers do not permit much space for new ideas and fresh thinking. Communication between NGOs and governmental institutions is furthermore not highly developed. 'The old infrastructure of public institutions must first be changed in the minds of the new managers,' Simjanovska sighs.

Despite such difficulties, NGOs have begun to play an important role in the democratization of Macedonian society. Simjanovska and her allies have succeeded in establishing a public initiative together with the Ministry of Culture where they decided to have six national debates and two regional debates about cultural policy issues. In Simjanovska's eyes, the debates held so far are a success. They have discussed the decentralization of power; the reconstruction of the Ministry of Culture; the development of market-oriented culture and art; the education of professional managers; the denationalization of cultural institutions; and the involvement of civil society in formulating cultural policy. The hope is that these debates can contribute to a more wholesome notion on what culture means to national self-esteem and self-development. 'Transforming a way of life and changing society's norms, values and spiritual patterns is a long process,' Simjanovska admits. But she is also optimistic: 'Our experience since Macedonia became independent in 1991 proves that the civil sector must fight for these new values to prevail.'

Revisiting Macedonia some years later we find that Simjanovska's work has paid off. Performing Arts Centre Multimedia from Skopje started a project in 2005 aimed at strengthening local cultural institutions. The project was supported by the Ministry of Culture of the Republic of Macedonia and the European Cultural Foundation and, in part, through a US Embassy grant. The implementation of the project started in a period when the democratization and decentralization of national cultural institutions in Macedonia was set as a priority within the four-year National Programme for Culture and as an obligation set by the new Law for Culture introduced in 2003 and the new Law for Territorial Organization of Local Self-Government in Macedonia in 2005.

Until June 2005, the Ministry for Culture was the sole institution responsible for all of the state cultural institutions, creating a strong centralized system in which the institutions depended largely on the decision-making mechanisms that existed in the Ministry for Culture. With the process of decentralization, the responsibility for 48 cultural institutions (houses of culture, museums, libraries and working universities) in 29 municipalities in Macedonia was transferred to the local authorities, and from that moment onward local government was formally in charge of the creation of its own, local cultural policy and local cultural institutions had chief responsibility for what was available to the community in terms of culture, especially important in small places and villages where these institutions are the only cultural spots.[51]

How stories about the European are told

Like writing the history of Europe, making sense of European culture is something of a policy minefield. From an analytical point of view this may offer us a valuable lesson. Recall the review of Geert Mak's book from earlier in this chapter, and then look at the 'Museum of Europe'[52] exhibition in Brussels, brought together at the request of the European Parliament. It aims 'to take Europeans back to the roots of their shared civilisation' and seeks to be 'the "place of memory" that Europe needs'.[53] Arguing that the project omits such events as the Round Table at which the Polish negotiated the end of Communism in 1988–9, Piotr Semka wrote in December 2008 in the conservative newspaper *Rzeczpospolita* that such omissions 'are very sorely felt by Poland'. Semka further writes that of course he is aware that someone will always feel that some European event is missing. 'The problem lies elsewhere,' argues Semka, 'beyond individual historical events. The perspective of this project strongly reflects Western Europe, in particular the events that were of key importance for Germany and France.'[54]

It is not always popular to bring this debate into the open. When the Polish version of *Fear*, the book about 'how Polish anti-Semitism was possible after Auschwitz', written by Princeton historian of Polish origin Jan Tomasz Gross, was published, it set off a blistering debate. Gross is particularly critical of the Polish Catholic Church, maintaining that with the exception of the Bishop of Czestochowa, clerics not only did nothing to protect Jewish survivors from assaults after the war, but even sought explicitly to justify these attacks to a greater or lesser extent. As a reaction, the radical Catholic League of Polish Families has officially demanded that the Polish Foreign Ministry deny Gross entry into Poland. Other critics have pointed out that this is old news, and that the Poland of 2008 cannot be compared to the 1950s, neither in terms of societal structure nor regarding the role of the Catholic Church. But Gross by no means denies these tremendous changes in Polish society. According to a reviewer of the debate, Jakub Kloc-Konkolowicz, Gross simply believes that uncomfortable topics of the past must be discussed openly. Also, one must add, Gross's controversial book was printed in Poland by a respectable Catholic publisher.[55]

Clearly, not all historical events and perspectives on them can be included in every story about Europe, neither does there exist One True Storytelling Idea of Europe. However, there is a need for closer scrutiny of what's forgotten as European, what's emphasized as typically European, and what is not considered European at all, not least in the light of the persistent claims of Eurocentrism. In a thought-provoking essay Norwegian authors Stian Bromark and Dag Herbjørnsrud write that in the 1700s 'European intellectuals hailed China for everything from philosophy to porcelain and painting. In the 1800s Persia and Egypt

were the great models – a long series of philosophers from Goethe
to Nietzsche and Schopenhauer recognised that our common human
civilisation had been developed by Asians, and that we Europeans could
barely stand on the shoulders of what they had created for us.' Today,
sadly, the image has changed. They claim that we have developed a
self-glorifying image of Europe which is possibly the most Eurocentric
ever, and forgotten our transnational heritage.[56]

Basically the same idea was instigated by art historian and
former Romanian Minister of Culture and Minister of Foreign Affairs,
Andrei Plesu: 'The past must be demythologised, and all its mistakes
must be corrected.'[57] Not that this is something that could be done in
a hurry; in their 2005 Varna Declaration, Ministers of Culture of the
countries of South-east Europe proposed the creation of 'cultural
corridors' to revive the historical links in the region – the lines of
interaction between people who have left their cultural marks on
territories, landscapes, settlements and traditions. Three years later the
governments concerned had only reached the stage of a pilot project.[58]
'Official' EU history books such as Jean-Baptiste Duroselle's *Europe:
A History of Its Peoples* from 1990 also merit closer scrutiny. Published
in about a dozen languages with a preface by the then leader of the
Commission, Jacques Delors, it gives a convoluted indication approved
by Brussels on what Europeanness is – or was at the time.

More than anything, these examples show the necessity of
investigating how Europeaness is 'invented'. By 'invented' I don't imply
that anything European is made up, only that it is the result of a selective
process in which the methods should not be taken for granted. What
is hidden under the carpet, and what is given a parade? Argentine
philosopher Enrique Dussel claims that if 1492 is the moment of the
birth of modernity as a concept, it also marks the origin of a process
of concealment and misrecognition of the non-European.[59] Exploring
these issues, mainly in reply to Duroselle's book, Professor of Social
Anthropology Thomas Hylland Eriksen wrote that 'Europeans define
their community in contrast to something different, namely the
non-European (whatever that is).' Writing this in the mid-1990s, Eriksen
refers to the philosopher Georg Simmel (1858–1918). More than a century

ago, he showed how the internal cohesion of a group is contingent on external pressure, also known as 'Simmel's law'.

'Looking back on history, this is truly European,' Eriksen adds. 'The more barbaric Muslims can be made to seem, the more alien the Japanese, the more hopeless the Africans, the more childish the Americans; the stronger will be the sense of being European.'[60] Another Professor of Social Anthropology, Cris Shore, author of several books on the EU's cultural policies, is even more hostile towards Duroselle's book: 'This book is both teleological and highly selective in what it includes and excludes from this canon of elite references. The result is a sanitised and extremely Eurocentric construction of the past, which largely ignores the darker side of European modernity, including Europe's legacy of slavery, imperialism and racism.'[61]

Perspectives on how to avoid such criticism and recontextualize European history were the basis for EUSTORY – an international network where organizations from 14 countries, on the initiative of the Körber Foundation, teamed up in 2001 to put forward a European approach towards history. Because, as the editors of one of the three published volumes from the project write, it 'is not at all clear what "Europe" means as a dimension of Historical Consciousness'.[62] As soon as this is agreed, the real challenge comes into view. Books from the EUSTORY project come up with a lot of good and interesting views, answers and claims. Having said that, it is not so much about underlining the right answers as circling in the right questions. Fencing in a continent or a country culturally by comparing it to others could in itself be quite harmless. Cultural variation of course exists.

But the devil lies, as it were, in the general representation. Whereas Europeans might find the idea of Europe in American movies like *Eurotrip* or Japanese theme parks completely distorted (which in turn can be ridiculously funny),[63] their own conceptions could easily be as coloured by stereotypes and misrepresentations. When the attempts at defining Europe are made on behalf of more or less stereotypical ideas of non-Europeans, while simultaneously giving one's own culture – national or European – a high profile, essentialist identity without asking any questions about how this is done,[64] something is bound to fall out of rhythm. Not least if we accept – not everybody agrees with me on this one – that transnational realities have always been, and will always be, an intrinsic part of European countries.

Reading letters by European emigrants to the US, gathered by the Culture 2000 project EMILE (early EMIgrant LEtter stories),[65] or attending one of the events by the Culture Programme project 'Shaharazad – Stores for life',[66] is highly illuminating in this respect. As a final point, Shore writes in line with Eriksen that it is not only black, Asian, Muslim or Third World peoples who are excluded from the canon of European culture, but also those from the United States, 'which is somewhat surprising given the appetite European consumers seem to have for Americana'.[67] A renewed idea of how Europeanness is told, acknowledging the transnational histories all Europeans are a part of, and which can be traced far back in time, is thus needed.

Broadening the European public

What can be done in the name of change? Public coursework on topics touched upon in this chapter are central to educational institutions, but they are just as central on a daily basis when speaking of the European media. The memory that Europe needs, writes Italian political theorist Debora Spini, is a shared memory rather than a common memory. While the latter is merely aggregating memory, a shared memory requires communication.[68] Here we run into trouble. Even though media niches, where people from all European countries can meet up and communicate, are myriad, it is hard to see this adding up to a European space.

Thierry Chervel, the publisher of *signandsight.com*, the English language service of *perlentaucher.de*, the largest cultural online magazine in German language, therefore makes an important point when he claims that the weak presence of Europeanness is rooted in a weak public. Underpinning this argument is the notion that a viable public sphere is a central precondition for democracy because it enables widespread public debate.[69] Despite substantial magazine efforts like *Eurozine* (for the intellectual),[70] *Herald of Europe* (for the conservative),[71] *Frieze* (for the arty),[72] *European Voice* (the only one having the EU as its main target),[73] eurotopics[74] and The Budapest Observatory (for academicians who enjoy straight talk)[75] or Café Babel (for the likes of Erasmus students and such),[76] there is no real pan-European media to speak of. Further, when an attempt is occasionally made to produce one, it resembles the Tower of Babel more than well-ordered media pluralism.

The most famous attempt to create a pan-European media was Robert Maxwell's newspaper The European, launched in 1988. Maxwell saw the paper as a counterweight to the US titles Newsweek and Time and it had three sections: news, business and 'Elan', a tabloid arts review. Articles were written in English, French and German. In July 1990, sales were claimed as 340,000: 187,000 in the UK and 153,000 in Europe. Then things began going down the drain. Maxwell died from drowning, numerous owners with shifting competence brought the magazine into an identity crisis, money was lost, the number of readers plummeted, and despite various attempts to lift the magazine back on its feet, it was never resurrected.[77]

The history of The European typifies the debate in some kind of way. It is extremely difficult to reconfigure national hegemonies of intelligentsia and media affairs into a European blend. In Chervel's opinion the ignorance is greatest in large Western European countries where public debate is little more than globalization critiques, a fixation on 'the latest evil deed of bad boy Bush', or 'self-contented thumb-twiddling'. Almost ignored by Western European media, Ukrainians were for instance in 2008 attending the 75th anniversary of the Holodomor, the famine caused by Stalin's collectivization programme which left millions of Ukrainians dead.

Instead of transnational issues, 'talk is . . . of political leaders, late night comedy stars and football scandals,' Chervel rounds off with a sneer.[78] In contrast, Chervel has managed to engage a variety of intellectuals in what he considers to be a truly European debate. With a fiery polemic against Ian Buruma's Murder in Amsterdam and Timothy Garton Ash's review of this book in the New York Review of Books, French philosopher Pascal Bruckner has kindled an international debate: should Europeans or should they not ally with democratic Muslims in order to cope with tensions running through a multi-religious Europe? Bruckner, who thinks 'absolutely not', has got his share of followers, while Buruma, being more pragmatic about it, also received a lot of support.

Evidently, the idea of developing a European public sphere is a much larger undertaking than quantitatively improving the coverage of the actions of the European Union. Professor of Sociology Hans-Jörg Trenz defines the European public sphere as 'the communicative infrastructure that is used for debating the legitimacy of the project of European integration'.[79] That could honestly be a lot. The European Commission, on their side, adopted the White Paper on a European Communication Policy on 1 February 2006.[80] According to the White Paper, communication should become a policy in its own right and be based on a dialogue between citizens and policymakers as well as among citizens themselves. These debates should eventually result in a development where Europeans could address issues of common interest in parallel to the discussions already ongoing in the Member States. Thus citizens would achieve stronger influence on the decision-making process at the EU level.[81]

A subsequent Eurobarometer survey set out to test perceptions regarding some of the major initiatives contained in the White Paper and its underlying concepts: what are the chances of a dialogue between European institutions and citizens of the Union and how could the Commission facilitate this?[82] The findings were interesting. For the majority of citizens, political participation was confined to voting in elections, especially local or national ones. Other forms of political participation (signing petitions, attending demonstrations or discussing issues in online forums) were of marginal interest. The heart of the issue in regard to EU-level participation – besides the fact that there is only moderate interest in participating in politics of any kind – seems to lie in the logistics: 78 per cent of European citizens are not sure about the structure of the EU and uncertain as to whom they could turn to if they had an issue or concern. They do not know who is making the decisions. For two-thirds of Europeans, it was unclear who represents them in the European Parliament (66 per cent).

Even more interesting is that citizens across the EU are most inclined to show interest in the opinions of fellow Europeans regarding issues that are transnational by nature; environmental protection and the fight against organized crime/terrorism (both 89 per cent). Three other issues of above average cross-border interest are the emerging problem of secure energy supplies for Europe, the topic of creating jobs across the Union, and the issue of multicultural/religious tolerance, with more than eight out of ten Europeans mentioning these as well. Regarding the sources of information about the EU that people might use, television and newspapers tie in first place (75 per cent). The internet comes in third position (68 per cent) and radio, fourth (58 per cent). A large number of Europeans say they would watch 'European content' on TV in their national language (76 per cent). But at the EU level, only 7 per cent followed TV programmes from another country on a *daily* basis.[83]

Speaking European

To engage in a debate about the European public sphere is, however, not only a matter of what you think of the European Union. It also includes the notions of what to put into the phrase 'European media'. Is it about European issues, European takes on those issues, or simply Europeans writing about them? Research done by the Swedish anthropologist Ulf Hannerz on foreign news correspondents concludes that contrary to what one may think, in the era of globalization, coverage has been shrinking. Adding the traditionally partial views of journalism, merely because most of contemporary media (with the exception of the internet)[84] is closely interlinked to the functional set-up of the nation-state and the demands from domestic readers, the restricted scope of communication may in fact be a constraint on a more transnational outlook.[85] According to the Adequate Information Management (AIM) project, a three-year (May 2004–June 2007) and 11-country study which aimed to better understand the daily news machinery of reporting Europe, the researchers state that 'the editorial offices lack manpower and knowledge for EU coverage. Newspapers and private television almost exclusively fall back on stringers, pool correspondents and newswire services. Therefore consideration of individual readerships or a regionalization of EU news is largely impaired.'[86]

Questions like those discussed above were also central to the 2008 annual conference of the Centre for European Studies, University of Oslo (ARENA): 'Media and the public sphere in Europe'.[87] Generally, it was clear that Eastern Europe again was wiped off the European map (with the exception of Professor John Erik Fossum, who in his concluding remarks bemoaned this very fact). No speakers from the 2007 EU enlargement countries were present, nor were there any perspectives heard on what enlargement eastwards could mean for the European public sphere. An important point made by the publicist Arne Ruth, former chief editor of Swedish daily newspaper *Dagens Nyheter*, was that some issues are best covered with a transnational outlook. The Eurobarometer survey mentioned above also showed that EU citizens were most interested in hearing from fellow Europeans on issues that were transnational, like organized crime. Journalistic style was another element being considered. Trine Eilertsen, editor-in-chief at Norwegian newspaper *Bergens Tidende*, said that if journalists manage to combine the grand scheme of things, like 'European integration', with everyday stories people can identify with, elitism is watered out and a much larger market of readers will buy the paper. The flipside of this kind of journalism is high costs – an ever-present concern among newspaper editors.

Finally, virtually every participant at the conference singled out language barriers as a challenge to creating a European public sphere. Ruth described it precisely when he wrote in a 2007 article that 'there are literally hundreds of specialized journals that carry the epithet European or an equivalent in their title. But when it comes to general cultural and political reviews, there may be no more than a dozen that achieve a genuine European distribution, and almost all of these are in English.'[88] English was also the keyword when European magazine *signandsight. com* presented in 2007 'Let's talk European! Beyond provincialism – Towards a European public', a panel discussion with representatives from European media.[89] A very large portion of globally distributed news comes in English, most of it from media that are based in an English-speaking country.

There are reasons galore mentioned for this, but evidence points in several directions. First, the translation rate of books between non-English speaking European countries is extremely low. In 2006, 58 per cent of French translations came from English originals, as compared to 7.2 per cent from German, or a mere 0.2 per cent from Polish. Between neighbouring countries such as Poland, the Czech Republic and Hungary, the flow of books is a tiny trickle, making up on average less than 1 or 2 per cent of all translations in those countries. In the year before, in 2005, a mere 9.4 per cent of all translations into German came from French originals. Yet this still brought French comfortably to second place in the overall translation statistics in Germany, as compared to 2.7 per cent for Italian (number 3), or Dutch (2.5 per cent, number 4) or Spanish (2.3 per cent, number 5). Sixty-two per cent of all translations were of English originals.[90]

The internet is also dominated by the use of English. But, in addition to following traditional economic power lines in the same way as the transnational publishing business and hence relegating the finer cultural perspectives, the internet is far more user-generated than the literature world – both technologically and linguistically. Take email delivery services. In the 1990s, hotmail was king. Now gmail has overthrown it, largely due to changes in consumer taste. Google, the most popular search engine in the world, is currently available in 40 languages, chosen statistically to reach 98 per cent of the world's internet population. Much more interesting, though, is the global *expansion* of users. A wave of blogs has populated cyberspace with opinions and voices from all over the world. In Albania and Bosnia and Herzegovina, growth in usage of the internet between 2000 and 2008 has been 18,748 per cent and 14,971 per cent, respectively, compared to 87 per cent for Finland and 145 per cent for Switzerland.[91] Looking at internet users by world region, Asia leads the way with 39.5 per cent, followed by Europe (26.3 per cent) and North America (17 per cent).[92]

This dispersion of users can also be seen in the decrease of internet content in English, which fell below 50 per cent in 2003. And as web-crawling spiders (accumulating the numbers used in internet statistics) increasingly include new domain names containing Russian characters, the 11,000 Chinese signs, and other non-Latin languages, many believe a further decrease will be measured.[93] Another interesting

feature is the increased multilingualism of popular web services such as
YouTube. Although it began its life as an English-speaking community,
domains in 2007 became available in Spanish, Portuguese, French,
Italian, Dutch, Japanese and Polish. Each new site is fully translated
and localized for each country including content (featured videos,
director videos, promotions), as well as the interfaces, search, user
support, and such community features as video ratings, sharing, and
content flagging.[94]

    With the internet acquisition curve pointing upwards across the
globe still, English remains the majority language. Whereas some point
to Americanization and imperialism theories to explain this, it might
as easily be a historical coincidence. As Anthony D Everitt has pointed
out, Latin was the universal language for a long time, followed by French
from the 17th century on. The 20th century was the first time that English
had taken on such a strong position as global lingo.[95] Grammatical
flexibility is one keyword, or as Naomi Buck says: 'English has been
sashaying, reconnoitring and kowtowing its way around the world
for a long time. It knows how to beg, borrow and steal but also how to
integrate, share and age – with grace and not.'[96] With increasing global
interdependence (and, of course, the history of British imperialism),
English has for such reasons gained a global reputation as a simple
means of communication, not least if we include internet translations.

    Mario Queiroz at Google illustrates some of the quandaries
with other alternatives: Hebrew or Arabic are written from right to
left. An Arabic speaker may search for [world cup football 2008]. Part
of the query will be written from right to left in Arabic [كأس العالم
لكرة القدم. 2008], while the numbers will be written from left to right.
Sometimes the right-to-left difference can mean having to change the
entire layout of a page, as with gmail. Or take Russian, where words
change depending on their position and role in a sentence. In Russian,
for example [pizza in Moscow] is [пицца в Москве] but [pizza near
Moscow] is [пицца рядом с Москвой].[97]

    What consequences do these developments have for a European
public? During the signandsight panel discussion mentioned above one
captivating suggestion arose. As the deputy chief editor of the Dutch

daily *Trouw*, Gerbert van Loenen, pointed out, if a Dutch person's ideas of Romania are based on the *Wall Street Journal*, this might produce an Anglo-American bias. On the other hand, use of English has the possibility to enable non-English speakers to know more about each other. Hans Maarten van den Brink, director of the Dutch Cultural Broadcasting Fund, went even further and proposed that 'if we all spoke English, it would in fact stop the Anglicisation in the media and in our culture. If we don't, we'll all read what they think, and hear it and see it. But if we do, they'll also hear us.' Using English as a means of communication without taking the long road via American (or English) newspapers may potentially increase awareness of what's going on in Europe.

Arne Ruth nevertheless raised concern about romanticizing English. According to him there is no way of defining in advance what interpretation of what's going on will eventually become a universal perspective. He did, however, say that journalists will find increased use of English in Europe relevant, resulting in better stories in people's first language, giving them a better chance of knowing what's going on. In an article, Ruth extends this argument by saying that 'from the perspective of European integration, the problem seems to be that national media are both reflecting and strengthening particularities, with journalists rarely acknowledging insular tendencies in the value system on which they base their coverage. A truly European discussion would still mean a multiplicity of views and arguments.'[98] As mentioned before, this also has a lot to do with the enlargement of the EU eastwards. If a European public is to evolve, one must – at least to some degree – conform to a certain updated idea of Europe.

Similar observations are posed by Polish writer Adam Krzeminski. He fears that English will simplify the debate radically. 'Even fairly good school or tourist English is rarely sufficient when it comes to holding a qualified discussion or in some cases even delving into the psychology of someone from a neighbouring country.' Ironically, he sees no viable alternative: 'And yet this is a bitter necessity in a Europe whose national histories have often been bloody ones, and in a Europe of carefully cherished collective self-interest and a degree of ignorance that is arrogant.' This is not merely confined to celebrities, Eurovision Song Contests or art exhibitions. For a country like Poland, which longs for European belonging, Krzeminski continues, 'Europe is not only the norm, but also a kind of insurance policy against the abstruse antics of their own political class.' The way I read Krzeminski, Poland must be allowed to enter Europe on their terms, culturally and politically, not restricted by arrogant old European conceptions of the continent's cultural treasure on the one hand, or the 'Stalinist model underlying the Russian philosophy of history' on the other.[99]

Perhaps the question of whether we should use English or native languages to create a less nation-stuck public debate is a sidetrack. Most interesting during the panel discussion arranged by *signandsight.com*, in my view, was a question from the audience. The argument was that the world is globalized, and talking about a European public sphere thus meant that we were closing our eyes to the rest of the world. Adding the difficulties of defining Europe culturally, my initial response to the questions 'What Europe? Whose Europe?' based on the discussions in this chapter, then, is to point at how the European story is told. 'Europe needs a bold new story – and to invent new ways to tell it,' Timothy Garton Ash wrote in 2007,[100] and I reckon he's correct. In the next chapter, we will check out the EU's response.

[1] Delanty and Rumford, 2005: 60.

[2] Bundt and Fosse, 1996. See also Delanty, 1995; Jordan, 2002.

[3] McCormick, 2008: 145; cf also Glenny, 2008.

[4] www.ina.fr/europe-des-cultures/En/Html/PrincipaleAccueil.php

[5] From the presentation text at www.worldvaluessurvey.org

[6] McCormick, 2008: 32. For the record, the EU has 23 official languages.

[7] Loomba, 2005.

[8] www.berlinerkonferenz.eu

[9] www.berlinerkonferenz.eu/uploads/media/A_SOUL_FOR_EUROPE_Concept_of_the_initiative_April_08.pdf

[10] Barroso, 2004.

[11] In Romano Prodi's *Europe as I See It*, the former Commission President argues that Christianity provides a cultural unity across Europe. Not everybody agrees. See Prodi, 2000, Delanty and Jones, 2003: 192, Bromark and Herbjørnsrud, 2004, and Shore, 2006, for debates.

[12] McCormick, 2008: 62.

[13] Ahnström, 1996.

[14] McCormick, 2008: 24.

[15] Beunderman, 2005.

[16] Wagner, 2008.

[17] www.euractiv.com/en/enlargement/eu-turkey-relations/article-129678

[18] Eurobarometer, 2006a: 223–4.

[19] Uffe Østergaard (1999: 52) claims that the use of Europe, at least as a secular concept, first appeared in the 15th century. Leif Ahnström (1996: 20) claims that a European identity didn't come around until the 18th

century along with capitalism, nation-states and so on and so forth.

[20] McCormick, 2008: 24–6.

[21] McCormick, 2008: 27.

[22] Eriksen, 2002.

[23] Anderson, 1991.

[24] Gellner, 1983.

[25] Davies, 1996: chapter 11; see also Palmer, Colton and Kramer, 2002.

[26] Said, 1994: 10.

[27] McCormick, 2008: 45–6.

[28] De Rougemont, 1961.

[29] http://europa.eu/abc/12lessons/lesson_1/index_en.htm

[30] www.europeana.eu/portal

[31] Davies, 1996: 1076.

[32] Davies, 1996: 1076–8.

[33] For an academic version of this viewpoint, see Spini, 2003.

[34] Goldblatt, 2007.

[35] Švob-Ðokić and Šmejkalova, 2004; Marushiakova, 2008.

[36] Keulemans, 2005: 22.

[37] Švob-Ðokić, 2004: 3.

[38] Klamer, Petrova and Mignosa, 2006: 50.

[39] Bognar, 2007.

[40] http://palinstravels.co.uk/static-206

[41] www.mk.gov.pl/english/english.html. See also www.culturalpolicies.net/down/poland.pdf

[42] The policy document is available at www.mk.gov.pl/website/document/?docId=215

[43] http://ec.europa.eu/culture/portal/sites/members/poland_en.htm

[44] www.culturalpolicies.net/down/poland.pdf

[45] www.culture.pl/en/culture

[46] www.culture.pl/en/culture/artykuly/wy_wy_mediations_biennale_2008

[47] Antoine, 2007.

[48] Antoine, 2007.

[49] Mach and Pozarlik, 2008: 1.

[50] Simjanovska, 2002.

[51] See http://multimedia.org.mk/cultural_policy_projects.html and

www.policiesforculture.org/administration/upload/Web-Macedonia_info.doc

[52] www.expo-europe.be

[53] www.expo-europe.be/en/site/musee/musee-europe-bruxelles.html

[54] www.eurotopics.net/en/presseschau/kultur

[55] Kloc-Konkolowicz, 2008.

[56] Bromark and Herbjørnsrud, 2004.

[57] Plesu, 2005: 47.

[58] De Vries, 2008: 47.

[59] Dussel, 1993: 66.

[60] Eriksen, 1995: 257–8.

[61] Shore, 2006: 18. See also Shore, 2000; 2001.

[62] Pók, Rüsen and Scherrer, 2002: 9. See also www.eustory.org

[63] Hendry, 2002.

[64] The Mercator map, where Europe is located at the centre of the world, is one example. For a provocative and informative view on Eurocentrism, see Shohat and Stam, 1994.

[65] www.emigrantletters.com

[66] The Shahrazad project is a literary offshoot of the International Cities of Refuge Network (ICORN). For more information, see www.icorn.org and www.shahrazadeu.org

[67] Shore, 2006: 1.

[68] Spini, 2003: 71.

[69] Fossum and Schlesinger, 2007.

[70] www.eurozine.com

[71] www.heraldofeurope.co.uk

[72] www.frieze.com

[73] www.europeanvoice.com

[74] www.eurotopics.net

[75] www.budobs.org

[76] www.cafebabel.com

[77] For the complete story, see www.magforum.com/european.htm

[78] Chervel, 2005.

[79] Trenz, 2008: 1.

[80] http://ec.europa.eu/communication_white_paper/doc/white_paper_en.pdf

[81] For recent developments, see http://ec.europa.eu/commission_barroso/wallstrom/communicating/policy/index_en.htm

[82] Eurobarometer, 2006b.

[83] Eurobarometer, 2006b.

[84] In fact, there are possibilities for those who want to engage. At the website 'Debate Europe' (http://europa.eu/debateeurope/index_en.htm), which was awarded the European eDemocracy Award for 2006, anyone with web access can join debates on several hot topics.

[85] Hannerz, 2004; see also Trenz, 2006.

[86] www.aim-project.net

[87] www.arena.uio.no/news/News2008/%C3%A5rskonferanse_08.xml

[88] Ruth, 2007.

[89] A summary of the evening's discussion is available at www.signandsight.com/service/1374.html

[90] Wischenbart, 2007.

[91] www.internetworldstats.com/stats4.htm#europe

[92] www.internetworldstats.com/stats.htm

[93] Marling, 2006: 65.

[94] Arsiwala, 2007.

[95] Everitt, 2008: 62.

[96] Buck, 2006.

[97] Queiroz, 2008.

[98] Ruth, 2007.

[99] Krzeminski, 2007.

[100] Ash, 2007.

3 The European Union in the age of culture

The EU has paid more attention to cultural policies than critics allow.[1] The institutional infrastructure associated with today's EU cultural policies shows impressive variety.[2] Nina Obuljen, research fellow at Zagreb's Institute for International Relations, and Assistant Minister for International Relations and EU Affairs at the Croatian Ministry of Culture, argues that cultural policy does not necessarily mean implementing a grand vision. The sum of small things can be just as effective. Cultural policies also depend on provisions and rules in other spheres of public policies.[3] As I will discuss in this chapter, this has to some degree been the case with the EU. But a wholehearted effort from the inner corridors of Brussels has yet to emerge. The 2007 Communication may be a turning point.

The 2002 film *L'Auberge espagnole* is both excellent and enlightening. Directed by Frenchman Cédric Klapisch, it brings warmth, joy and a visualization of what for me is the essence of Europeanness. Briefly, here is the plot: as part of a job that he is promised, Xavier, a French economics student in his twenties, signs on to Erasmus – a European exchange programme – to gain a working knowledge of the Spanish language. Pledging that they'll remain close, he says farewell to his girlfriend, then heads to Barcelona. Upon his arrival, Xavier is

thrown into a cultural stew when he moves into an apartment full
of international students, who join him in a series of life-initiating
adventures.

In addition to intelligent lampooning of the EU and amusement
caused by Xavier's fervent libido (unity in diversity?), the film
sympathetically shows how everyday multiculturalism pervades the
students' apartment. It brings them together as Europeans. As Xavier
says: 'I'm French, Spanish, English, Danish. I'm not one, but many. I'm
like Europe, I'm all that. I'm a real mess.' Add to the story cosmopolitan
scenery from a funky Barcelona and music by artists such as Radiohead,
Daft Punk and Ali Farka Toure, along with flamenco, Afro-pop and even
Chopin, and we come to see Xavier as representing modern European
life.

The European Union, by contrast, has for various reasons
traditionally had a slightly different take on European cultures. Brussels
has never messed around, but rather faithfully stuck with the idea
of Europe as being a well-defined mosaic of nations, where cultural
policies has been left to Member States themselves. With the 2007
Communication, we may reasonably ask whether transnational cultural
policy harmonization is about to bloom.

A brief history of the EU and culture
At the heart of the thinking of French statesmen Jean Monnet (1888–1979)
and Robert Schuman (1886–1963), frequently called the founding fathers
of the EU, was the idea that successful cooperation in some core areas
of the EU would create a spillover effect. Economic cooperation would
lead to political union, then to social cohesion and so on.[4] Culture came
in last in this equation.

In 1957, Belgium, the Federal Republic of Germany, France,
Italy, Luxembourg and the Netherlands (which six years earlier had
established the European Coal and Steel Community (ECSC)), signed
the Treaty of Rome, intended to build a European Economic Community
(EEC) based on a wider common market covering a whole range of
goods and services. While there was discussion of cultural aspects
in the early attempts at creating a European community, the Treaty

contains only two minor sentences referring to culture. The first related to 'non-discrimination', and the second to exceptions to the free movement of goods where a special case can be made for 'the protection of national treasures possessing artistic, historical or archaeological value'. Thus, prior to the Maastricht Treaty in 1992, the EU 'had no legal basis for direct involvement in cultural affairs'.[5]

Despite what one may think reading the history of nationalism in works like A D Smith's *Nationalism and Modernism*,[6] cultural policies in the early postwar years were not a high priority in the countries of Europe, either. However, in the 1960s, cultural policies began to attain status as tools for societal coherence, supporting the arts and fostering national identity. Emphasis was laid on increasing public access to cultural works. Throughout the decade, cultural policy in Europe became less random and more integrated into public visions by institutional means. The postwar Nordic cultural policies, for instance, were basically designed to regulate economic institutions in order to ensure artistic freedom and cultural diversity.[7]

The heightened status of culture began to reach the roundtables of international politics in the late 1960s. One moment of great importance was the first conference of European Ministers of Culture in Helsinki in 1972, organized by UNESCO. Here Jacques Duhamel (1924–77), then French Minister of Culture, in many ways defined the language that would govern not only European, but also global cultural debates in upcoming decades. In his speech poignantly entitled 'The Age of Culture', the distinctively European-minded Duhamel began by saying that 'there is hardly a country in Europe without an awareness of a diffuse but crucially important phenomenon, concerning the place of culture as both an agent and an object of the great transformation affecting contemporary societies.'[8]

This sounds very much like the political talk of today and even more so when we consider what Duhamel had to say about the basis for this view. The cultural transformation of Europe finds expression in a generalized questioning of the notion of culture, which has lost its erstwhile clarity and has become elusive. When classical culture – in Duhamel's eyes, the works of Greek philosophers and 'men like

Galileo' – became unable to master the material development for which it had provided the means and designated the paths, culture no longer represents exclusively the moulding of the individual through the practice of the fine arts. Culture is also knowledge, existence and communication. As a result, he concludes that we can establish a cultural policy only by changing the view of culture: 'only a broadened conception of culture can respond to the current situation where, in every country, almost all the population are now affected by cultural development and the sense that it is intimately bound up with economic development.'[9]

I have no direct evidence that, after Duhamel's speech, European politicians or EU officials actually went home and began pondering a European cultural policy. But it is reasonable to believe that the conference had some impact on the political climate in Europe. The European Council, after a meeting in Copenhagen on 14 and 15 December 1973, published a Communiqué highlighting the importance of culture and cultural identity for further integration at the European level. It stated: 'the nine member countries of the European Communities have decided that the time has come to draw up a document on the European identity.'[10] Unfortunately, the Council did not elaborate on this intrepid statement. Nevertheless, it is a clear signal of where things were going. Historian Bo Stråth, for one, argues that this turn towards identity and culture marked an important shift in the official discourse of European integration.[11]

Records of EU activity in the cultural policy arena during the 1970s indicate that Stråth is correct. According to the historical timeline presented by Nina Obuljen, in 1976 the European Commission submitted to the Parliament a document articulating for the first time the need for coordination of cultural activities. By the end of 1977, the Commission published *Community Activities in the Cultural Sector*,[12] primarily dealing with regulations in favour of free circulation of goods and cultural exchange. In 1976 and 1979, the European Parliament adopted two resolutions inviting the Commission to submit formal proposals for the treatment of culture at community level. In 1982, the first conference of the Ministers of Culture of the EC adopted the declaration, signed in

1983, which sought to explore the possibilities of cultural cooperation with special emphasis on audiovisual media.[13]

Not surprisingly, the wording of these documents was very vague. In contrast the rhetorical underpinnings were less indistinct. At Mondicult, an international conference of culture ministers organized by UNESCO in 1982, French Minister of Culture, Jack Lang, voiced concern about the growing link between economy and culture as referenced by Duhamel, above: 'We want this conference to provide the platform for the peoples of the world, through their governments, to call for a true cultural resistance, for a true crusade against this domination, or – let us resist other people's terms and call things by their real name – this financial and intellectual imperialism.'[14] Lang never mentions the US directly, but refers to 'a great power' and drops in Reagan's name.[15] He exhorts this crusade against a nightmarish dystopia where everybody wears the same clothes and listens to the same music and national cultures are replaced by a uniform lifestyle with no real value.

Lang was not alone in seeing things this way. Tobias Theiler, author of *Political Symbolism and European Integration*, summarizes the debate by writing that:

> 'while the aim of promoting a European identity continued to resonate throughout the various audiovisual production initiatives by the Commission and the EP, it became complemented by increasingly vociferous calls to reduce the Community's audiovisual trade deficit with the United States. With a growing sense of urgency, both bodies depicted Europe's reliance on US films and television programmes as costly not only in economic terms but also as a source of serious cultural damage to European audiences and as a threat to the survival of European culture – so much so that by the late 1980s the anti-Americanisation theme had become the predominant discursive frame for their various audiovisual initiatives.'[16]

Possibly reacting to Lang's inflammatory speech and the climate in general, the European Council between 1984 and 1986 adopted several resolutions dealing with cultural matters, including European films, the mobility of artists and networking of libraries, among others. Worth mentioning in particular is the Addonino Committee on 'A People's

Europe', established by the European Council in 1984 to look at a number of measures towards strengthening and promoting the European Commission's identity and image among its citizens and the rest of the world. It supported the adoption of initiatives which included an EC passport, an EC driving licence, an EC emergency health card, EC border signs and an EC flag, and the financing of an EC TV channel (Eurikon) to promote 'the European message'.

In addition, 1984 was also the year when the European Declaration on Cultural Objectives was adopted by the European Ministers Responsible for Cultural Affairs. Giving fairly new directions on how the EU perceived the sociological relationship between culture and individualism, it aimed to 'develop opportunities for creative activity and self-expression, to encourage the free exchange of artists and the democratic use of new communication technologies, so that everyone may utilize their abilities and make their contribution to the development of society by realizing their full potential.'[17]

The 'European Capitals of Culture', one of the best known and long-running culture projects of the European community, was launched in 1985 by the Council of Ministers on the initiative of the then Greek Minister of Culture, Melina Mercouri.[18] Starting with Athens, more than 30 cities have been designated Capitals of Culture, from Stockholm to Genoa, Stavanger to Glasgow, Cracow to Porto. Over the years, this event has highlighted the richness of European cultures and the features they share, and fostered a feeling of European citizenship. According to the European Commission, which awards the title annually, a city is not designated a Capital of Culture solely for what it is or what it does. It is awarded the title principally on the strength of the programme of specific cultural events it proposes to organize during the year in question, which is meant to be an exceptional year. A good example is the festival 'A Voyage through Europe', organized in Genoa in 2004. This festival took the European theatre as its theme. Three European theatre companies were invited to perform a play written by an author from their country, in its original language.[19]

According to Obuljen, 1987 was a watershed in EU cultural history. That year the EC officially established the Council of Ministers of Culture and the ad hoc Commission for Cultural Issues. The 'Television without Frontiers' Directive, which abolished most legal barriers to the transmission and reception of television signals between the Member States, was adopted two years later. Moreover, it imposed an (albeit non-binding and highly controversial) quota regime which was intended to aid European producers by curtailing the inflow of audiovisual material from overseas.[20] In 1991 the first framework for the financial support of the audiovisual industry, MEDIA I, was established. In 1992 article 128 (later article 151 of the Treaty of Amsterdam from 1997) was included in the Maastricht Treaty, representing the first time a treaty article explicitly related to culture. Paragraph 1 provides that 'the Community shall contribute to the flowering of the cultures of the Member States, while respecting their national and regional diversity and at the same time bringing the common cultural heritage to the fore.' While Paragraph 4 states that 'the Community shall take cultural aspects into account in its action under other provisions of this Treaty, in particular in order to respect and to promote the diversity of its cultures.'

Even if this was a big step forward for the EU, many critics felt that it didn't make any difference as long as the Union had no deeper financial obligations to help European culture thrive and foster integration.[21] Apart from the treaty text itself, this article paved the way for new programmes and ideas, and put culture explicitly on the EU table.

In 1995, the Erasmus programme was included in Socrates I, aimed at creating a European educational network from kindergarten age to university levels. In 1996 and 1997, the EU implemented three new programmes with financial support: Kaleidoscope (contemporary creation), Ariane (books and reading, including translation), and Raphael (cultural heritage). There was also a new framework programme called MEDIA II, to support the production and distribution of European audiovisual works.

As the millennium approached, the Culture 2000 programme was established, offering economic support to inter-European collaboration on cultural projects. With a five-year budget of €167 million, the purpose of Culture 2000 was to simplify action by using a single instrument for financing and programming cultural cooperation.

The programme aimed to promote cultural diversity and dialogue between European peoples, cultural activity, transnational dissemination of culture and exchanges of artists. The results were mixed. The 2008 evaluation report finds that 'although there is no evidence that Culture 2000 led to the establishment of new regional or national intercultural cooperation initiatives, the programme had a clear impact on cultural policies in some participating countries.'[22] In 2001 the so-called Ruffolo report stated that 'it is time for the EU to replace numerous declarations about the importance of culture with taking concrete responsibilities.'[23] One of these responsibilities was to enable artists and cultural workers from all over Europe to come together. The establishment of the European Cultural Parliament in 2001 is one example,[24] where some 40 cultural personalities from 25 European countries participated at the first conference in 2002. In 2003 the programme was extended unchanged for the years 2005 and 2006.

More significant, however, were developments following President Barroso's strong endorsement of culture as a binding element of an expanding EU at the 'A Soul for Europe' conference in 2004. After years of tough discussions on how to continue from Culture 2000, the EU finally settled on a budget of €400 million for its Culture Programme 2007–2013.

As we will explore later, this programme aims to achieve three main objectives:

- to promote cross-border mobility of those working in the cultural sector;
- to encourage the transnational circulation of cultural and artistic output;
- to foster intercultural dialogue.

To achieve these objectives, the programme supports three strands of activity: cultural actions, European-level cultural bodies, and analysis and dissemination activities. Closely related to the Culture Programme is the €755 million MEDIA 2007–2013 Programme, described as 'a big push for Europe's audiovisual industry', supporting production, distribution and promotion of European audiovisual products.[25]

In addition to these, but in many ways just as important, are the EU's actions and programmes that strive to integrate culture and its related issues into the wider policy framework. For example:

- Projects supported under the EU's Citizenship Programme promote dialogue between different cultures and support efforts to forge a common European identity.
- The link between education and culture runs through the EU's educational policies. For instance, many projects funded under the Socrates Programme and its predecessors have supported educational or training projects in the cultural field, and this will continue under the Lifelong Learning Programme.
- One of the objectives of the previous Youth Programme was to foster better understanding of Europe's cultural diversity. The new Youth in Action Programme also seeks to promote linguistic and cultural diversity.
- Culture plays a key role in the development and social cohesion of the territory by acquiring financial support under the EU's Structural Funds.
- The rural development aspect of the Common Agricultural Policy has a cultural dimension under the 'Leader +' initiative which helps rural communities make the best use of natural and cultural resources.
- Information technology has an important role in making cultural information widely accessible. In August 2006, a Commission Recommendation was adopted on the digitization, digital preservation and online accessibility of cultural materials.
- The Seventh Framework Programme for Research (FP7) supports culture directly and indirectly through various specific programmes, in particular in the realm of the social sciences and humanities.
- There is a strong link between the promotion of culture and creativity and EU copyright and related rights legislation, and also rules governing state aid.

In the context of this overlapping policy mesh, the European Commission has committed itself to deepening its analysis of the interface between cultural diversity and other Community policies. The aim is to strike the right balance between different public policy objectives when making decisions or proposals of a regulatory or financial nature.

Of particular importance in this respect are the regional policy funds. For the period 2007–13, regional policies received a budget of €348 billion including €278 billion for the Structural Funds and €70 billion for the Cohesion Fund. This amounts to over 80 per cent of the Community's expenditure for culture. Because other Community programmes are unable to meet its financial needs, the culture sector has benefited considerably from these funds. Funding for culture from the Structural Funds is mainly based on the recognition of the 'transversal' quality of culture. In other words, culture interrelates with a variety of other fields and almost every aspect of contemporary life and society, for example, the cultural industries, media and new technologies, tourism and leisure, urban planning, regional development, education and training. It takes into account that the cultural sector generates employment and contributes to social cohesion, innovation, sustainable development and other common objectives in the EU.[26]

Empowering the 'heart of human civilization'
From this brief account of the evolution of the EU's cultural policy work, we see that the institution has been careful to define in detail its cultural motives and programmes. However, the European Union's new 'European Agenda for Culture in a Globalising World',[27] prepared following an extensive public online consultation, may signal a change. As stated in chapter 1, the agenda was approved by the cultural sector during the Lisbon Forum in September 2007, and endorsed by the Council in its Resolution of November 2007 and then by the European Council in December 2007.[28] The agenda has no budget of its own, but is subsumed by the Culture Programme 2007–2013 and MEDIA, the EU support programme for the European audiovisual industry.[29]

The Communication opens with the assertion that 'culture lies at the heart of human development and civilization'. In the following press release, Commission President Barroso argued that culture and creativity 'are important drivers for personal development, social cohesion and economic growth'. He also stressed how cultures encapsulate a broad spectrum of history: 'they are the core elements of a European project based on common values and a common heritage – which, at the same time, recognizes and respects diversity.'[30]

From this general overview, we see three missions emphasized that together make up the strategy shared by EU institutions, Member States and the cultural sector in Europe. The first mission is 'promotion of cultural diversity and intercultural dialogue'. A multicultural continent such as Europe requires multicultural policies. Specific objectives are the promotion of the mobility of artists and professionals in the cultural field and the circulation of artistic expression beyond national borders. The EU also wishes to promote and strengthen intercultural competences and dialogue, in particular by developing 'cultural awareness and expression', 'social and civic competences' and 'communication in foreign languages', which are part of the key competences for lifelong learning identified in 2006 by the European Parliament and Council. 2008 was heralded as the European Year of Intercultural Dialogue.

Second, the agenda emphasizes the promotion of culture as a catalyst for creativity in the framework of the Lisbon Strategy for growth and jobs. Cultural employment in 2005 was estimated at 4.9 million people in EU 27 and accounted for 2.4 per cent of total employment.[31] The Communication highlights the importance of this sector stating that 'these industries and the creativity which they generate are an essential asset for Europe's economy and competitiveness in a context of globalization'. Of particular interest is the objective of developing 'creative partnerships between the cultural sector and other sectors (ICTs, research, tourism, social partners, etc) to reinforce the social and economic impact of investments in culture and creativity'. In view of the tensions between culture and the economy, and to protect cultural diversity and enhance media pluralism, the EU has always taken the position in WTO trade negotiations that certain cultural and audiovisual sub-sectors should not be liberalized (the so-called 'cultural exception').

Third, the EU seeks to promote culture as a vital element in the Union's international relations. Closely following the 2005 UNESCO Convention on the Protection and the Promotion of the Diversity of Cultural Expressions, the Community and the Member States have reaffirmed their commitment to developing a new and more proactive cultural role for Europe in its international relations and to integrating the cultural dimension as a vital element in Europe's dealings with partner countries and regions. The EU's intention here is 'to use its external and development policies to protect and promote cultural diversity through financial and technical support for, on the one hand, the preservation of and access to cultural heritage and, on the other, the active encouragement and promotion of cultural activities across the world.'

Additionally, the Council resolution includes five specific priority areas of action for the 2008–10 period:[32]

- to improve the conditions for the mobility of artists and other professionals in the cultural field;
- to promote access to culture, especially by promoting cultural heritage, cultural tourism, multilingualism, digitization, synergies with education (in particular arts education) and greater mobility of collections;
- to develop data, statistics and methodologies in the cultural sector and improve their comparability;
- to maximize the potential of the cultural and creative industries, in particular that of SMEs;
- to promote and implement the UNESCO Convention on the Protection and Promotion of the Diversity of Cultural Expressions.

Policy meetings will be held in European cultural forums in mid-2009 and at the end of 2010, when the first three-year cycle will be assessed.

The working plan for the agenda is based on the Open Method of Coordination (OMC), an intergovernmental framework for cooperation.

This, in turn, is based on benchmarking and spreading best practice, and works in four stages.[33] First, EU ministers agree on policy goals in the area concerned. Second, Member States translate these guidelines into national and regional policies, with specific targets. Third, the ministers agree on benchmarks and indicators, to measure and compare best practice within the EU and worldwide. Finally, through evaluation and monitoring, Member States' performances are assessed – relative to each other and to their declared goals. Advocates of this 'soft' (that is, not law-based) approach argue that it allows coordinated action in areas where it would be politically difficult, or even impossible, to move forward through a common policy or legal framework.

Hence every two years, the Commission and each Member State will jointly assess efforts made to achieve the objectives of the culture strategy. This approach does not challenge the cultural exception in the Treaty or the principle of subsidiarity (see chapter 1) in the field of culture. Today the OMC, which is a key mechanism in the Lisbon Strategy, is already used in other fields such as education, social protection and youth.

Critics fear, however, that the OMC is at best a talking shop and at worst a weapon against the traditional 'Community method' of European integration. The European employment strategy, established by the European Council in November 1997, provides an example of the OMC achieving positive results. The unanimously agreed guidelines cover policies ranging from active labour market measures to help for the long-term unemployed, to equal opportunities. In some cases, such as Spain and its labour market, the EU-wide policy consensus has helped governments to push through difficult reforms.[34] Only time will tell whether the OMC will be effective in the case of culture.

A short guide to the Culture Programme
If you want to discover your funding options under the EU's Culture Programme, you should do two things: first, go to the European Union's webpage for cultural matters.[35] Next, you *must* read the 73-page *Programme Guide Culture 2007–2013 from A to Z*,[36] with particular emphasis on eligibility criteria, selection criteria and award criteria,

and perhaps the most important thing: deadlines. There you find out
under which of three 'strands' your application may fall.[37] Receiving
funding under these strands, which cannot exceed 50 per cent of the
total budget, is based on cooperation between partners in different
countries participating in the Culture Programme. Since it is sometimes
hard to find appropriate foreign partners, the EU suggests you contact
your so-called 'Culture Contact Point' (CCP) [38] or visit the website
www.labforculture.org, which is a gathering spot for actors on the
European culture scene.

Strand one: supporting cultural action[39]
The thrust of this strand is to help organizations, such as theatres,
museums, professional associations, research centres, universities,
cultural institutes and public authorities from different countries
participating in the programme to cooperate so that different sectors
can work together and extend their cultural and artistic reach across
borders. Cooperation among cultural organizations receives the largest
share of the overall programme budget (approximately 77 per cent).

This strand is further divided into three sub-categories. The first
sub-category seeks to create multi-year, transnational cultural links
by encouraging a minimum of six cultural operators from at least six
eligible countries to cooperate and work across sectors to develop joint
cultural activities over a period of three to five years. EU support for
the actions is limited to half of the total eligible cost, up to a maximum
of €500,000 a year. The funding is intended to help set up or extend the
geographical reach of a project and make it sustainable beyond the
funding period.

The second sub-category concerns actions involving at least
three cultural operators, working across sectors, from at least three
eligible countries over a maximum period of two years. Actions that seek
to develop long-term cooperation are especially targeted. EU support
is limited to half of the total eligible cost and is set between €50,000
and €200,000. Literary translation projects are supported under this
sub-strand.

The third sub-category refers to high-profile actions of 'substantial scale and scope'. They should make an impact on European citizens and promote a sense of European identity. These actions are supposed to raise awareness and appreciation among citizens of the richness of Europe's cultural diversity and to contribute to intercultural dialogue. The European Capitals of Culture programme, supported within this sub-strand, has grown over two decades into one of Europe's major cultural events. A further aspect of this sub-strand is the award of prizes to celebrate artistic talent among young Europeans.

Strand two: supporting cultural organizations[40]
This strand is aimed at promoting a sense of shared cultural experience. To be eligible, applicant organizations must show 'a truly European dimension', whether individually or as a network, association or federation. Their influence should be felt in at least seven European countries, and preferably at the EU level as a whole. With a budget of approximately 10 per cent of the programme's overall budget, it provides co-financing for the permanent work of these organizations. Support is available for organizations engaged in providing representation at EU level, collecting or disseminating information to encourage trans-European cultural cooperation, networking at European level for cultural bodies, participating in cultural cooperation projects or acting as ambassadors for European culture. Festivals can also be funded. Implicitly the EU hopes that the work of these bodies will become a permanent feature of European cultural life. They produce publications, recordings and other products which means that their work can continue to circulate even after a specific event, tour or conference is over.

Strand three: supporting analysis and dissemination activities[41]
Representing about 5 per cent of the programme's budget, this strand supports analysis and dissemination activities in three ways. First, it funds studies to improve understanding of European cultural cooperation and the conditions that help it to flourish, including the mobility of cultural workers, the circulation of works of art and artistic and cultural products, and intercultural dialogue. Second, the

programme supports Cultural Contact Points (CCPs) in participating countries. CCPs promote the Culture Programme locally and raise awareness of its activities and the opportunities it offers among potential participants and citizens at large. Finally, by funding the collection and dissemination of information on the various EU-funded cultural activities and projects, this strand seeks to raise public awareness across the EU.

Grant criteria and procedures
In the Programme Guide we read that the award criteria form the basis for assessing the artistic and cultural quality of the proposals in relation to the general and specific objectives of the Programme as well as the focus and characteristics of each strand. There are two types of award: one for projects and one for operating costs, and the award criteria are defined for each strand. Eligible proposals are assessed by an evaluation committee composed of the Culture Unit of the Education, Audiovisual and Culture Executive Agency (EACEA) and Commission officials, assisted by independent experts from participating countries. The evaluation committee makes recommendations for the distribution of grants. It proposes a list of organizations or projects meriting a grant based on the scoring received. For all selections, the list of proposals to co-finance is submitted to the Programme Committee, composed of representatives of the eligible countries, for their opinion, and subsequently transmitted to the European Parliament for its 'right of scrutiny'.[42]

The final selection is made by the Programme Committee on the basis of qualitative and quantitative award criteria.[43] Just to give an example, for strand one, these are:
- the extent to which the project can generate real European added value as well as the European dimension of the proposed activities;
- the relevance of the activities to the specific objectives of the Programme;
- the extent to which the activities proposed are designed and can be carried out successfully with a high level of excellence;

- the quality of partnership between coordinator and co-organizers;
- the extent to which the activities can produce outputs which achieve the objectives of the Programme;
- the extent to which the results of activities proposed will be appropriately communicated and promoted;
- the extent to which the activities can generate a long-lasting impact (sustainability);
- the international cooperation dimension (only for cooperation projects in non-EU countries, strand 1.3).

Taking a closer look at these criteria, my attention is drawn to the first one, concerning 'real European added value as well as the European dimension of the proposed activities'. In this respect, general factors assessed by the EU are:[44]

- the extent to which the objectives, methodology and nature of the cooperation among cultural operators demonstrate an outlook that goes beyond local, regional or even national interests to develop synergies at European level;
- the extent to which proposed activities may have a greater effect, and their objectives can be better achieved, at European level than at national level;
- the extent to which cooperation and partnership are based on mutual exchange of experiences and would lead to a final result that differs qualitatively from the sum of the several activities undertaken at national level.

These assessment factors echo Dubravka Ugrešić's arguments for a European cultural policy we encountered in chapter 1. They aim to advance a less nationalistic concept of cultural expression.

Projects are assessed on scales from 0 to 25, 30, 35 or 40 points, depending on combinations of strand and project types. To be eligible for grants, projects must achieve a defined minimum score. Between the deadline for submission of applications and publication of selection results, consultations by groups of experts in a given application area take a minimum of six weeks.[45]

Cultural Contact Points – a helping hand

I have already mentioned the CCPs. With the exception of Liechtenstein, CCPs have been established in all countries participating in the Culture Programme. Their function is to promote the Culture Programme nationally and locally, and raise awareness of the funding opportunities it offers.[46] In Norway, the CCP is incorporated into Arts Council Norway both administratively and financially. According to its 2007 activity report, the Norwegian CCP essentially works as a European office devoted to dissemination of information and the implementation of the Culture Programme. The CCP is responsible for Culture Programme information seminars, which are followed by sessions of individual advisory meetings. There are three types of topic which usually arise during these sessions: is a project eligible to apply for EU Culture funding? If yes, how should it proceed? If no, where can it find other support? How does it find cultural operators and potential co-organizers? Most urgent, seemingly, is the need for technical assistance, especially in the weeks before application deadlines. CCPs also assist candidates in understanding EU vocabulary and award criteria, checking the budget's eligibility and considering project proposals.[47]

But in practical terms, how much help can a CCP provide? CCP Norway employs one person full time, Astrid Bjerke. When I met her at the CCP office, she clarified the role of a CCP: 'We never write the application directly, but assist the applicant through all stages of the process – exchange of ideas, finding partners and giving technical assistance to those who need it. People come to me at all stages in the process, from having loose ideas, to presenting almost ready applications. Some of them I work with for years. Some need help to understand the programme criteria, others are looking for partners. A few also want help to check the budget or other technical details. Not everybody uses the CCP service before they apply, though.' According to Bjerke, nearly all cultural fields are represented among applicants.

'Some regions are, however, more active than others, Bergen and Stavanger in particular. If I had to choose one sector that is especially active it would be literature; Norwegian publishers have been very active. In the latter years the dance sector also has been very well represented.'

In my view, the number of applications sent annually – about 15 – seems fairly low. But in Bjerke's view this is where the number should be. Assisting applicants and giving them hope while simultaneously providing them with a reality check is apparently an act of balance. 'It is very, very difficult to get funding from the Culture Programme. Even though the application process itself has been simplified, the criteria for funding are still quite intricate. Moreover, it's not merely a matter of applying; familiarity with routines and regulations in Brussels is almost obligatory. I guess that's why it is relevant for them to be directed towards other funding options that CCPs often know about. Not all of those we assist end up applying under the Culture Programme, some go elsewhere.'

This fact is reflected in the CCP's wider network. Although Arts Council Norway is the official CCP, Bjerke mentions several organizations and groups cooperating with Arts Council Norway that communicate the content of the Culture Programme to their respective environments, including the Ministry of Culture and Church Affairs, ABM-utvikling (Norwegian Archive, Library and Museum Authority), the Directorate for Cultural Heritage in Norway, other EU programmes that Norway participates in, the delegation of the European Commission to Norway and the Nordic Culture Fund.[48] Bjerke further informs me that one of the reasons why it has become more difficult to get funding from the EU is the increased popularity of the money pool, which has become way too small for the many big fish who want to swim in it. Hence, 'the independent cultural experts'[49] who evaluate the project proposals have little choice than to select the most professional and thorough applications and projects.

Could this lead to an elitist proclivity in the Culture Programme? Do popular culture projects, in the strict sense of the term, decline as a result of heightened professionalism at the EU's cultural offices? 'Let me put it this way,' says Bjerke, 'despite the fact that the EU wants to embrace a wide range of cultural operators and activities, developments in recent years have made it difficult for small actors to strike through in the competition. The big multi-annual projects consume a lot of the money, while most cultural actors in Europe are small and medium-sized and have to apply for the smaller so-called "cooperation measures".' Bjerke also points out, as the Programme Guide for the Culture Programme says, that the EU may also require any organization awarded a grant to provide a bank guarantee. The purpose of this guarantee is to make a bank or a financial institution, a third party or the other beneficiaries stand as irrevocable collateral security for, or first-call guarantor of, the grant beneficiary's obligations.

It is not easy to determine how influential a CCP is in the process of getting money from the EU. Even a highly qualified CCP, like Norway's Bjerke, is still only one person – a small staff to deal with the artistic variety of applications and potential number of applicants. The practical range of CCPs also varies from country to country, adds Bjerke. 'Some countries with low costs are perhaps able to be more active than those with higher expenses. The European Commission decides the co-financing ratio for the CCPs based on population, not staff and living costs in each country, which obviously vary significantly.'

As mentioned in chapter 1, cultural policies are instrumental on some level one way or another. But reasons differ. Does Bjerke, as a CCP, think it's possible to spot which objectives of the Culture Programme – grand ideological visions, cultural diversity, or art for art's sake – are decisive when committees select projects for financial support? 'My impression is that it is undoubtedly the artistic and professional qualities that are emphasized when applications to the Culture Programme are considered, and that the European added value is decisive for the outcome. The EU funding doesn't replace local, regional and national culture funds but has its own rationale; the money is intended to stimulate value beyond the national and to offer more than the sum of efforts by each country alone.'

Thoughts from Place Madou

At first glance, the text of the new agenda for culture seems very similar to former EU policy documents. So apart from more money, what's new? Let us return to Brussels and Xavier Troussard, acting Head of Unit for Culture, Directorate-General for Education and Culture, European Commission, whom I introduced in chapter 1. Troussard represented the EU in the negotiations concerning the UNESCO Convention on the Protection and the Promotion of the Diversity of Cultural Expressions from 2005 and led the negotiations deciding that 2008 would be heralded as European Year of Intercultural Dialogue (EYID).

Troussard explains to me that taken as a whole, the really big shift in European cultural policy is the changed attitude among Member States themselves. 'Before, what Member States did on culture was their thing,' he says with a smile. 'Now, what we say, and what has been accepted by the Member States and by the sectors is that, despite differences in respective competences – and precisely because national competences play a central role – we can recognize that we have common objectives.'

Since the early 1990s, anthropologist Cris Shore has criticized the EU for being culturally conservative and even Eurocentric. After revisiting the EU's cultural policies in a 2006 article, he concludes: 'Clearly "high culture" (opera, classical music and grand architecture) features prominently in EU conceptions of cultural action.' He further argues that 'in practice, ideas of popular culture, multiculturalism, cultural pluralism, and hybridity appear to be anathema to official conceptions of European culture.'[50] Troussard, on the other hand, claims that Shore exaggerates and that there are no obvious signals of conservatism in EU programmes. But, as Shore says, what about popular culture? Isn't the EU – supported by influential organizations like Europa Nostra,[51] the pan-European Federation for Cultural Heritage – more concerned about old buildings and museums than folk-punk-rockers like The Pogues or video exhibitionists on MySpace?

Troussard disagrees: 'I don't see how this could be substantiated. We are not here to say "rap is better or worse than Bach". I think it would be very dangerous to start with even a very positive idea such as that we should do more for popular culture or that we should do more for video games. If you look at the Culture Programme, there is nothing in it which could justify the formulation of criteria for judging the content of a project. Nor do you have anything which says that there is a priority for heritage or serious culture. It would be total suicide for an organization like the EU to begin selecting things on the basis of their content. And when you look more closely at the projects that have been selected, there is a lot of popular culture and a lot of contemporary expression.'

Although Shore may have a valid argument based on the general history of cultural policies at the EU, Troussard is right in describing where things are going. For years, the EU has supported the European Border Breaker Festival,[52] which truly covers pop music. The EU has no similar awards for opera. A new EU prize for contemporary literature, sponsored by the Culture Programme, will be awarded for the first time in 2009. Culture Programme statistics for 2008 also support Troussard's argument that the EU is not staunchly conservative.

Culture Programme: 2008 projects by theme

Theme	Number of projects
Literature, books and reading	113
Performing arts	90
Interdisciplinary	58
Cultural heritage	45
Visual arts	38
Design and applied arts	17
Multimedia and new technologies	15
Architecture	14
Innovation and creativity	6

Source http://eacea.ec.europa.eu/culture/infoday/documents08/pres/statistics.pdf

There are 45 awards for cultural heritage projects, for instance, and twice as many in performing arts.

It is clear, Troussard argues further, that popular culture is addressed, at least indirectly, in two of the EU's messages: 'One is about cultural industries and creativity, because most popular culture is linked to the economy of culture. The second is related to intercultural dialogue. We have recognized that one of the issues is to give a voice to those who are the most deprived on cultural expressions means. It leads to a preference given to activities or projects for those who are deprived of means of expression. Some of the expressions that come out from that will be popular culture, for example, rap and slam, as they are widely used for people to voice their own experiences, anger or whatever.'

It is reasonable to connect the new agenda for culture with previous EU initiatives on how to perceive and retell stories of the European experience, as discussed in chapter 2. According to Robert Stradling, author of *Teaching 20th Century European History*, published by the Council of Europe, much of the recent thinking about teaching European history has been influenced by a wider debate about whether Europe is best defined by its common cultural heritage or by its diversity.[53] Troussard thinks the one does not rule out the other: 'There is a need for contemporary reviews of heritage in the sense of showing what is common, what we may share, and what the meaning of our heritage is in our society today. You cannot create a thriving culture if you forget where you come from. This is also something we ask the sector to work on, because one of the clear distinctions and often a clashing tendency in the cultural sector, is between heritage people who want money for restoring beautiful pieces of architecture, who are not always interested in the educational process needed to transmit its value on the one side, and on the other side the contemporary creation sector, which often looks at heritage as a thing of the past we can forget about. So I think, at the European level, you need both sides.'

Related to this issue is CLIOH.net (Creative Links and Innovative Overviews to Enhance Historical Perspective in European Culture). This is a Socrates-Erasmus Thematic Network founded in 1988 to address the task of bringing the study of history and a critically founded historical perspective to bear on the challenges facing European society and education today.[54] Also related is CLIOHRES.net (Creating Links and Innovative Overviews for a New History Research Agenda for the Citizens of a Growing Europe),[55] a Sixth Framework Programme Network of Excellence organized by 45 universities, many of which are CLIOH.net members.

Geir Atle Ersland is a historian working at the Centre for Medieval Studies (CMS), University of Bergen, which, since 2004, has been a member of CLIOH.net. He says that CLIOH.net is an active network: 'While Western Europe has left behind the period where national identity was developed, history is still a profession open to national interpretation for the new European countries.' Moreover, since the EU is instrumental in the project, it opens up, according to Ersland, methodological possibilities: 'A supranational history project like this may function as a counterweight to history as a national identity builder.'[56]

Such reflections upon critical questions of teaching and learning history are interesting in light of that part of the Communication concerning intercultural dialogue. Multiculturalism brings along a series of challenges, says Troussard, in particular how to deal with European diversity itself: 'In intercultural dialogue we're looking at two different challenges. The first is that there are 27 countries rooted in different histories. We need to know each other better to understand the richness of diversity, but we also need to discuss it, since we do not necessarily have the same feelings about the things we may have to decide on. Leaving immigration aside, cultures rooted in European history are different. Our model is not the model of the melting pot; our model is that we keep our identities, and we feel that it is very important to keep them.'

The second set of challenges relates to integration and migration. With apocalyptic warnings about 'Eurabia' at one extreme, naïve embrace of multiculturalism at the other, and a very large space to fill in the middle, the EU has a difficult task. Troussard reflects this difficulty when he observes: 'diversity is growing due to migration from within the EU but also from outside the EU. The positive is totally different, depending on the country. In some countries there is immigration – some countries have second or third generations of immigrants – and others have historical minorities like the Roma. This is also a concern in the cultural sector itself, because the cultural sector should be able to provide a space for expression for all those living in a society. There is a problem of inclusiveness in the cultural sector itself.'

Both of these aspects, as we will explore in greater depth in the next chapter, affect discussions about values. 'For us,' Troussard says, 'cultural diversity embraces to some extend diversity of values. Of course, to live together in any society, you need to strike a deal, recognizing some fundamental values. It is true that on a European level we don't have a real formulation of those common values, but we have a transcription of some of them into rights – human rights and fundamental freedoms. Should we go further? I don't know, but in any society you have a permanent discussion about values.' On a more philosophical level, Troussard points out the difficulties with the concept of culture itself: 'The problem is to move from an essentialist vision of cultures to a conception of culture where we recognize that any individual is a mosaic of different heritages and influences, and to make this hierarchy of values decide our lifestyle. We are all different but with a major point of connection: we're all citizens. And as citizens, of course we have to debate whenever an element of this diversity may have an impact on the life of the community.'

Bridging the social capital of Europe

Central in invigorating cultural life in Europe is civil society. As defined by the London School of Economics Centre for Civil Society, it refers to 'the arena of uncoerced collective action around shared interests, purposes and values'.[57] In theory, its institutional forms are distinct from those of the state, family and market. In practice, the boundaries between these arenas are often complex, blurred and negotiated. Therefore, since the EU seems reluctant to create supra-national efforts in the cultural area, and since most Member States seemingly have little intention yet of transferring more decisive power to the EU, one unifying cause could be reinforcing the potential of civil society.

The American political scientist, Robert D Putnam, for one, has argued that non-political organizations in civil society are vital because they recharge democracy, so to speak, by building social capital, trust and shared values. These are transferred into the political sphere and help to hold society together, facilitating an understanding of the interconnectedness of society and interests within it. Putnam, however, distinguishes between bridging and bonding social capital. The latter means getting involved with people like ourselves. In the worst case, bonding social capital can serve to reinforce our pre-existing beliefs including our prejudices.[58] Bridging social capital, on the other hand, develops when you get involved with people who are less like yourself. Charles Hauss writes that it may be as simple as getting involved in your neighbourhood association or organizing interfaith dialogues on divisive political issues. By doing this, Hauss argues, we can discover not only the issues we disagree about, but also areas where we do agree and can work together. We develop trust and toleration. Our community's social life literally becomes more civil.[59]

In this connection, a project worth attention is the Swedish foundation Fryshuset. When it began in 1984, sports and music were the dominant activities, but as young people began to shape and influence the place, social engagement started to grow as a reflection of the needs of society at large.[60] One of the projects supported by Fryshuset is called Sharaf's Heroes (Sharafs hjältar), a project of the Swedish anti-racism organization Elektra.[61] Founded in the wake of the tragic honour-killing murder of the Swedish-Kurdish girl Fadime Sahindal in 2002, Elektra, through Sharaf's Heroes, focuses on how young Muslim men can be helped to change patronizing attitudes and conduct inside patriarchal cultures such as honour-related repression and violence. Based on research showing that young men are often imbued with honour culture attitudes by their peers and by family members, the most effective way of combating these attitudes would be by engaging young men themselves. Put simply, the strategy is to ally with liberal Muslims and have them fight undesirable attitudes from within.

Concentrating on working class Muslim men aged 17 and older, representatives of Sharaf's Heroes offer real-life alternative role models in contrast to street gangsters or violent fathers, without abandoning their Muslim heritage, beliefs and values. Sharaf's Heroes arrange well-attended courses, plays and lectures. In March

2008, the organization received an award from the Swedish Minister
for Integration and Gender Equality. Internationally, Sharaf's Heroes
has established bonds with radical French feminist organization 'Ni
Putes Ni Soumises' (Neither Whores Nor Submissives, founded by
French-Algerian Fadela Amara),[62] Transact and New Scotland Yard.

Certainly, these efforts confirm the value of bridging social
capital and the view of Odile Quintin, Director General for Education
and Culture, who maintains that 'it is decisive that the work [in creating
an intercultural dialogue] begins and evolves in local communities'.[63]
There are many difficulties in actually making this work as a European
integration asset, including cultural things, like languages. Xavier
Troussard explains why: 'As soon as you look at any problem from the
perspective of 27 Member States, things are complex. And you have
to be able to translate this complexity in a way that is understandable
for people.' Troussard's solution is not only voices and direct
communication, but also mediators and translators: 'We have to bring
in people from grassroots organizations to explore commonalities
and explain that they can have a say when moving in the direction they
wish,' he says. 'But the tendency is for them to get stuck in a kind of grey
area. As soon as external stakeholders have specialized to understand
what is going on in Brussels, a gap opens up between them and the
grassroots; so called "lobbies" have a big problem translating the
grassroots language to Brussels and vice versa.'

Civil society actors have attempted incrementally to come to
grips with these perplexities. In October 2006, the European Culture
Foundation and European Forum for the Arts and Heritages (EFAH,
now Culture Action Europe, CAE) began an effort to draw the wider
cultural sector into their thinking on diversity issues and to forge
crucial links with other organizations with related concerns. The Civil
Society Platform for Intercultural Dialogue's effort is based on the
conviction that the arts and culture can facilitate intercultural dialogue
and reduce tensions and conflicts. The Platform seeks to organize an
exchange of best practice in intercultural dialogue and to formulate
policy recommendations for the political system from which the EYID
initiative emanated.

A group of seven foundations – the Culture Cluster of the
Network of European Foundations (NEF)[64] – initiated the project. A
small secretariat was set up within EFAI and operations began. In
its first year the Platform organized two plenary meetings, conducted
a Europe-wide consultation, held a three-day evaluation seminar and
undertook a multi-stage drafting process which led to the first edition
of The Rainbow Paper ('Practice Makes Perfect: A Learning Framework
for Intercultural Dialogue'), presented at the EYID opening in Ljubljana
on 7 January 2008. The Platform also contributed to the Council of
Europe's consultation for its White Paper, and is part of the European
Commission's Contact Group for the EYID, together with the European
Youth Forum[65] and the Social Platform. In 2007, the Civil Society Platform
conducted a European-wide consultation in four languages, which asked
eight questions on how to improve and encourage intercultural dialogue.
The mobilization efforts of the networks active in the Platform were very
successful: over 120 contributions were made from 28 countries in two
and a half months. Organizations from Azerbaijan to Portugal gave their
ideas and experiences on intercultural dialogue. The response from
Eastern and South-eastern Europe was 'unexpectedly strong'.

The results of this consultation confirm that those concerned
with intercultural dialogue work on many different issues, including
diversity due to migration, East-West rapprochement, and reconciliation
after violent conflict. Others refrain from a problem-oriented approach.
They posit that intercultural dialogue should be a natural process
that emphasizes education, civic participation, social responsibility
and dynamism, good communication and creativity, and they make
proposals for additional progress in these fields.[66] By the end of 2007,
over 200 organizations from various levels and sectors (youth, culture,
migration, anti-discrimination, lifelong learning, etc) had participated
in one or more of the Platform's activities. Requests for participation
continue to grow, especially since the European Commission has
proposed that the Platform become part of the 'structured dialogue'
between the EU and civil society.

On 25 September 2008, Platform coordinator Sabine Frank
presented the final version of The Rainbow Paper ('Intercultural

Dialogue: From Practice to Policy and Back') for EU endorsement. What distinguishes this document from academic research, like that carried out by experts on cultural policies in the EU, is that it is a 'participatory exercise' and a 'complement to the raft of policy documents'.[67] Additionally, The Rainbow Paper should be commended for its insight that we should stop identifying conflicts in our interaction with others as culturally and ethnically motivated when they are often actually rooted in socio-economic and political inequalities. Also laudable is its acknowledgement that organizations, private or public, require time and effort to build the necessary capacities for change, despite an impatient political environment.

One can argue that trying to bridge socio-economic disparities with intercultural dialogue, while arguing that cultural differences are not at the centre of the problem, is somewhat contradictory. However, The Rainbow Paper argues in a matter-of-fact way that political differences and conflicts can be mitigated through cultural collaboration. A much-quoted example elsewhere is the East-West Divan Orchestra, founded by Argentine-Israeli conductor Daniel Barenboim and the late Palestinian-American academic Edward Said. The young musicians are Israeli, Palestinian, Lebanese, Syrian, Jordanian and Egyptian. Through its activities the Orchestra gives hope that the Arab-Israeli conflict – one of the worst in human history, and at the time of writing still drowning in death and tragedy with the war on the Gaza strip – can be resolved.[68]

Returning to my conversation with Troussard, he concluded by emphasizing the desire among his colleagues at Place Madou to be a driving force in developing European culture: 'It is a clear commitment by the Commission not to invent a new bureaucratic or talking process, but to drive it to concrete results. We want this development to be time-bound; it shouldn't be an open-ended process that you never evaluate. Therefore we have a forum where we test ideas and recommendations in mid-2009 and a kind of wrapping-up forum at the end of 2010 to look at the progress in all areas and map the next steps, if any. We are very keen on evaluating, through this work plan, whether we really have succeeded in identifying ideas that Member States and the cultural sector can incorporate into their policies, and to better understand where there could be a community added value.'

Will they make it? After my meeting with Troussard, I went out into the streets of Brussels with a feeling that the EU has never been more dedicated to giving culture a real chance. It may be a long walk, as I will discuss in the following chapters, but the very fact that culture is acknowledged as an important dimension of a successful European Union is fertile ground for those optimistic about the future of European integration.

[1] Remember that EU architect Robert Schuman (1886–1963), for instance, was also one of the founding fathers of the European Cultural Foundation in 1954.

[2] See for instance www.culturalpolicies.org

[3] Obuljen, 2004; see also Banús, 2007.

[4] McCormick, 2008: 8–9. See also Monnet, 1976.

[5] Shore, 2006: 12.

[6] Smith, 2003.

[7] Duelund, 2008a.

[8] Duhamel, 2002: 83.

[9] Duhamel, 2002: 85.

[10] European Council, 1973.

[11] Stråth, 2002.

[12] European Commission, 1977.

[13] Obuljen, 2004: 129.

[14] Lang, 2002: 114.

[15] Lang, 2002: 116.

[16] Theiler, 2005: 96–7.

[17] www.inclusiveeurope.hu/index. php?page=declaration_en

[18] http://ec.europa.eu/culture/our-programmes-and-actions/doc413_en.htm

[19] Conceptually related to Capitals of Culture is the Alliance of European Cultural Cities (AVEC). Among other things, it has launched the RESIDE project which has allowed five partners in Europe and one in Tunisia to create a cooperation network to ensure the quality of the products for tourists on Roman archaeological sites. See www.avecnet.com

[20] Theiler, 1999.

[21] See Theiler, 1999, and Mokre, 2006, for discussions.

[22] http://ec.europa.eu/culture/archive/sources_info/evaluation/pdf_word/culture2000_final_report/COM_2008_231_1_EN_ACT_part1_v4.pdf

[23] Ruffolo, 2001: 8.

[24] www.kulturparlament.com

[25] European Commission, 2007c.

[26] http://ec.europa.eu/regional_policy/funds/prord/sf_en.htm. For an introduction to how they work, see www.cultureactioneurope.org/advocate/glossary?p=structural-funds

[27] European Commission, 2007a.

[28] http://ec.europa.eu/culture/focus/focus1087_en.htm

[29] European Commission, 2007c.

[30] http://europa.eu/rapid/pressReleasesAction.do?reference=IP/07/646

[31] EuroStat, 2007: 51.

[32] http://europa.eu/rapid/pressReleasesAction.do?reference=IP/07/1709&format=HTML&aged=0&language=EN&guiLanguage=en

[33] Hughes, 2001.

[34] Hughes, 2001.

[35] http://ec.europa.eu/culture/index_en.htm

[36] European Commission, 2007b.

[37] http://ec.europa.eu/culture/our-programmes-and-actions/doc411_en.htm

[38] http://ec.europa.eu/culture/annexes-culture/doc1232_en.htm

[39] http://eacea.ec.europa.eu/culture/guide/strand_1_1/funding_en.htm

[40] http://eacea.ec.europa.eu/culture/guide/strand_1_2_1/funding_en.htm

[41] http://eacea.ec.europa.eu/culture/calls2007/strand_3_2/index_en.htm

[42] European Commission, 2007b: 20.

[43] European Commission, 2007b: 37–40.

[44] European Commission, 2007b: 38.

[45] European Commission, 2007b: 13. In the past, the names of these experts were publicly disclosed. Under the current Culture Programme, their identities are secret.

[46] http://ec.europa.eu/culture/annexes-culture/doc1232_en.htm

[47] Arts Council Norway, 2007.

[48] www.nordiskkulturfond.org/?sc_lang=en

[49] About these experts, see: http://eacea.ec.europa.eu/about/procurement/eacea_2007_experts/index_en.htm

[50] Shore, 2006: 18–19.

[51] www.europanostra.org. They describe themselves as 'the representative platform of over 250 heritage NGOs active in 45 countries across Europe. It is the voice of this vast movement of European civil society active in the field of heritage towards international bodies concerned, in particular the European Union Institutions, the Council of Europe and UNESCO.'

[52] www.european-border-breakers.eu

[53] Stradling, 2001: 230.

[54] www.clioh.net

[55] www.cliohres.net

[56] Cited in Espeland, 2008.

[57] www.lse.ac.uk/collections/CCS/what_is_civil_society.htm

[58] Putnam, 2000. See also Hauss, 2003.

[59] Hauss, 2003.

[60] www.fryshuset.se/archive/pdf/english_version2.0.pdf

[61] *Sharaf* is Arabic for honour.

[62] For more about this organization, see Hillauer, 2005.

[63] Isaksen, 2008.

[64] These are Compagnia di San Paulo, European Cultural Foundation, Evens Foundation, Freundenberg Stiftung, King Baudouin Foundation, Riksbankens Jubileumsfond and the Van Leer Group Foundation. In March 2008, the Bernheim Foundation joined the partnership. Other members of NEF can be found at www.nefic.org/members.php

[65] The European Youth Forum (YFJ) is a platform made up of 96 National Youth Councils and international youth NGOs from across Europe. See www.youthforum.org

[66] ECF, 2007b.

[67] LabforCulture, 2008.

[68] Allow me a small globalization anecdote here: the orchestra is named after an anthology of poems by Johann Wolfgang von Goethe (1749–1832), *West-östlicher Divan* (1819) or *West-Eastern Divan*. This *Diwan* (poetry), or collection of lyrical poems, was inspired by the 14th century Persian poet Hafez. The famous Indian poet Muhammad Iqbal (1877–1938) wrote his *Payam-i-Mashriq* (*The Message of the East*) as a reply to Goethe's Diwan.

4 The ambiguity of intercultural dialogue

The first point on the EU's agenda for culture is intercultural dialogue. Looking at the way people across Europe eat Indian food and drink Czech beer, and write academic essays in EFL (English as a Foreign Language) about the oil industry in South America on Japanese computers with American software, such an element seems nothing short of mandatory in any cultural policy. But how does the EU's map for intercultural dialogue fit the cultural landscape of contemporary Europe? And what should we think when a survey which sought a reaction to the phrase 'Intercultural dialogue in Europe' found quite a large percentage (36 per cent) could not attribute any particular meaning to it?[1] With reference to thinkers such as Thomas Hylland Eriksen, Ian Buruma and Francis Fukuyama, I use this chapter to discuss how to embark upon these issues.

To cope with cultural complexity in the 21st century all European countries have engaged in some form of multicultural policy. There are, however, great variations in how they are carried out. Sociology Professor Stuart Hall pins down no less than six multiculturalisms: conservative, liberal, pluralist, commercial, corporate and critical or 'revolutionary' multiculturalism. Each has its own distinctive approach to the central problem in modern societies, namely how to reconcile cultural diversity with societal solidarity.[2] At the same time, as Professor of Social Anthropology Thomas Hylland Eriksen points out, concerns about gender roles, political loyalties, democratic values and religious rigidity have turned 'the question of integration' into a political issue of the first order.[3] No wonder that multiculturalism has become an open sesame in some milieus and a four-letter word in others. So what about the EU?

In order simultaneously to bring European cultural heritage to the fore and recognize the contribution of all cultures present in European societies, the agenda for culture states that cultural diversity needs to be nurtured in a context of openness and exchange.[4] A few specific policy aims have been identified to ensure that Europe exploits its cultural diversity to the full. These include using public and private resources to promote the mobility of artists and professionals in the cultural field, as well as their works. Intercultural competences can, according to the EU, be enhanced by developing cultural awareness and expression, by cultivating social and civic competences and by improving communication in foreign languages. The agenda will also support European cultural bodies and stimulate creativity by giving recognition to major European cultural achievements through European prizes in architecture, cultural heritage and music, as well as supporting the well-established European Capitals of Culture.

Moreover, the EU designated 2008 as the European Year of Intercultural Dialogue (EYID) to raise the profile of such exchanges and to help establish a sustainable strategy. Due to the fact that 'Europe is becoming more culturally diverse', the EU states on EYID 2008's website that 'intercultural dialogue has an increasingly important role to play in fostering European identity and citizenship'. Following an open call for proposals, the Commission therefore co-financed a small number of 'emblematic actions' on a European scale in order to raise awareness of the objectives of the EYID and underline the benefits of intercultural dialogue. A total of €2.4 million was dedicated to the co-financing of these actions. The Commission received almost 300 proposals competing for a small number of flagship project grants.[5] These, in turn, came out of a variety of cultural expressions from all over Europe.[6]

Odile Quintin, Director General for Education and Culture, is one of many who refuse to equate dialogue with agreement. Dialogue, in her eyes, is to listen to the other and understand what he or she is saying. 'One can agree to disagree,' she says, 'that's also part of a dialogue.'[7] Nevertheless, some disagreements can't last forever, and over the last couple of years, this progressively worn topic has engaged Europeans in a variety of forms and as a result been made flesh in a variety of issues. Hijabs, Muhammad caricatures, uproar in the French suburbs, female circumcision, the killing of filmmaker Theo van Gogh, abortion issues, childcare, welfare discussions, secularization debates – all are examples of how not all borderlines within multicultural countries are given. Neither are the judgements on how to define them unanimous, nor the means for dealing with them to be found in everyday life.

Obviously, immigration to, and within, European countries is of vital importance. In 2007 the European Commission launched a new programme to cooperate with countries outside the EU (so-called 'third countries') in the areas of migration and asylum with a budget of €380 million for 2007–13. The focus will be countries along the southern and eastern migratory routes towards the European Union, although other migratory routes as well as south-south migrations will also be covered. Commissioner for External Relations and European Neighbourhood Policy (ENP), Benita Ferrero-Waldner, believes that the programme will 'contribute to a better and more balanced management of migration in a true spirit of partnership with other countries, which for us also includes the fruitful exchanges between our citizens and cultures'.[8] Thematically speaking, the programme covers all the essential aspects of migration. For the first four years (2007–10), the programme will dispose of an allocation of €205 million. Following an evaluation that will take place in 2009, the programme will enter its second and final phase in the period 2011–13 with an additional allocation of €175 million.[9]

Difference versus diversity
Much of this effort (rightly) concentrates on the socioeconomic aspects of migration. On a more fundamental, cultural level, the strategy for culture is suffering from its reluctance to take a stand in more

controversial cases than Finns munching tapas or Norwegian teenagers flocking to Spanish fashion chain Zara. A precondition for making intercultural dialogue work, it seems, is a clearer notion of how the dialogue is set, and under which circumstances dialogue is no longer an option.

In general, celebrations of 'cultural diversity' are considered politically uncontroversial. Opposition, with a few exceptions, to what pejoratively has been nicknamed 'the multicultural project' is left in the hands of right-wing politicians, conservative commentators and blogs. But there is another side of this that has been surprisingly understated in the European debate. Allowing a variety of cultural expressions to burgeon has been recognized as a fundamental value in most societies. Values are not independent of culture, as we have discovered in the previous chapters, and which is obvious from reading Hall's harangue on multiculturalism.

Eriksen therefore proposes a simple contrast in order to highlight two fundamentally distinctive ways of dealing with, and identifying, cultural variation.[10] Diversity, he concludes, is largely associated, by organizations like UNESCO and in the European debate on immigration and multiculturalism, with phenomena such as rituals, food, folktales, arts and crafts, as well as a 'few traditional economic adaptations which are either threatened by modernity or proven to be consistent with it (and should by that token be given a chance)'. The organization of society, including its political structure and voting rights, human rights, its kinship structure and rules of inheritance, its gender roles and educational system, its labour market and its health service – in other words signifiers of *difference* – are kept separate from the notion of diversity. 'There is in fact nothing in the report,' Eriksen writes, 'which suggests that its authors regard child marriages, political despotism or religious intolerance as expressions of creative forms of diversity.'[11]

Broadly speaking, we may state that diversity is seen as a good thing, while difference is not. While there is considerable support for diversity in the public sphere, difference is increasingly seen as a main cause of social problems associated with immigrants and their descendants.[12] This is more than an academic concept. Social

psychologist Sandra Jovchelovitch writes that in the contemporary
matrix of multiculturalism 'difference loses a certain idealised and
abstract character to become real and something to deal with, upsetting
usual parameters of self-understanding and the enactment of social
practices'.[13] As documented through a series of surveys by Human
Rights First and the Pew Research Center, unfavourable opinions, hate
crimes and violence against religious minorities and homosexuals have
proliferated in Europe in the last years.[14] A 2008 survey done by Pew
reveals that fully half of Spanish (52 per cent) and German respondents
(50 per cent) consider Muslims unfavourably.[15] In plays like *The Veiled
Monologues* and *Is.Man*, written and directed by Adelheid Roosen and
based on a collection of real-life testimonies by women from a variety of
Arabic countries now living in the Netherlands, the schism is illuminated
by stories of love, sex and relationships.

In this case it can be useful to take a closer look at an essay by the
conservative American political scientist Francis Fukuyama. Looking at
Europe as an outsider, and in a different style from like-minded European
thinkers like Pascal Bruckner and Bernard Henri-Levy, he offers some
challenging insights on matters of European identity.[16] His point of
departure is how, after the Second World War, European institutions
like the EU have made a lot of effort to integrate the European nations.
Being a product of elites, this effort has nevertheless failed to resonate
among the European public. His view is that modern identity is
'inherently political, because it demands recognition'. Unfortunately,
Fukuyama continues, it appears that universal recognition based on
a shared individual humanity is not enough. In particular this goes for
groups that have been discriminated against in the past. Hence modern
identity politics revolves around demands for recognition of the group
identities of 'formerly marginalized groups', from the Québécois to
African-Americans, women, indigenous peoples and homosexuals.
Migration and EU enlargement add another layer of difficulty to this, in
particular when it comes to Muslims, Fukuyama argues.

Interpreting Fukuyama this way, the outcome of intercultural
dialogue is not multicultural synchronization, but destabilizing
ambivalence. Together with a traditional reluctance among European

politicians to deal with sensitive cultural issues (excepting those who are completely lunatic about them), which increase as politicians continue to avoid the difficult questions, the result seems to be a seeping polarization. Scepticism about whether Muslim immigrants really want to adopt the majority values increases in direct proportion to the growing suspicion with which Muslims who actually want to become a part of their new home country are greeted. Meanwhile, in the battle for recognition, Muslim culture, in all its richness and aesthetic miscellany, sometimes becomes perverted into radical identity politics. In some the struggle for identity even inspires terrorist acts, as documented by Olivier Roy in his study *Globalized Islam*.[17]

Fukuyama, though, ignores the furore created by the early versions of the Treaty establishing a Constitution for Europe (TCE), so famously rejected by the Irish by referendum in 2008. These versions said that the EU was inspired by the cultural, religious and humanistic heritage of Europe. Countries like Poland, Ireland and Spain argued that the text should be changed and that Christianity was the right thing to emphasize as expressing the collective European identity.[18] It was but one sign that these countries have strengthened the influence of Catholic and orthodox churches upon European politics, and extended the conservative dimension to issues like Treaty texts, women's rights, stem cell research, homosexuality and HIV/AIDS in Europe.[19]

Fukuyama is also less concerned about the internal cultural transitions that have become apparent with the latest EU enlargement. Although he mentions Poland as an example of the new face of migration (to Western Europe, mind you), the fact that cultural divides and transitions in Eastern Europe – as I presented glimpses of in chapter 2 – are more complex than 'getting back in', is relegated in favour of Fukuyama's eagerness to point out the threat of Islam. While some studies give a negative view of Europeans in terms of levels of intolerance, a 2007 Eurobarometer survey on intercultural dialogue shows other aspects of the picture.[20] Almost three-quarters of the 27,000 respondents (72 per cent) believe that people with a different background (ethnic, religious and national) enrich the cultural life of their country; while roughly a quarter (23 per cent) of citizens disagree with that idea. At the same time a majority of Europeans found intercultural dialogue beneficial; two-thirds also said that carrying on cultural traditions is equally important.

To me, this complexity surrounding the term 'intercultural dialogue' begs the question of what to do about the diversity-difference axis. At a seminar arranged by the research programme Cultural Complexity in the New Norway (Culcom) at the University of Oslo, Ian Buruma, author of *Murder in Amsterdam*,[21] suggested from a politically liberal point of view that the line should be settled in court. The reason was that most European countries have legislation which protects individuals as well as groups from acts of aggression and slander. Basically, if you're insulted, sue'em. However, this argument is unsatisfactory inasmuch as it doesn't concern power differences. Not everybody has the money or the time to go to court if they feel they are being discriminated against. Fear of losing their jobs is another factor here. Discrimination also has 'silent' effects. A scene from Marjaneh Bakhtiari's *Kall det hva faen du vil* (literally, 'Call it what the fuck you want'), an 'immigrant novel' as they are called in Scandinavia for some reason, illustrates this with tender precision. When three young boys with Asian backgrounds enter a bus, it suddenly becomes claustrophobic inside; moans fill the air and hands take firm grips of purses and wallets. Prejudice, without anything being said, results in suspicion and bigoted practice.

The culturalizing syndrome

Any way we look at it, European identity and culture, as discussed in chapter 2, is based on comparison with others. Establishing a self-understanding requires difference. In light of Buruma's book it is, however, not easy to see what kind of difference should be given immediate notice: economic, social or cultural. The story of Mohammed Bouyeri, the murderer of Theo van Gogh, is distinctively Dutch, but, at the same time, disturbingly similar to the stories of the 7/7 and the Madrid bombers and even to that of 9/11 man Mohamed Atta, who was radicalized in Hamburg. Geraldine Bedell wrote in a review of *Murder in Amsterdam* that 'you can see the same initial attraction to European lifestyles: sex and drugs and alcohol and partying; the same sense of rootlessness, of feeling neither one thing nor the other; the same influence of a radical imam and the seeking out of Islamist tracts on the internet; the same global sense of Muslim victimhood.'[22]

To get some more answers, I took the train from Brussels to Amsterdam to meet Gottfried Wagner, Director of the European Cultural Foundation (ECF). With its atmospheric network of canals and brick houses, this 'Venice of the North' is quite a contrast to the somewhat faceless Brussels. It quickly becomes clear that Wagner, being in possession of a hawk's-eye view of what's going in Europe, thinks the situation is too intricate for simple answers. 'The notion of violence is complex,' Wagner says, and gives an example from Rotterdam: 'Recently there was an uprising there when the government was blamed for violating human rights, because they constantly made their way into the homes of immigrant families to observe how they behaved. In fact, in most societies of Europe, there is no neglect of rules. On the contrary, there is an increase of surveillance and the enforcement of rules has become tougher. Increasingly the state enforces alarmist views that overlook other reasons for integration problems.'

Wagner is right that fear is a keyword in European immigration politics. According to the political scientist Ulrik Pram Gad, one could argue that nearly all majority solutions for improving integration are based on the following caricatured scenario: generally, the discussion begins with defining us and them. 'They' are the immigrants, or to be more precise *the Muslims*, since the Chinese and Poles are usually left out of the discussion if Muslim examples are available. 'We' are the ethnic Norwegians or Danes or whatever, claiming – with UNESCO approval – the right to protect 'our' culture the way we have defined it. In order to preserve this, they need education (or else they will abuse the welfare state that we have built), society needs to disperse ghettos (thus dissolving the threat to national homogeneity) and we need to fight excessive crime statistics among immigrants (to keep our society peaceful).[23]

According to Wagner, and reading Buruma's book once more, social disruption is by any measure more complex than relatively eye-striking cultural variations. Referring to a speech by Dutch Minister for European Affairs Frans Timmermans, Wagner believes it has a lot to do with neglecting other factors. 'The middle class is mesmerized by the fear of losing what they have rather than striving for something more. And that has to do with globalization and consumption and production around the globe. He [Timmermans] pleads for a reinvention of the social democratic analysis of the socio-economic ruptures caused by diversity. Unfortunately there are no answers within political parties. Because of the silence of the political class when it comes to real questions and answers, changes make people afraid and drive them to culturalize differences.'

It is, however, not only the alarmist attitude of the political right that contributes to 'culturalization', that is, in the words of philosopher Slavoj Zizek, social variations conditioned by political ideologies and economic inequality that are naturalized into 'cultural differences'.[24] Many on the left and in the centre of politics also uphold the idea of culture as the centre of all things, countering the populist right by defending a rather relativistic idea of multiculturalism. Both sides – on either majority or minority level – overemphasize the idea that 'individuals are determined by their culture, that these cultures form closed, organic wholes, and that the individual is unable to leave his or her own culture but rather can only realise him or herself within it.'[25] They also overlook what Gottfried Wagner has written elsewhere, that 'inequality of social and economic resources affects both individuals and groups; educational backgrounds determine the ability to deal with diversity, on "both sides".'[26] This mirrors much of the EU's stand on immigration. None the less, the cultural sides of the issue of what holds society together beyond formal agreements in our 'liquid times', as sociologist Zygmunt Baumann phrases it,[27] have begun to make their way into the political corridors and governments.

Developments like those in Denmark and Austria where the political right has gained voters by enforcing stricter immigration policies are illustrative. In the Netherlands, the Dutch government has launched a national cultural canon. In Great Britain, New Labour and political movements on the left discuss prospects of a 'progressive nationalism' in answer to the cultural policies of Anglo-Saxon conservatives and their nationalist investments in social and cultural discussions. In Serbia radical neo-nationalist movements are nourished by myths and propelled by demands to legitimize the return of lost territories. France has even given birth to a Ministry for Immigration and National Identity.[28] This revitalizing of national pride in some form or the other can be interpreted, as hinted at by Fukuyama above, as a reaction to what's perceived as a greater distance between the common people and the cosmopolitan elites and the (allegedly) cultural self-confidence of certain immigrant groups.

In order to regain control over their own fate some turn to 'strategic essentialism', that is, purposely activated rhetorical constructs that 'they' are threatening 'us' – as shown above – which, regardless of their level of realism, are nevertheless highly effective in mobilizing an 'us' identity. But there are also aspects like those posed by the above-mentioned Timmermans, who in his speech also said that 'I believe there should be more self-confidence in politics to stand for the rules of public space, to defend them and demand of everyone that they abide by those rules and don't use cultural differences as an excuse not to abide by those rules.'[29] Often, though, this political dish comes with a very vague sense of the gap between diversity and difference. Islam is often demonized, while the Alhambra palace in Spain – once the residence of the Muslim rulers of Granada and now one of Spain's major tourist attractions – is not.

The desire for recognition

The reason why I have chosen to write about this dualism at such length is that in search of a European identity and culture, I believe it to be a fundamental exercise of thought and policy path finding. What if we return to Francis Fukuyama? Despite his rather rudimentary idea of Europe touched upon above, he has a two-phased solution which principally draws on Buruma and gives practical nods towards Wagner. 'The first prong of the solution,' he writes, 'is to recognise that the old multicultural model has not been a big success in countries such as the Netherlands and Britain.' To continue the idea of cultural diversity as a common good needs more energetic efforts to integrate all sorts of people into a common liberal culture. To do this, Fukuyama argues, we need to get away from multiculturalism based on what's called the politics of group recognition and group rights. Professor John Erik Fossum contextualizes the argument by saying that within the politics of recognition there is a deep tension between the universalist thrust for equal dignity and the particularist thrust for difference and uniqueness, both of which are well entrenched at international, European and national levels.[30]

This also echoes the moral philosophy of Professor Axel Honneth, and before him G W F Hegel (1770–1831), where 'the struggle for recognition' (a universal right) is at the heart of social identity and social conflicts. Positive discrimination of minority groups, as it were, therefore poses an ethical contradiction when faced with claims of democratic equality.[31] Fukuyama's main response to this is that 'liberalism cannot ultimately be based on group rights, because not all groups uphold liberal values. The civilization of the European Enlightenment, of which contemporary liberal democracy is the heir, cannot be culturally neutral, since liberal societies have their own values regarding the equal worth and dignity of individuals.' As a result, people advocating cultural values that do not accept these premises do not deserve equal protection in a liberal democracy. The other prong of the solution, Fukuyama continues, 'concerns the expectations and behaviour of the majority communities in Europe'. To him, national identity continues to be understood and experienced in ways that sometimes make it a barrier for newcomers who do not share the ethnicity and religious background of the native-born. Examples are not hard to find. 'If a white person happens to meet an exotic-looking individual who speaks English with an Irish or an Oxford accent,' Professor of Sociology Ulrich Beck writes in a similar vein, 'the individual is grilled until the appearance of the assumed consonance between passport, skin colour, accent, place of residence and place of origin is re-established.'[32]

The construction of national identity, and the stories that a community tells about itself, need, according to Fukuyama, 'to be reopened in the light of Europe's new diversity'. Here the majority communities in Europe have the chief responsibility. Fukuyama illustrates this give-and-take approach by making a reference to the cultural reorientation debate in Germany around the millennium shift. His main example is the idea of *Leitkultur* – 'core culture', or the notion that German citizenship entails certain obligations to observe standards of tolerance and equal respect. This is not a term invented by Fukuyama, but was brought on to the agenda by Bassam Tibi, a German academic of Syrian origin, in his 1998 book *Europa ohne Identität: Die Krise der multikulturellen Gesellschaft* as a non-ethnic, universalist conception of citizenship that would open up national identity to non-ethnic Germans.[33] Although by neutral standards it mirrors much of Jürgen Habermas's idea of 'constitutional patriotism',[34] the debate got out of hand and when politicians appropriated Tibi's proposal for their own purposes, Paul Spiegel, president of the Central Council of Jews in Germany, caustically asked if German *Leitkultur* included burning synagogues.[35] Geert Wilders, the right-wing Dutch politician and producer of anti-Islam film *Fitna*, interpreted *Leitkultur* as a shield against the islamization of Europe.[36] Tibi eventually protested and declared the debate a failure.[37]

In 2005, the new presiding chairman of the German Bundestag, Norbert Lammert from the Christian Democratic Union (CDU), proposed a reopening of the debate by moving the discussion to a European level. In an article in *Die Welt*, he wrote that if Europe wishes to preserve the multiplicity of national identities, and yet establish a collective identity, it must develop a political core ideal, a set of foundational values and convictions. Such a European core ideal must necessarily be based on the common cultural roots of Europe, on its shared history and on shared religious tradition.[38] Right away, this implies finding out where the core ends. Buruma's primary suggestion, when things got rough, was to strike the line in court. This sounds reasonable, but does it solve the problem?

Compare the reaction to the Muhammad caricatures, where the publication of 12 satirical cartoons depicting the Prophet Muhammad in the Danish newspaper *Jyllands-Posten* in 2005 led to a global debate about the right to offend and freedom of speech,[39] and the reaction to caricatures printed in French satirical magazine *Charlie Hebdo* in 2006. In the latter case, under the title 'Mahomet débordé par les intégristes' ('Muhammad overwhelmed by fundamentalists'), the front page showed a cartoon of a weeping Prophet Muhammad saying 'C'est dur d'être aimé par des cons' ('it's hard to be loved by idiots'). The newspaper also reprinted the 12 cartoons from *Jyllands-Posten*. As with the case last time, reactions from both religious and intellectual milieus were harsh. But in addition to verbal protests, the Grand Mosque of Paris and the Union of French Islamic Organizations (UOIF) sued the magazine, claiming the edition included racist cartoons. When the case came to trial, Executive Editor Philippe Val was acquitted by the court. The court followed the state attorney's reasoning that two of the three cartoons were not an attack on Islam, but on Muslim terrorists, and that the third cartoon with Muhammad with a bomb in his turban should be seen in the context of the magazine in question which attacked religious fundamentalism.

This case is particularly interesting because of its sheer complexity. Reporters without Borders (RSF), for example, hailed the decision and said that 'the court's verdict accords with the French republic's values and is good for French society as a whole'.[40] Former President Jacques Chirac offered the UOIF the services of his personal lawyer, Francis Szpiner, while Nicolas Sarkozy, President to be, announced that he preferred 'an excess of cartoons to a lack of cartoons'.[41] While *Jyllands-Posten* belongs on the political right, *Charlie Hebdo* is undoubtedly leftist. In the past, the magazine has made a mockery out of the Pope, Jesus, Buddha and other religious figures. Approval has been voiced across Europe of the Muslim organizations for using the tools of democracy to convey their discontent.

Philippe Val himself, who called the trial victory a 'revenge' for the murder of Theo van Gogh and the cancellation of Mozart's *Idomeneo* by the Berlin Opera,[42] can hardly be described as a right-wing islamophopbe; rather, he's more of an anarchist. A collection of his writings has been published under a title that may be translated into English as *Good Screwings with bin Laden*. Alas, as conclusively stated by Carolina Boe and Peter Hervik who analysed the two cases comparatively,[43] simply taking the issue to court did not unravel the underlying conflict. And if we had a series of lawsuits across Europe, I am pretty convinced that it would strengthen rather than ease the disagreements at issue.

Strategies for dealing with intercultural dialogue should therefore explicitly include such reflections. All things considered, I think Fukuyama's questions are more resolving than his answers. But as the information gathered from my presentation of the EU in the beginning of this chapter illustrates, diversity seems to be more about food and language than conflicting morals and divergent interpretations of freedom of speech. Maybe Xavier Troussard, whom we met in the previous chapter, can help us out. During our conversation at Place Madou, he said that 'for us, cultural diversity embraces diversity of values, while of course, to live together in any society, you need to strike a deal, recognizing some fundamental values. It's true that on a European level we don't have a real formulation of those common values, but we have a transcription of some of them into rights – human rights and fundamental freedoms. Should we go further? I don't know, but anyhow, in any society you have a permanent discussion about values.'

In fact, there is a permanent discussion. One of the most promising initiatives related to these challenges, also connected to the EYID 2008, is the so-called Brussels debates.[44] Chaired by Shada Islam, a Brussels-based journalist and Senior Programme Executive at the European Policy Centre (EPC), the idea is basically to arrange seven debates through the year canvassing a range of issues. Arranged jointly by EPC and the European Commission, the debates first and foremost aim at providing platforms for airing thoughts on how to improve intercultural dialogue. Now, most of these debates circle around familiar topics like immigration, citizenship and multilingualism, but my eyes were quickly drawn to the second debate: 'Negotiating differences. A responsibility of artists and cultural institutions.' In the pre-event background paper for the debate on 2 April 2008, provided by the European Cultural Foundation (ECF) and European Forum for the Arts and Heritage (EFAH)/Culture Action Europe (CAE), we can read that 'in a situation where "cultural differences" are constantly being blamed for human tensions and divisions, and where inequalities, complicated by global power struggles, are put on the bill of "culture", we need to find some new ways to engage with each other and learn from each other.' [45]

Enthused by this brave statement, I was correspondingly disappointed when I discovered that the term 'differences' is not discussed in the paper at all. Jette Sandahl, founding director of the new Museum of World Culture in Gothenborg, however, came up with some interesting thoughts during the debate. She explained how museums had got stuck with 'freezing people into static concepts of ethnicity', and that museums can nowadays 'only afford a limited sense of nostalgia for what once was'. Among the prerequisites for intercultural dialogue in cultural institutions she thus outlined that cultural institutions had to 'let go of monocultural traditions and monopolies of interpretations'. As an alternative, Sandahl made a powerful plea for the museum to face identity riddles in two ways. 'A contemporary museum has to reflect and span both of these trends – identity as accumulated history, as tradition and preservation of continuity, and, on the other hand, identity as aspiration and hope, as a striving towards the future.' Artists and cultural institutions need to be aware of the social, political and historical context in which they work and this includes hopes for the future. Museum professionals have to move from being experts to being facilitators, and society needs to learn to 'become comfortable with difference and respect what we don't understand'. [46]

To meet this need the organizers of the EYID have established a Brussels debate forum, which allows you, one week prior to each of the seven debates, to make public your opinions about this. [47] Although the number of reads is OK (some 20,000) after six debates (where four of them are open for comments at the time of reading), the number of posts is low (just short of 20). Yet, it is a fact, as documented by the closing conference of the EYID 2008, 'New Perspectives for Intercultural Dialogue in Europe' in Paris, from 17 to 19 November, that a considerable portion of stakeholders, policymakers and grassroots civil society organizations have been mobilized throughout Europe. Counting at the conference date, there had been 524 national events and 406 projects, while 91 national 'ambassadors of intercultural dialogue' had been nominated by the Member States. Behind these numbers there is a variety of interesting actions.

Dialogue from below

The majority of these projects, like 'Cultures from around the Block' (seven local media projects across Europe in Berlin, Prague, Bucharest, Coventry, Warsaw, Bratislava and Brussels, offering a virtual tour of European neighbourhood culture seen through the eyes of youth), organized by Multicultural Center Prague, have strong ties to civil society.[48] As I discussed in the previous chapter, the EU has, with The Rainbow Paper, made some considerable efforts in this respect. It gets particularly interesting when we find out that there is a growing field of cultural exchange from below in the civil sector, consisting of what Troussard calls 'mediators' and platforms. This is best illustrated by a brief tour of the websites of the numerous organizations working for the cultural effervescence of Europe. Many of them are young and have yet to realize their true potential. Sites like www.rhiz.eu, aiming at connecting young Europeans, or blogs like A Fistful of Euros,[49] are still on the verge of breakthrough.

Considering the idea of a European public, discussed in chapter 2, I would in particular recommend visiting *cafébabel.com*. Describing itself as 'the European magazine', it has weight behind its words due to an impressive network of writers and local teams spread across Europe, including eastern Europe. Nine years after two Erasmus students, Nicola Dell'Arciprete and Adriano Farano, arrived at Strasbourg's Political Studies Institute (IEP) with a revolutionary idea in their baggage – creating the first pan-European media of participative European journalism – it is now a professional magazine (with more than 400,000 hits per month) covering culture, politics and the economy, most of it available in seven languages. It also has about 80 active blogs from about eight countries and eight forums. Unique is also the newly launched Europocket Television, a web-based platform of audiovisual content on the European Union and its institutions as well as culture, solidarity, environment, travel and entertainment, all operated by 'young people for young people'.[50]

Alongside these initiatives, a list of more institutionalized mediators, by no means exhaustive, provided by Culture Action Europe, gives some indication of the range of mediators and platforms for the cultural interest in Europe:

ACCR – European Network of Cultural Centres-Historic Monuments
The European Network of Cultural Centres-Historic Monuments gathers professionals exploring the interaction between heritage, research and contemporary creation.

AEC – European Association of Conservatoires
The AEC is a European cultural and educational network with more than 238 member institutions for professional music training in 55 countries.

Banlieues d'Europe
Banlieues d'Europe is a European cultural network bringing together cultural actors, artists, cooperative officials, social workers, researchers and local councillors, who are concerned with questions of artistic action aimed at excluded people in deprived neighbourhoods in Europe.

BJCEM – Biennal of Young Artists from Europe and the Mediterranean
The BJCEM Association is a network that gathers 71 members from 20 countries – local bodies, ministries, associations and cultural institutions – and is open to membership of local and national bodies from Europe and the Mediterranean.

CEATL – European Council of Associations of Literary Translators
CEATL is an international association that currently brings together 25 associations of literary translators representing 21 European countries. It promotes and guarantees literary translators' representation in European policies.

EFA – European Festival Association
EFA is an organization representing more than 100 quality festivals and 11 national festival associations in 38 European and non-European

countries. It is the voice of hundreds of festivals across Europe and beyond.

ELIA – European League of Institutes of the Arts

Founded in 1990, ELIA is an independent membership organization representing approximately 350 higher education arts institutions from over 45 countries. ELIA represents all disciplines in the arts, including architecture, dance, design, fine art, media arts, music and theatre.

EMC – European Music Council

The EMC is the leading professional organization in Europe dedicated to the development and promotion of all kinds of music. It contributes to a better mutual understanding among peoples and their different cultures and to the right for all musical cultures to coexist.

ENCC – European Network of Cultural Centres

ENCC is an international network of arts and cultural centres, founded in Turnhout, Belgium in June 1994. Multi-disciplinary cultural centres have their own way of acting, their own problems and fields of interest. The ENCC aims to be their platform, networking on a global level for stronger action in the local community.

ETC – European Theatre Convention

The ETC is a network encouraging international exchange of ideas, persons and performances between its 36 member theatres. The ETC also aims to support the creation of new plays and collaboration projects and wants to highlight and explore the role of theatre in the new Europe of today.

EUnetArt – European Network of Art Organizations for Children and Young People

EUnetArt is a place to meet, exchange and learn, a framework for developing cooperation projects, a platform to raise issues and a voice for arts for children and young people in Europe. Founded in 1991 in

Bologna, EUnetArt is a multi-disciplinary cultural network of over 100 organizations in approximately 28 countries.

Europa Cantat
Europa Cantat is a non-profit organization that exists to encourage and increase greater understanding and cooperation between Europeans by bringing them together in the common activity of singing, promoting the exchange and development of cultural heritage and education.

EWC – European Writers Congress
The EWC facilitates trans-European cultural and literary cooperation, the realization of common projects and the professional exchange of experience and good practice among 58 writers' associations in 30 countries.

IAMIC – International Association of Music Information Centres
IAMIC is a worldwide network of organizations that document and promote the music of our time. IAMIC currently supports the work of 43 member organizations in 38 countries.

IETM – International Network for Contemporary Performing Arts
IETM is a membership organization that exists to stimulate the quality, development and contexts of contemporary performing arts in a global environment, by initiating and facilitating professional networking and communication, the dynamic exchange of information, know-how transfer and presentations of examples of good practice.

IFEA – International Festivals and Events Association Europe
Founded in 1992, the International Festivals and Events Association Europe – IFEA Europe – is the European affiliate of IFEA World. For the past 50 years, IFEA has served as the global network organization for professionals who work in the cultural festivals and public events sector.

Opera Europa
Opera Europa is the leading service organization for professional opera companies and opera festivals throughout Europe. It currently serves 110 member companies from 33 different countries.

PEARLE – Performing Arts Employers Association League Europe
Created in 1991, PEARLE is the European trade federation of performing arts organizations. PEARLE represents through its member associations almost 4,000 theatres, theatre production companies, orchestras and music ensembles, opera houses, ballet and dance companies, festivals and other organizations within the performing arts sector across Europe.

RECIT – European Network of the Literary Translators' International Centre
The RECIT network offers services to European literary translators, organizes meetings between them and promotes literary translation as part of the cultural heritage.

Res Artis
Res Artis is the largest existing network of artist residency programmes, representing the interests of more than 200 centres and organizations in 49 countries worldwide that offer international artists facilities and conditions conducive for making art.

RESEO – European Network for Opera and Dance Education
RESEO's mission is to develop and promote the practice of opera and dance education in Europe. RESEO's strength lies in the number and diversity of its membership, which currently comprises over 50 opera and dance companies of all sizes from 20 countries in Europe.

Team Network
Developed in collaboration with several European partners, the TEAM Network – Transdisciplinary European Art Magazines – aims to encourage international cooperation and the exchange of ideas, to

enhance common thinking on priority issues and to define a programme of joint initiatives and actions, including workshops for young critics, meetings and translation support.

TEH – Trans Europe Halles
Trans Europe Halles is a network of independent culture centres. It was founded in 1983 and currently has 43 members in 24 countries.

Three other large platforms/mediators are the European Union National Institutes for Culture (EUNIC), Culture Action Europe (CAE) and European Cultural Foundation (ECF). The first is a partnership of national institutions for culture, engaged beyond their national borders and operating with a degree of autonomy from their governments.[51] It currently includes organizations from 25 EU countries and aims to include national institutes for culture from all the Member States. The total operating budget of the current EUNIC membership is more than €2.2 billion per year. EUNIC operates at two complementary levels: the first level consists of the Heads or Directors General of the national institutions. The second level comprises clusters of national institutions for culture, based in cities across Europe, cooperating together in common projects. Projects guided by the EUNIC Warszawa Cluster, for instance, involve at least three member institutes – though often more than that.[52]

While EUNIC is heading a variety of projects, I find Alter Ego to be one of the most appealing. It is one of the seven flagship projects chosen by the Commission to celebrate the intercultural year of 2008. It was a European-wide competition running in 22 Member States. Young people (14–18 years old) were encouraged to explore different and varied identities in their local communities, by creating a double portrait (in video, photo, text or music): a self-portrait alongside a portrait of a person from a different background and tradition.

Finally, all entries were gathered on a central web space,[53] offering the opportunity to vote on the submitted works. When voting closed, a jury of artists and media professionals in each country, with an emphasis on known artists of a minority or migrant background, then

One of the finalists from 'Me and My Alter Ego'

Artist Alise Popila, from Riga, Latvia
Source www.alterego-europe.eu/eu

selected a number of finalists. The young finalists were then invited to a five-day 'Intercultural Workshop' in Denmark in November, where they were coached by European artists from minority/migrant communities. At the end of the project (January–March 2009), the works generated during this final stage in combination with the works selected from the competition will be part of an exhibition travelling across Europe through the EUNIC network and available through the website as well as on DVD.[54]

Comparatively, Culture Action Europe (CAE) and European Cultural Foundation (ECF) are more independent organizations, although their objectives are similar to those of EUNIC. Currently CAE has more than 90 members,[55] representing in turn over 8,000 organizations spread across the EU countries and beyond at the local,

regional, national or European levels in more than 14 artistic disciplines. Members of CAE are from all domains of cultural activity, ranging from orchestras to writers' associations, research institutions to cultural contact points, national theatres to international cultural networks, conservatoires to choirs and festivals. Below these statistics there is a myriad of cultural activity too large to describe here. Regarding its role as mediator, notable benefits to members include:
  - privileged access to an exciting and informed network of peer groups and individuals;
  - a dedicated and attentive listening post for EU cultural policy;
  - use of the Culture Action Europe office in Brussels for meetings;
  - free entry to the Members' General Assembly;
  - the knowledge that you are contributing to its work to increase the importance of and funding for culture within the EU.

Next, joining CAE helps organizations across Europe to advocate their views to those with power. They have even written an advocacy toolkit,[56] free of jargon and boring treaties, free to for anyone use. One example of actual influence exposed is The Rainbow Platform, which I discussed in the previous chapter. And whereas CAE to some degree continues the UNESCO trail (see chapter 6),[57] they leave cultural creation fully in the hands of European citizens.

The European Cultural Foundation is in many ways a similar mediator and platform. Based in Amsterdam, and with a small staff of 25 people (speaking 15 languages in all), it has since its modest beginning in the mid-1950s grown to become a leading actor in European cultural policy. In my view, the greatest achievement of ECF is its ability to monitor cultural changes in Europe and accordingly to develop new and ingenious incentives for cultural action. Of particular prominence is www.labforculture.org, a 'cultural Ali Baba's cave', which is a networking platform for information on European arts and culture. Astonishingly simple in its function, it provides one meeting point for artists in search of collaboration projects or funding. As they put it themselves: 'Find Ideas. Find People. Find Money. Find Events. Find Debates. One website, 50 countries, 5 languages.'[58]

Positively experiencing the stranger

In *Modernity and Ambivalence* Zygmunt Bauman attempts to give an account of the different approaches modern society adopts towards 'the stranger'. He argues that, on the one hand, the stranger, because he cannot be controlled and ordered, is always the object of fear; he is the potential mugger, the person outside of society's borders who is constantly threatening those on the inside. On the other hand, in a consumer-oriented economy the strange and the unfamiliar is always enticing: in different styles of food, in different fashions and in tourism it is possible to experience the allure of what is unfamiliar.[59] It seems likely that the StrangerFestival – 'Europe's biggest event for young video makers and fans sharing stories' – has adopted the latter view and added a humanistic dimension which embodies the true spirit of what I think the EU wants to achieve with its efforts on culture.[60]

Making the video

Source European Cultural Foundation (ECF)

In the background paper for the festival it says that the impact at European level will be 'greater awareness of the diversity of values and norms amongst European youth' and 'tested methodologies on how visual culture functions as a tool for intercultural dialogue'.[61] On the ECF's website we can read that such 'debate is badly needed in a MySpace-and-youtube world of ready communication but little analysis. Young people are everywhere demonstrating their mastery of new media: now is the time to talk about what is being expressed. At Stranger, the debate will be led by young people themselves.'[62] The festival was held from 3 to 5 July 2008 in Amsterdam. Three days of socializing, fun, competitions and workshops in different categories brought in more than 1,000 videos and more than 250 participants. On Thursday night, the festival was set in motion by ECF President, HRH Laurentien of the Netherlands. Friday and Saturday were packed with workshops – 300 young people from all over Europe refined their skills and learned new ones. An expert meeting was also held, involving UK think-tank DEMOS, BBC, MTV and others. Saturday night was award night: 24-year-old Maciek Salamon from Poland was announced as the winner of the Official Stranger Award 2008 for his video 'The Walk'.[63]

Helped by strong press coverage, it is reasonable to believe that StrangerFestival gave a strong boost to the intercultural dialogue involving young people across Europe. Winner of the InsideOut Award, for instance, was 11-year-old Zarina Pashtova from Kabardino-Balkaria, a part of the Russian Federation located in the North Caucasus. This category was about the fine line between being included or excluded, about stereotypes and prejudices and ways to overcome them. In Zarina's video[64] we see the author herself blowing up a balloon against the background of various activities she does together with other kids. 'The meaning of my video,' says Zarina, 'is that a human being's inner world is extremely vulnerable, and you cannot leave people by themselves, because then they would get lost in their own solitude and forget about us. We have to value every human being.'[65]

Recognition to the young

Source European Cultural Foundation (ECF)

In the background paper it is explicitly stated that the StrangerFestival does not assume Europe to be a multicultural carnival: 'Cultural diversity does not only bring positive learning and discoveries, it can also trigger prejudices, drum up support for populism and create fear and hostility. The Stranger project deals with today's Europe and its challenges in the only way which works among young people: honestly talking about things with their real names.'[66] I asked Tommi Laitio, the Programme Coordinator of StrangerFestival and the 'One Minutes Junior' project together with Raya Ribbius,[67] to elaborate on this in light of the diversity-difference axis. He thinks the festival grabs the heart of European multiculturalism: 'The goal of StrangerFestival was never to find harmony or to make all the participants friends, it was to demonstrate to the participants and the organizations the creative potential there is in young people to solve situations there and then. We consciously chose to start the interaction with personal testimonies, that is, videos entered in the competition, and then moved on to focus on the physical encounter, making people work with each other. This way we recognized their personal accounts as valuable and started the interaction from the notion of self-definition.'

Maybe the fissure between diversity and difference is more visible than necessary due to the dominant idea of European cultural traditions and heritage, as discussed in previous chapters. 'A while back, I attended a British Council event in Stockholm that started from the question whether European culture exists,' Laitio recalls. 'The event gathered around 30 young diplomats and cultural operators under the umbrella of EUNIC. I was asked to write a provocation paper for the event in which I said that as a person coming from the most north-easterly corner of the EU, I find it much easier to associate with Pushkin than with Rembrandt and that many of the things that are addressed as our common heritage are Mediterranean, north-west European, male, white and heterosexual. This position irritated immensely many of the people representing Mediterranean cultural institutions.' In a speech at The Network Effect conference in Budapest in March 2008, Laitio raised a similar question: who defines the characteristics of an identity – the people themselves or the ones in power? To him, it is crucial that people themselves keep some space free of institutional instruction, free of governments trying to rebuild Britishness or Dutchness by starting 'national discussions', introducing citizenship tests, launching cultural canons and inventing traditions such as an obligatory citizenship ceremony. Identity is about becoming, not being; it's something one does, not something one is.[68]

[1] Eurobarometer, 2007b.

[2] Hall, 2000; Eriksen, 2006.

[3] Eriksen, 2006.

[4] European Commission, 2007a.

[5] www.interculturaldialogue2008.eu/339.0. html?&redirect_url=my-startpage-eyid.html

[6] For an overview of these projects, see www.interculturaldialogue2008. eu/354.0.html?&L=0

[7] Cited in Isaksen, 2008.

[8] www.delmda.ec.europa.eu/whatsnew/ press_releases_en.html

[9] www.delmda.ec.europa.eu/whatsnew/ press_releases_en.html

[10] See Muukkonen, 2002, for debates about diversity, difference and art.

[11] Eriksen, 2006.

[12] Eriksen, 2006.

[13] Jovchelovitch, 2007: 128–9.

[14] www.humanrightsfirst.org

[15] Pew, 2008.

[16] Fukuyama, 2007.

[17] Roy, 2004.

[18] Eriksen, 2004.

[19] Grindheim, 2007.

[20] Eurobarometer, 2007b.

[21] Buruma, 2006.

[22] Bedell, 2006.

[23] These remarks were made by Gad at a seminar arranged by the research programme Cultural Complexity in the New Norway (CULCOM) at the University of Oslo, 20 October 2008.

[24] Zizek, 2008.

[25] Eriksen and Stjernfelt, 2009.

[26] Wagner, 2006: 173.

[27] Baumann, 2007.

[28] Duelund, 2008b.

[29] Timmermans, 2008.

[30] Fossum, 2001.

[31] Honneth, 1996.

[32] Beck, 2006: 165.

[33] Tibi, 2000.

[34] Habermas, 2001. Primarily, the idea is that citizenship and civic binding is created by submission to shared values, not ethnicity, religion or a sense of common history.

[35] Cited in Mrozek, 2000.

[36] *Der Spiegel*, 2008.

[37] Tibi, 2001.

[38] Lammert, 2005.

[39] A must-read here, covering many parts of the world, is Kunelius et al, 2007.

[40] RSF, 2007.

[41] Sarkozy, however, demanded as late as October 2008 a ban on a Sarkozy doll and voodoo manual that encourages readers to stick pins in it. A French court rejected Sarkozy's argument that the doll violated his right to his own image and said the voodoo doll was within the authorized boundaries of freedom of expression and the right to humour. For more details, see Chrisafis, 2008.

[42] Boe and Hervik, 2008: 225.

[43] Boe and Hervik, 2008.

[44] See www.interculturaldialogue2008. eu/408.0.html

[45] www.interculturaldialogue2008.eu/ fileadmin/downloads/documents/230-brussels%20debates/Arts%20%26%20 Culture_Concept%20Paper.pdf

[46] A summary of what was said at the debate can be read at www.interculturaldialogue2008. eu/fileadmin/downloads/documents/230-brussels%20debates/080411_Wrap-up_paper_formatted_2_NH.pdf

[47] The Forum can be accessed at www. interculturaldialogue2008.eu/156.0.html

[48] www.mkc.cz/en/news-90/cultures-from-around-the-block.html

[49] http://fistfulofeuros.net

[50] www.europocket.tv. Although unique today, it has its predecessor in the Eurikon experiment, which was conducted under the auspices of the European Broadcasting Union (EBU) with the participation of 15 European broadcasters and the European Community in the early 1980s. Eurikon was, however, never intended to be a permanent European television channel. Instead, it was designed as an experimental prototype. See Theiler, 1999, for more.

[51] www.eunic-europe.eu/EUNIC-website/index.php

[52] www.britishcouncil.pl/eunic

[53] www.alterego-europe.eu/eu

[54] www.eunic-europe.eu/EUNIC-website/fileadmin/user_upload/What_we_do/Docs/Alter_Ego.doc

[55] For an overview, see www.cultureaction europe.org/network/our-members

[56] www.cultureactioneurope.org/advocate/advocacy-and-lobbying-at-eu-level

[57] Yudhishthir Raj Isar, president of CAE, was formerly Executive Secretary of the World Commission on Culture and Development, director of Cultural Policies and of the International Fund for the Promotion of Culture at UNESCO.

[58] www.labforculture.org/en/About-Us

[59] Bauman, 1991.

[60] www.strangerfestival.com

[61] ECF, 2007a.

[62] www.eurocult.org/news-events/?article_id=42

[63] Salamon's video – and a number of other videos – can be watched at www.eurocult.org/media-library/videos

[64] The video can be seen here: www. theoneminutesjr.org/index.php?thissection_id=10&movie_id=200800032

[65] Pashtova is also an alumna of UNICEF peace and tolerance camp of 2007 and her thoughts can be read at www.unicef.org/russia/media_9359.html

[66] ECF, 2007a.

[67] www.theoneminutesjr.org

[68] Cf Mach and Pozarlik, 2008.

5 The creative Europe

The second point on the EU's new agenda for culture is about utilizing culture as a catalyst for creativity. Most of the industries of the cultural economy survive by their innovative edginess. With the Lisbon strategy as leitmotif, I suggest in this chapter that if a strategy focusing on the cultural economy is to be successful, it must better adapt to the terrain in which the creative industries thrive. In today's world, I find it particularly odd that the EU should maintain a nation-state approach to filmmaking even though it implies a European dimension as a condition for support. As an alternative, I present some lessons from the most successful film studio ever: Hollywood. Finally, I argue that the EU should implement a more proactive stance in developing one of the most promising areas of the cultural economy, namely video games.

To me, a sentence like 'using culture as a catalyst for creativity' directly translates to the video games industry. I admit it: I am a die-hard fan of video games. Ever since my little brother and I got our first NES (Nintendo Entertainment System) in the latter half of the 1980s, playing *Pro Wrestling* or *Super Mario Bros* until our fingers were completely numb, I have been absorbed by the excitement, poetry and drama in games like *WRC Evolved*. Popping on the start line, revving the engine to its maximum, and then blasting through the frozen wastes of Finland, the

ains of Australia and the sun-kissed mountain roads of Corsica –
that's what I call entertainment!

Statistics show that I'm not alone. In spite of the recurring moral
panics about addictiveness, gaming is more than antisocial teenage
loners sitting in front of their computers and TVs. It is also a socializing
activity, both online and in the real world. In the era of broadband
expansion, 2003–08, the annual computer festival 'The Gathering'
(TG) in Norway still managed to get full house every year, attracting
more than 5,000 participants.[1] A new report shows that among those
European gamers who are parents to children under 16 (36 per cent
of the sample), over eight in ten play video games with their children.
Furthermore, reading the reasons for doing so, we find that it ranges
from children requesting that their parents play with them to being a
fun activity for all the family and a good opportunity to spend some time
together.[2] The average age of game players in Europe is between 26 and
33 and rising.[3]

The cultural economy

Video games are only one example of what is known as 'the cultural
economy'.[4] Surely, being a vast field, there are numerous ways ('models',
as some researchers call them) to understand the relationship between
the cultural economy and the rest of the economy, that is, how a change
in one affects the other in a market in which cultural goods and services
are produced and traded globally. In this book, however, I concentrate
on what is called *the growth model* and *the innovation model*, which in
my view overlap to a great deal, given my chosen examples. The first
proposes a positive economic relation between growth in the creative
industries and growth in the aggregate economy. The creative industries
are a growth driver through their new creation of value. This model
thus accommodates digital content, from games to mobile content or
aerospace simulators, as an input factor into the economy. The latter
model suggests that economic value from creative industries does not
stem from their relative contribution to economic value, but from their
contribution to the coordination of new ideas or technologies and thus
to the process of economic and cultural change.[5]

It is also these models, at least to someone untrained in the cultural economy lingo, that most resonate with the second part of the EU's new agenda for culture, where it says that the EU aims to develop 'creative partnerships between the cultural sector and other sectors (ICTs, research, tourism, social partners, etc)', and to 'reinforce the social and economic impact of investments in culture and creativity, in particular with regard to the promotion of growth and jobs and the development and attractiveness of regions and cities'.[6] In a broader perspective this links to the so-called Lisbon Strategy for growth and jobs.[7] In March 2000, European leaders committed the EU to become by 2010 'the most dynamic and competitive knowledge-based economy in the world capable of sustainable economic growth with more and better jobs and greater social cohesion, and respect for the environment'. The results so far achieved have been unconvincing.

From the European Parliament Fact Sheet on cultural policy we can read that, apart from support through particular programmes for the EU's approximately 7 million people professionally active in the cultural sector, the Union supports the creative industries through many provisions of the EU Treaty. Examples here are directives on copyright, intellectual property and legislation concerning resale rights, and rental and lending rights. As a way of supporting artistic and intellectual creativity, the EU allows Member States to apply reduced rates of VAT to certain goods and services such as the supply of books and periodicals, access to cultural events and reception of radio and TV broadcasts (minimum standard rate: 15 per cent; reduced rate: 5 per cent). The EC Treaty also guarantees workers freedom of movement, at least to some degree. In the case of workers in the cultural sector this right, and therefore artists' mobility, is often hampered by national administrative barriers, which still need to be removed.[8] (I will return to this issue in chapter 7.)

The question is whether this is enough to harness the many industries of the cultural economy as defined above. KEA Affairs concludes, in a 2006 study prepared for the European Commission, that 'the role of the cultural and creative sector within this context [the European economy] is still largely ignored.'[9] A 2004 report from the so-called High-Level Group chaired by Wim Kok, former Prime Minister of the Netherlands, depicts an even gloomier picture: 'External events since 2000 [like 9/11 etc] have not helped in achieving the objectives but the European Union and its Members States have clearly themselves contributed to slow progress by failing to act on much of the Lisbon Strategy with sufficient urgency. This disappointing delivery is due to an overloaded agenda, poor coordination and conflicting priorities. Still, an inveterate issue has been the lack of determined political action.' The High-Level Group further concludes that 'the Lisbon Strategy has become too broad to be understood as an interconnected narrative. Lisbon is about everything and thus about nothing. Everybody is responsible and thus no one.'[10]

Creative cities
Apart from this harsh critique of the organizational inefficiency in implementing the Lisbon Strategy, there are also more substantial links between economy, creativity and innovation that should be further examined in light of the EU's new agenda for culture. Above, I cited the EU stating that one of the specific objectives in using culture as a catalyst for creativity is to reinforce the attractiveness of regions and cities.[11] It is reasonable to assume that one precondition for attracting people to come to work in any given company is that it is located somewhere good to live.

Surprisingly, there is very little in the Lisbon Strategy, even in the relaunched edition from 2005, about such an objective. A closer relationship between the two might concretize what historian Peter Hall writes in his *Cities in Civilization: Culture, Technology and Urban Order* (an 1,169-page venture into the comparative cultural history of cities, which investigates the exceptional cultural creativity which distinguished the world's great cities in their golden ages): 'the biggest and most cosmopolitan cities, for all their evident disadvantages and obvious problems, have throughout history been the places that ignited the sacred flame of the human intelligence and the human imagination.'[12] Ultimately, the challenge is how to take advantage of this 'sacred flame'.

Professor Richard Florida's book *The Rise of the Creative Class* gives us a useful framework in this respect. By analysing comparatively the list of technological hotspots in the US with the geography of creative talent and his own rank indexes of tolerant places receptive to diversity and having plenty of cultural amenities, Florida found a correlating pattern – and suddenly he had the premises for his theory of 'a creative class'. The Creative Class consists of people who add economic value through their creativity. Florida explains: 'Their property – which stems from their creative capacity – is an intangible because it is literally in their heads.'[13]

Additional research has confirmed that Florida's theory and findings are transferable to Europe. A 2004 report showed that the Creative Class made up 25 per cent of the workforce in seven of the 14 European countries examined, and comprised nearly 30 per cent in three – Finland, Belgium and the Netherlands. Sweden was the top performer on the so-called Euro-Creativity Index, ahead of the US (the only nation outside Europe included, just for comparison), while Ireland outpaced all nations in Creative Class growth, with a 7 per cent annual growth rate since 1995.[14]

Florida's theory is controversial. His argument that cities that rank high on 'the Bohemian Index' – that is, environments being open to immigrants, artists and gays, and those which are less segregated – are the most creative and innovative has received a lot of criticism. Some of it is uncalled for. The point is not that these characteristic groups literally cause economic growth, but that their presence indicates an underlying culture that is open and conducive to creative minds. Benefits of having a clever immigration policy to attract 'brainware' are easily found. Kevin Robins is just one of many who claim there is a productive interrelation between pluralism and innovation.[15] Peter Hall emphasizes that 'probably, no city has ever been creative without continued renewal of the creative bloodstream'.[16] A similar picture is usually drawn of American ICT haven Silicon Valley. Other than prestigious examples like Indian-born Sabeer Bhatia and Russian-born Sergei Brin, co-founders of Hotmail and Google, respectively, roughly one-third of all new high-tech businesses in the 1990s were founded by immigrants.[17]

Linkages between innovational capabilities and the challenges of intercultural dialogue are thus obvious. In this context it is important to realize that those who either praise immigration as a magic key to economic growth or see immigration as the inevitable cause of the fall of a nation are both wrong. Political articulations of immigration pros and cons, as Philippe Legrain makes clear in his 2007 book *Immigrants: Your Country Needs Them*, need to be more precise and more adaptable to the fast-changing nature of urbanization and globalization.[18] Tom Bentley, former Director of British think-tank DEMOS, is not impressed by the efforts of the EU: 'While several countries have recently liberalised their immigration policies to encourage the managed flow of skilled entrants, the backlash has left the debate unresolved and EU progress towards a coherent policy framework is excruciatingly slow.'[19]

More important than immigration debates, in my view, is Florida's underlying question of why some cities thrive while others stagnate. Why do creative people cluster in specific cities? The essential units in this debate are *places* because they provide so-called 'thick labour markets' that help match people to jobs, mating markets that enable people to find life-partners, the amenities that allow people to pursue the lifestyles they wish and the ability to construct and validate their identities. Florida resumes this view by constructing a term which sums up the factors that go into Creative Class location decisions: *quality of place*. The characteristics defining the quality of place are in three groups:[20]

- What's there: the combination of the built environment and the natural environment, a proper setting for pursuit of creative lives.
- Who's there: diverse kinds of people, interacting and providing cues that anyone can plug into and make a life in that community.
- What's going on: the vibrancy of street life, café culture, arts, music and people engaging in outdoor activities – altogether a lot of active, exciting, creative endeavours.

Examples of why this is important can be found in *The Creative City* by Charles Landry, Director of British think-tank Comedia. After examining a handful of successful cities in the 1990s, Landry came to the conclusion that they demonstrate 'an appreciation of cultural issues' and that expressing values and identity is the key to the ability to respond to change – especially organizational culture. According to Landry, they discovered how the cultural sector had a direct impact on inward investment by attracting international companies who seek a vibrant cultural life for their employees.[21] In a newer book, published in November 2007, Landry together with Phil Wood still argues that these ideas are valid.[22]

Retaining the European dreams

As far as purely industrial policy recommendations go – and returning to the basic elements of the overlapping cultural economy models presented above – it is highly interesting to note that the High-Level Group demands more specific objectives in a renewed Lisbon Strategy. This conclusion also resonates with the ones arrived at by the EU itself. In its Communication from 2005, 'Working together for growth and jobs. A new start for the Lisbon Strategy', Commission President Barroso writes that 'Europe's actions need more focus. We must concentrate all our efforts on delivering on the ground policies that will have greatest impact. This means keeping existing promises, building on the reforms already underway in every Member State and launching new action where it is needed to keep us on target.'[23]

One way to achieve this is suggested by KEA. Their advice is to break down cultural/creative industries into subcategories and steer policies more head-on towards any given subject.

Delineation of the cultural and creative sector

Circles	Sectors	Subsectors
Core arts field	Visual arts	Crafts, paintings, sculpture, photography
	Performing arts	Theatre, dance, circus, festivals
	Heritage	Museums, libraries, archaeological sites, archives
Circle 1: Cultural industries	Film and video	
	Television and radio	
	Video games	
	Music	Recorded music market, live music performance, revenues of collecting societies in the music sector
	Books and press	
Circle 2: Creative industries and activities	Design	Fashion design, graphic design, interior design, product design.
	Architecture	
	Advertising	
Circle 3: Related industries	PC manufacturers, MP3 player manufacturers, mobile industry, etc	

Connected to the EU's agenda for culture, I see two main areas in Circle 1, Cultural Industries, where a heightened sense of exactness in outlining objectives could ease the criticism. The first is the Film and Video industry. Economically, the range is endless. Motion Picture Association of America (MPAA) states that worldwide box office receipts reached an all-time high of $26.7 billion in 2007, a 4.9 per cent increase compared with 2006.[24] The lion's share of this money goes back to the Hollywood companies. Emotionally, nothing seems to be more liberating for creativity, culture, identity and mass appeal than films. Filmmaker Wim Wenders made an authoritative contribution to the fate of the European film business during the conference 'A Soul for Europe' in Berlin in 2006.

Source Adapted from KEA, 2006

....

Characteristics

....

– Non-industrial activities

– Outputs are prototypes and 'potentially copyrighted works'

....

– Industrial activities aimed at mass production

– Outputs are based on copyright

....

– Activities are not necessarily industrial, and may be prototypes

– Although outputs are based on copyright, they may include other intellectual property inputs (trademark, for instance)

– The use of creativity is essential to the performance of these non-cultural sectors

....

– This category is loose and impossible to circumscribe on the basis of clear criteria. It involves many other economic sectors that are dependent on the previous 'circles', such as the ICT sector

....

'Why is it that today, not only in Europe, but all over the world, "going to the pictures" is synonymous with "seeing an American film"?! Because the Americans realized long ago what moves people most and what gets them dreaming. And they radically implemented that knowledge. The whole "American Dream" is really an invention of cinema, and it is now being dreamed by the whole world. I don't want to discredit this, but merely ask the question, "Who is dreaming the European Dream?" Or better: how are we encouraged to dream it?' [25]

By retaining and creating our own myths, many of which don't belong to us any more, Wenders answers. Many of the fairytales gathered in Europe in the 17th century are known only through American film versions. When tourists visit Neuschwanstein Castle in Germany, rumour has it that many think it's a replica of Sleeping Beauty Castle in Disneyland. For Wenders, the true role of European cinema is to place European stories once more at the heart of people's dreams. 'Those images of European cinema,' he said, 'could help a whole new generation of Europeans to recognize themselves, they could define what Europe is all about in emotional, powerful and lasting terms. These films could convey European thinking to the world. We could communicate our most valuable asset, our culture.'

Wenders is right when he says that Hollywood movies dominate the world. However, he's wrong when he attributes this dominance merely to the US. Before I explain why, it is necessary to take a closer look at the EU's conditions for film funding in order to see what we may learn from the Hollywood industry. Since the early 1990s, MEDIA, the EU's support programme for the European audiovisual industry, has supported the development and distribution of thousands of films as well as training activities, festivals and promotion projects throughout the continent. The new MEDIA 2007 programme (2007–13) is the fourth multi-annual programme since 1991 and has a budget of €755 million. From the outside, the scope of this EU programme is quite impressive. Its objectives are:

- to strive for a stronger European audiovisual sector, reflecting and respecting Europe's cultural identity and heritage;
- to increase the circulation of European audiovisual works inside and outside the European Union;
- to strengthen the competitiveness of the European audiovisual sector by facilitating access to financing and promoting the use of digital technologies.

What's more important, it has produced actual results, not least when it comes to developing what is often perceived as the real strength of Hollywood – distribution chains.[26] From 2001 to 2006, more than half a billion euros were injected into 8,000 projects from over 30 countries.[27] However, there are some funding rigidities that if removed could spur creativity in new directions and even transform the EU into a pioneering cultural policy actor. The application process is too weighty. Application for so-called slate funding, that is support for the development of drama, animation and creative documentary, demands that the applicant read 18 densely written pages of guidelines and fill out an advanced application form of 22 pages. Moreover, there is the condition that projects applying for money must seek to reflect 'European cultural identity'. As discussed in chapter 2, that's not as easy as it might look.

A question like this catches fire also when we look at Eurimages – the Council of Europe fund for the co-production, distribution and exhibition of European cinematographic works.[28] The co-production part is interesting. They support full-length feature films and animation as well as documentaries of a minimum length of 70 minutes, and all projects submitted must have at least two co-producers from different Member States of the Fund (which by 2008 was 33 states). The participation of the majority co-producer must not exceed 80 per cent of the total co-production budget, and the participation of the minority co-producer must not be lower than 10 per cent. In addition – and this is the strange part – we find in paragraph 1.6 of the guidelines, 'European origin and character of the project', that 'projects must be European in terms of origin, investments and rights'. In the case of fiction projects, the European character will be assessed on the basis of the points system included in the European Convention on Cinematographic Co-production. These projects must score at least 15 out of 19 points, according to the scheme of points set out in the table on p126.

Defining 'European character' (or even European dreams, mentioned by Wenders) by utilizing such mathematical requirements poses to me a major problem. This is not only because the film's story is excluded from the scheme, or that I have a very hard time seeing the difference between a European film (15 points) and a non-European film (14 points), but also because it ignores the transnational network of culture, production and economy which comprises the modern film business. For instance, European Audiovisual Observatory, a non-profit public service institution within the legal framework of the Council of Europe which gathers relevant information on the audiovisual sector in Europe, demonstrates in a report with the intriguing title 'Making

and Distribution of Movies in Europe: The Problem of Nationality'
substantial variation in what counts as national identity within Europe.[29]

European character of the project – Eurimages

European elements	Name	Nationality	Permanent residence	Points	Points system of the Convention
Director					3
Scriptwriter					3
Composer					1
First role					3
Second role					2
Third role					1
Cameraman					1
Sound recordist and mixer					1
Editor					1
Art director and costumes					1
Studio and shooting location					1
Post-production location					1
Total					**19**

Source Eurimages (www.coe.int/T/DG4/eurimages)

Accordingly, there are good reasons to question the idea that films – or
the people making them – in general necessarily have to be national or
even European by default. Some of them are put forward by Associate
Professor of English and American Studies at MIT, Christina Klein:

'Which criteria should determine its identity? The citizenship or ethnicity
of its talent? The source of its financing? The location of its production? Its
language? Its audience? Its visual style, themes, or story? Today, the notion of
a distinctly American or Chinese or Indian cinema is breaking down, as film

industries around the world become increasingly integrated with one another in ways that make them simultaneously more global and more local.'[30]

We can see Klein's pondering in light of the Films from the South (FFS) festival in Norway. Between 9 and 19 October 2008, more than 140 'films of quality from the non-western part of the world'[31] were screened in Oslo's cinemas. Among them were Dana Nechushtan's road movie *Dunya and Desie*, moving back and forth between the Netherlands and Morocco, Gariné Torossian's *Stone Time Touch*, a documentary about Canadians with Armenian roots, and *It's hard being loved by idiots*, covering the Muhammad cartoon controversy in France discussed in the previous chapter. All these films underline how tricky it is to understand and categorize films within a national frame. No less easy is the term 'from the South'; the film ending last year's festival was *Flight of the Red Balloon*, directed by Taiwanese Hou Hsiao-hsien, but cut in Paris with French actress Juliette Binoche as the star. As one film critic wrote: 'this film is but one example of the fact that "from the South" is not necessarily what you imagine. What do you imagine, really? Or do such terms really say more about the position from which things are seen?'[32]

Difficulties also arise when it comes to statistical matters. Nils Klevjer Aas, senior adviser at the Norwegian Film Fund, a board member at Eurimages and former Secretary General at European Audiovisual Observatory (EAO), once told me that 'the definition of nationality is one of the most difficult methodological questions of all in film statistics'. He pointed to the variety of different national conditions and criteria for EU/state aid to culture projects, including film.[33] After just glancing at them, I feel Aas's words ring true. He pulls out *Harry Potter and the Philosopher's Stone* as an example: 'When the first Harry Potter movie got made the problem was that nobody was able to define its nationality. It was made by a company registered in Great Britain, with British people and artists. Financing, however, was taken for granted as American, and the movie was distributed internationally by an American company. Because the producer refused to reveal its financial deals to the public, MEDIA had to withdraw its support from a lot of distributors who distributed Harry Potter as a European movie.'

Other wrangles concern artistic content. Alejandro González Iñárritu, the Mexican director of *21 Grams* and the Academy Award-winning *Babel*, has a clear opinion on the nationality question: 'You know, I just make films. Just that. Not Mexican films, not Japanese films, just films. I hate it when people want to nationalize art. It's like saying to someone who's French and is a painter, "Do you paint French?"'[34] Sometimes the fixation on nationality reaches almost ludicrous heights. When the French director Jean-Pierre Jeunet wanted to make *Un long dimanche de fiançailles* with financial support from the American company Warner Bros (who owned the rights to Sébastien Japrisot's novel) and applied to the French Centre National de la Cinématographie for a grant (less than one tenth of what Warner spent), a group of personalities in the world of French culture became very upset. Not only did they bring the case to court, they also insisted that the movie was no longer French. It did not matter, apparently, that the story was French, or that the movie was shot in France, in French, and with French actors.[35]

Lessons from Hollywood

Hollywood is, in contrast to what many people think, not at all as American as it may appear. Hollywood is just as European – or perhaps even more – and as cosmopolitan as Europe itself. How could this be? Look at history. Transnationality can be considered as a long-term paradigm in Hollywood, not least because the audience, according to film historian Geoffrey Nowell-Smith, has always been 'very cosmopolitan'.[36] In the early 20th century both Sidney Kent of Paramount Pictures and Will Hays, the first president of the Motion Picture Producers and Distributors of America (MPPDA), hired foreigners to make sure that producers did not picture 'in an unfavorable light another country's religion, history, institutions, prominent people and citizenry'.[37]

Immigrants even founded or co-founded some of the best known Hollywood companies. Carl Laemmle came from Germany and created Universal Pictures; Adolph Zucker was Hungarian and created Paramount Pictures; William Fox, another fellow Hungarian, founded Fox Film Corporation; Louis B Mayer was from Russia and founded

Metro-Goldwyn-Mayer together with Samuel Goldwyn, who came
from Poland. Benjamin Warner, also from Poland, founded Warner Bros
in 1923. Neal Gabler, author of *An Empire of Their Own: How the Jews
Invented Hollywood*, writes that a common explanation of their success
is that they originated from the same social level as the core group of
early moviegoers; working class immigrants. He furthermore writes that
'by making a "shadow" America, one which idealized every old glorifying
bromide about the country, the Hollywood Jews created a powerful
cluster of images and ideas – so powerful that, in a sense, they colonized
the American imagination.'[38]

   Some claim that the real change of direction came in the 1970s.
With the economic successes of blockbusters like *Star Wars* (George
Lucas, 1977) and the development of a more or less similar production
structure to other businesses driving economic globalization,
Hollywood became an open invitation to all kinds of investors, even
to those usually situated far from the entertainment industry. Crédit
Lyonnais, for instance – a bank owned by the French government
until 1982 – became one of the leading sources for financing several
Hollywood blockbusters, among them *Platoon* (Oliver Stone, 1986). A
new watershed came in 1989, when Sony bought Columbia Pictures,
provoking *Newsweek* magazine to place the Statue of Liberty dressed
in a kimono under the headline 'Japan Invades Hollywood' on one of
its covers. The following year Japanese company Matsushita Electric
Industries Co took over MCA, which included Universal Studios. Two
years later, Crédit Lyonnais acquired MGM/United Artists, before
Canadian company Seagram Co Ltd purchased 80 per cent of MCA,
including Universal, while Matsushita kept the last 20 per cent. In 2000
the French company Vivendi bought Seagram, still including Universal,
before the merger between the American NBC and French-American
Vivendi Universal Entertainment created NBC Universal in 2004, in
which the American company General Electric owned 80 per cent of
the shares. In 2005 a consortium led by Sony acquired MGM/United
Artists.[39]

   Greg Elmer and Mike Gasher, editors of *Contracting Out
Hollywood*, write that '*Hollywood* still denotes a place in Southern

California, a community within the city of Los Angeles, even the site of the annual Academy Awards pageant, but it has become a progressively inappropriate label for a film and television production industry that comprises a global network of locations, technical services, acting pools, even remote affiliate studio facilities.[40] Together with the financial globalization of Hollywood, large parts of the actual production have been outsourced from the US since the Second World War. In 1998, for instance, out of a total of 308 made-for-television movies, 139 were shot abroad and characterized by the American ITA (International Trade Association, US Department of Commerce) as 'runaway productions'.[41] Basically, this means relocating US-based movie productions outside the US for creative and economic reasons. Creative incentives might be exotic locations or specially designed studio complexes, which are often connected and come with a cheaper price than locations in the US.

Italian film and television production facility Cinecittà – advertising that 'you can walk in with your script and walk out with a completed film'[42] – on the outskirts of Rome is a good example. Among big-budget movies shot here are *Hudson Hawk* (Michael Lehmann, 1991), *Cliffhanger* (Renny Harlin, 1993), *Daylight* (Rob Cohen, 1996) and *Mission Impossible III* (J J Abrams, 2005). Even more interesting is it that Cinecittà Holding SpA, the largest shareholder in Cinecittà Studios SpA (25 per cent), is owned by among others the Italian government, the movie production company Filmauro Srl and Vittorio Cecchi Gori, the owner of Italy's largest distribution and production company.[43] Economic geographers like A J Scott also point to the fact that Hollywood has an unrivalled ability to get a film 'to a theatre near you'.[44] All of the Hollywood majors include subsidiaries and mergers in their distribution chains. United International Pictures (UIP), for instance, is co-owned by Universal and Paramount, based in London, and has a network of licensing deals and local offices in 127 countries.[45] Hollywood majors also contribute to an enhanced cinematic infrastructure, a particularly noticeable strategy in countries like India and China.[46]

However, it is true that the economic globalization of Hollywood 'does not fully account for the unpredictability of the cultural reactions that can make or break a film shown in another country'.[47] Why do

American movies become so popular in other countries? Is it not 'in the movies that America itself finds love and comes to adore its own self-image?'[48] To some extent, probably, but there are good reasons to disagree that Hollywood is typically American and American film synonymous with the worst of Hollywood. American Michael Medved, for one, writes in his 1993 book *Hollywood vs America* that 'tens of millions of Americans now see the entertainment industry as an all-powerful enemy, an alien force that assaults our most cherished values and corrupts our children'.[49] *The Economist* declared, from a radically different point of view, that Hollywood movies 'eschew fine-grained cultural observation for generic subjects that anybody can identify with regardless of national origins. There is nothing particularly American about boats crashing into icebergs or asteroids that threaten to obliterate human life.'[50]

These views demand that Hollywood be looked at from a more analytical angle. In this respect, one seminal study is Scott J Olson's *Hollywood Planet*. His main argument is that 'narrative transparency' is the key characteristic of Hollywood films, with 'the capability of certain texts to seem familiar regardless of their origin, to seem a part of one's own culture, even though they have been crafted elsewhere'.[51] The myth itself is not universal, only the recognition of *mythotypes*, which are narrative structures created to 'inspire awe, wonder, purpose, joy, and participation, hence denying the absolutism of reality'.[52] Local cultures then weave these emotional intentions from the mythotypes together with specific plots, heroes, crooks, environments and stories known as myths, or *monomyths*. Role-functions create a narrative structure which is recognizable to the viewer, even if the stories differ.[53] George Lucas, the director of the *Star Wars* series, among other things, is one of the most outspoken users of the monomyth.[54]

But even if mainstream Hollywood movies have structural similarities, it still doesn't answer the question: isn't Hollywood all-American? Not if we include the fact that the US, as illustrated above, is a nation of immigrants and that Hollywood has been a reflection of this. Film historian Andrew Higson argues that Hollywood through history has met its audience with 'an almost ruthless disregard for the nationality (as well as class and gender) of the spectator'.[55] Professor Richard Pells even states that 'the influence of immigrants and African-Americans on the United States explains why its culture has been so popular for so long in so many places. American culture has spread throughout the world because it has incorporated foreign styles and ideas' and specialized 'in selling the dreams, fears, and folklore of other people back to them'.[56] Personally, I believe it also has a lot to do with the continuous stream of European-born Hollywood directors and their share of 'blockbuster' films of the 1990s:[57]

- Harald Zwart (Norway): *One Night at McCool's*, *Agent Cody Banks*, *Pink Panther 2*
- Mikael Håfström (Sweden): *Derailed*, *1408*
- Renny Harlin (Finland): *Die Hard 2*, *Cliffhanger*, *The Long Kiss Goodnight*, *Mindhunters*
- Wolfgang Petersen/Roland Emmerich (Germany): *Outbreak*, *Air Force One*, *The Perfect Storm*, *Troy*, *Poseidon*, *Independence Day*, *Godzilla*, *The Patriot*, *The Day After Tomorrow*, *10,000 BC*
- Jan de Bont/Paul Verhoeven (Netherlands): *Speed 1* and *2*, *Twister*, *Tomb Raider: The Cradle of Life*, *Robocop*, *Total Recall*, *Basic Instinct*, *Starship Troopers*
- Ridley Scott/Sam Mendes (UK): *G I Jane*, *Gladiator*, *Black Hawk Down*, *Kingdom of Heaven*, *American Beauty*, *Jarhead*
- Luc Besson (France): *Leon*, *The Fifth Element*, *Kiss of the Dragon*, *Bandidas*, *Love and other Disasters*, *Transporter 1, 2* and *3*

This list confirms that the competitive advantage of Hollywood is its ability to attract talent from all over the world (something which is also reflected in the European sweep of the acting awards at the Oscars 2008) and that it doesn't need to bother about dubious scoreboard systems in order to make a good movie. It is, on the other hand, not unreasonable to question the importance of the director's nationality. Earlier I cited Alejandro González Iñárritu, who preferred to leave the whole concept of nationality out of the question. Wolfgang Petersen, the German director of epic dramas like *Troy* (2004) and *Poseidon* (2006), has a different opinion:

'I hope that a lot of my European roots, cultural background, and
upbringing translate into the films I do here (. . .) What I've learned in school
and wherever else is also very much part of my work here. It gives it the special
Wolfgang Petersen feel to it, instead of being very typical American styled. I
know I'm quite a bit under attack from Germany these days. But that's very
typical: when you leave your country for Hollywood, they say, "Now he's lost
soul and it's all very American." I think that's complete bullshit. Simply look at
my films or films of other European directors who work here: they bring their
heritage and their upbringing all with them.'[58]

None the less, Petersen thinks that his ethnic background is
insignificant for the Hollywood companies: 'To tell you the truth: I think
most of the executives and people of the studios don't think much
about it anymore. German or not, I'm just the filmmaker Petersen.'[59]
Petersen's comment is hence in many ways conclusive about what the
EU can learn from the contemporary Hollywood industry. Cosmopolitan
productions make movies for a cosmopolitan audience, even when
it's not intentional, because of their 'nation-blind' market orientation.
Together with a globalized production industry, transnational impulses
(economic as well as cultural) make Hollywood a unique film cluster.
'Hollywoodization' – yes indeed, but Americanization, no.

The future is digital
At the beginning of this chapter, I confessed my enthusiasm for
video games. As I said, I am not alone. The EU ICT Task Force writes
in a 2006 report that the EU, in its current strategies for the cultural
economy, must consider the global landscape for ICT investments.[60]
That means, among other things, acknowledging the growing role
of video games. Because 2009 is designated as the European Year of
Creativity and Innovation,[61] I believe that bringing a more strategic
approach to this area is urgently needed to fulfil the goals of the Lisbon
Strategy. In many ways the EU's new agenda for culture continues
the ideas from the so-called Essen Declaration, hailing from the EU
Presidency Conference 'Culture Industries in Europe: A Comparison of
Development Concepts' in Essen in 1999 (subtitled 'Ten Axioms for the

Culture Industries in Europe').[62] Two axioms especially deserve further elaboration: 1) culture industries are future-oriented, and 2) culture industries deploy Europe's historic heritage.

Regarding the former, the Declaration states that culture industries are distinguished by high levels of creativity and innovation, developing both substantive content and new technologies. Regarding the latter, the Declaration states that 'in the competitive global marketplace Europe's greatest potential is its history and traditions. Europe's rich and diverse cultural landscape are [sic] the product of centuries of creativity on the part of artists, craftsmen and women, technicians and their clients.' Both these maxims are invaluable to the cultural economy, economically (as potential growth sectors) as well as culturally (as an arena for unfolding creativity), and add up to a certain kind of 'amusement economics' where digital innovation plays a major part. Markets are growing, and because they are less conventionally attached to national cultures, the opportunities are potentially larger than with the nationally inclined film industry in Europe.

Economically, the gaming industry is growing. KEA Affairs estimates that games will see the greatest growth of the cultural industries from 2005 to 2010, increasing their market-size revenue from €699 million to €2,300 million.[63] According to a 2006 study, European revenues from online content are expected to reach €8.3 billion by 2010, a growth of over 400 per cent in five years.[64] Similar findings are evident across the Atlantic. Entertainment Software Association (ESA) announced in 2007 that US game industry growth was outstripping the growth of the US economy by a large percentage. In 2006, the entertainment software industry's value to the US Gross Domestic Product (GDP) was $3.8 billion. The industry also makes a disproportionate contribution to the real growth of the US economy as a whole. For example, in 2005–06 the industry's contribution to real growth exceeded its share of GDP by more than four to one. US computer and video game software sales grew 6 per cent in 2007 to $9.5 billion – more than tripling industry software sales since 1996.[65]

Looking at findings compiled by the NPD Group, a global market research company, and released by the ESA in January 2008, computer and video game companies posted record sales in 2007. The industry sold 267.8 million units altogether, and game console software sales totalled $6.6 billion with 153.9 million units sold. *Halo 3*, the best-selling title of 2007, took in more revenue in its first day of sales than the then biggest opening weekend ever for a movie (*Spiderman 3*) and the final *Harry Potter* book's first day sales. The entertainment software industry also stimulates complementary product purchases of roughly $6.1 billion a year. For example, approximately $73 million in HDTV sales can be attributed to the introduction of the XBox 360 game console.[66]

Culturally, today's video games exhibit a variety of challenges, themes, intertextual references and narratives, all appealing to a broad spectrum of players. Sports, strategy games, first-person adventures, historical battles and fantasy games are the most popular genres. Consider for instance *Grand Theft Auto*. Originally developed by Scottish firm DMA Design in 1997 (in 1999 the firm was purchased by American multinational Take-Two Interactive and later renamed Rockstar North), founded by David Jones, the series of GTA games has become wildly popular. As of 26 March 2008, the franchise had sold over 70 million copies worldwide. In the latest edition, *Grand Theft Auto IV* (*GTA IV*), the story about Niko Bellic entering Liberty City, getting involved in myriad controversies, unfurls in an almost novelistic manner. Playability is great, graphics amazing, music cool and assignments intricate: no wonder people are excited. A Norwegian gaming journalist, after playing *GTA IV*, explained that he had felt narrative greatness, no less, right up there with movies like *The French Connection* or TV series like *The Sopranos*. His conclusion was that *GTA IV* 'is truly one of the greatest things you can encounter in modern entertainment, regardless of genre or format'.[67]

Video games also offer possibilities for the creation of historical meaning and consciousness. Because, as historian Stefan Haas argues, in games one can put oneself more easily in someone else's place. As an example he mentions the classic strategy game *Age of Empires II: The Age of Kings* (1999), in which the player can choose between different peoples like the Normans, British or Mongolians, or between William Wallace, Friedrich Barbarossa, Genghis Khan or Joan of Arc. Different episodes from each life can be played in the basic environment of the game, and they are fitted together by a narrator telling the story. Even though most games or movies do not strive to be 100 per cent historically correct, as with the recently premiered blockbuster *Max Manus*, dealing with civil resistance groups in Norway during the Second World War, some allow a rather sophisticated – even contra-factual – view of history. Most of all the new media, writes Haas, include the recipient as part of the sense-creating process, giving up monocausal explanation in favour of complex, pluralistic models.[68]

The general reasons for games' growth in popularity are a mix of escalated individualism, technological literacy and a specific type of consumer economics – dubbed by *The Economist* 'the Bridget Jones economy'.[69] Sociologist Frank Furedi once wrote, exemplifying what we could call the cultural expansion of adolescence, that '28-year-old John Russell looks at me as though I am a lost cause. John, a well-paid lawyer, says he isn't interested in doing "adult stuff". He loves his PlayStation and spends a considerable portion of his disposable income on hi-tech toys.'[70] Game developer Richard Rouse has another take on the issue and believes that in a packed media environment it's all about emotional interactivity. 'The emotions that games are able to evoke in players are much stronger than what can be experienced in other media where the experience is less immersive and considerably less personally involving,' he writes. In addition, game players long for their own chosen forms of escapism: 'Many people want to be transported to a world more glamorous than their own.' At the same time there is a notable difference between this kind of escapism and those offered by books or movies. 'In games,' Rouse ends, 'players get the chance to actually be someone more exciting, to control a pulp-fiction adventurer, daring swordsman, or space-opera hero.'[71]

In reply to the financial downturn
During my conversation with Xavier Troussard, he claimed that video games are indeed covered by the MEDIA 2007–13 programme briefly discussed above. Reading it closely, we find below the heading 'Support for the development of on and off-line interactive works' that 'interactive

works for computer, internet, mobile phone, games consoles including handheld presenting a substantial degree of interactivity, scenario and innovation' are eligible for application.[72] But the maximum amount of money – €60,000 (€100,000 maximum to develop consoles, not games) – is like a drop in the ocean. Furthermore, only 20 per cent of the total budget is designated for development, traditionally a very large element of video games costs. Development costs for a top-of-the-line video game – and this was a couple of years ago, before PlayStation 3 and Xbox 360 – hover between $12 million and $35 million.[73] Remembering the table of chosen projects from the Culture Programme in 2008 (chapter 3), we also see that multimedia and new technologies are down the list.

Some of these issues are discussed in a recent press release from the European Council regarding education, youth and culture. Outlining challenges connected to media literacy in the digital environment and linking this to the European Year of Creativity and Innovation 2009, the EC briefly touches on the potential of the games sector. For example it says that the EC encourages Europeans 'to identify, access and appreciate content relating to or originating within different cultures, and to use new technological tools (software and hardware) to create and distribute their own cultural content'.[74] Yet, if this is all there is, and bearing in mind the financial crisis, I believe few are going to be very awed – even less so when they read that 'the Commission does not propose that a specific budget should be allocated for the Year, arguing that it can be organised by using existing EU programmes and planned administrative expenditure.'[75]

This is surprising given that focus areas have long been identified. A 1999 study identifies cultural industries such as design, fashion, multimedia and internet services as the fastest-growing sectors of the British economy. To an increasing degree these sectors are also run by 'independents': people mainly in their twenties and thirties, who run microbusinesses or are self-employed freelances, being often producers, designers, retailers and promoters at the same time. As in Florida's theory, their main asset is creativity. 'Across Britain,' the researchers state, 'thousands of young Independents are working from their bedrooms and garages, workshops and run-down offices, hoping that they will come up with the next Hotmail or Netscape, the next Lara Croft or Diddy Kong, the next *Wallace and Gromit* or *Notting Hill*.'[76] Another finding from this study is that policymakers, both national and local, know little about this new generation of entrepreneurs – how they work, where they come from, their distinctive needs – or how to interact with them.

Knowing that this study is a decade old, and having the disastrous effects of the economic downturn fresh in mind, the EU and Member States should switch from the conventional policy view and spotlight more explicit objectives under the umbrella of 'creative destruction' as outlined by Economics Professor Tyler Cowen.[77] My humble suggestion is that the EU should establish a separate programme for video games which aims at developing both platforms and software. Alternatively, it can be moved from MEDIA and connected to other cultural strategies that concern education, the movement of personnel, multiculturalism and urban planning – thus making it a part of the structural funds. Another alternative is to include it in the next framework programme, which are those EU programmes that 'bundle all research-related EU initiatives together under a common roof playing a crucial role in reaching the goals of growth, competitiveness and employment'.

Regardless of programme reorganization, video games are in this context a head-on target for concretizing the oft-mentioned 'knowledge triangle' – research, education and innovation – which is a core factor in European efforts to meet the ambitious Lisbon goals.[78] If successful, it will create an innovative network of skill centres, which already exist here and there, scattered across Europe (preferably in creative cities or even a branch at the European Institute of Technology[79]), where video games – and those who play them – will contribute both culturally and economically to the new Europe.

[1] www.gathering.org/tg08/tg08history.html

[2] ISFE, 2008.

[3] ISFE, 2008.

[4] See Anheier and Isar, 2008.

[5] Cunningham, Banks and Potts, 2008: 16–17.

[6] European Commission, 2007a.

[7] For a summary, see http://ec.europa.eu/ growthandjobs/faqs/background/index_ en.htm

[8] www.europarl.europa.eu/facts/4_16_4_ en.htm

[9] KEA, 2006.

[10] Kok, 2004.

[11] European Commission, 2007a.

[12] Hall, 1998: 7.

[13] Florida, 2004: 68.

[14] Florida and Tinagli, 2004.

[15] Robins, 2006.

[16] Hall, 1998: 285.

[17] Saxenian, 1999.

[18] Legrain, 2007.

[19] Bentley, 2004: 9.

[20] Florida, 2004: 232.

[21] Landry, 2000: 9. Among the European cities were Barcelona, Helsinki, Montpellier, Dublin and Strasbourg.

[22] Landry and Wood, 2007.

[23] European Commission, 2005: 5.

[24] www.mpaa.org/researchStatistics.asp

[25] Wenders, 2006.

[26] Miller et al, 2005.

[27] http://ec.europa.eu/information_society/ media/overview/index_en.htm

[28] www.coe.int/Eurimages

[29] Gyory, 2000.

[30] Klein, 2003.

[31] www.filmfrasor.no/en/about-us

[32] Moseng, 2008.

[33] http://ec.europa.eu/comm/competition/ state_aid/register/ii/by_primary_obj_culture. html

[34] Cited in Littger, 2006: 191.

[35] Lichfield, 2004.

[36] Nowell-Smith, 1985: 154.

[37] Miller et al, 2005: 67.

[38] Gabler, 1988: 7.

[39] Kunz, 2007: 31.

[40] Elmer and Gasher, 2005: 1.

[41] ITA, 2001: 1.

[42] www.cinecittastudios.it/public/_cfm/page/ page_454.cfm

[43] www.cinecittastudios.it/public/_cfm/page/ page_664.cfm

[44] Scott, 2004.

[45] www.uip.com

[46] www.timewarner.com/corp/newsroom/ pr/0,20812,669936,00.html

[47] Danan, 1995: 131.

[48] Sardar and Davies, 2004: 121.

[49] Medved, 1993: 1.

[50] *The Economist*, 1998.

[51] Olson, 1999: 18.

[52] Olson, 1999: 93.

[53] Campbell, 1972.

[54] Watch the interview with George Lucas explaining this at www.films.com/id/11017/ The_Mythology_of_Star_Wars_with_ George_Lucas_and_Bill_Moyers.htm

[55] Higson, 1989: 40.

[56] Pells, 2002.

[57] My source here is International Movie Database (www.imdb.com)

[58] Cited in Littger, 2006: 41.

[59] Cited in Littger, 2006: 41.

[60] EU, 2006.

[61] http://create2009.europa.eu

[62] www.ericarts.org/web/files/134/en/culture_ industries_essen_declaration.pdf

[63] KEA, 2006.

[64] Screen Digest, 2006.

[65] www.theesa.com/facts/econdata.asp

[66] www.theesa.com/facts/salesandgenre.asp

[67] Bryne, 2008.

[68] Haas, 2002: 186–90.

[69] *The Economist*, 2001.

[70] Furedi, 2003.

[71] Rouse, 2004: 6–7.

[72] http://ec.europa.eu/information_society/

media/producer/develop/interactive/
index_en.htm

[73] OECD, 2005: 25.

[74] EU, 2008.

[75] http://europa.eu/rapid/
pressReleasesAction.
do?reference=IP/08/482

[76] Leadbeater and Oakley, 1999: 11.

[77] Cowen, 2004.

[78] http://cordis.europa.eu/fp7/understand_
en.html

[79] http://ec.europa.eu/eit

6 Culture and foreign policy

The third and final point of the European Union's agenda for culture concerns 'external relations' – or foreign policy, if you will. While investigating various ways in which culture can be an integrated part of foreign policy, with exceptional emphasis on what's called 'soft power', I also discuss, with among others Gijs de Vries, former coordinator of anti-terrorism issues in the office of Javier Solana, the EU's High Representative in foreign policy, under which conditions such soft power is likely to be successful as an adjunct of European foreign policy. Arguing that the UNESCO trail is perhaps overdue for revision, replacing the idea of global politics as the will of powerful nation-states with a truly cosmopolitan baseline, I end this chapter with some examples of how this could be done.

At my first visit to the website describing the bonds between culture and the EU's external affairs, in the middle of August 2008, I was greeted with the message: 'Under construction'.[1]

Culture in the European Union's external relations

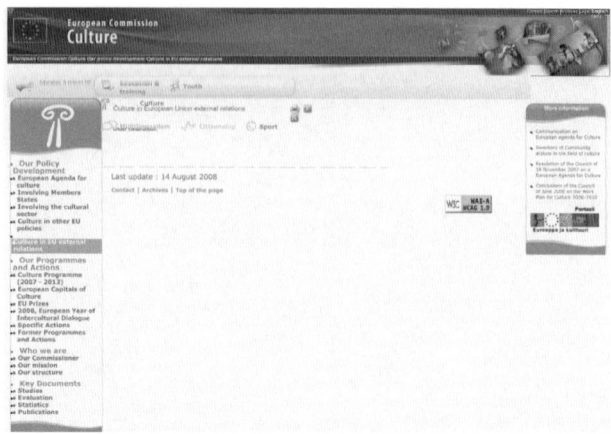

Source http://ec.europa.eu/culture/our-policy-development/doc1567_en.htm

Notwithstanding the possible irony of this message, the Communication states that 'worldwide, cultural diversity and intercultural dialogue have become major challenges for a global order based on peace, mutual understanding and respect for shared values, such as the protection and promotion of human rights and the protection of languages.'[2] Reflected by the fact that almost every country in the world now has diplomatic representation in Brussels, and that the Commission has opened more than 130 overseas delegations, the EU has a solid basis for foreign relations.[3] Still, orders seem tall, one might say. Traditionally, developing a common foreign policy has not been greeted with enthusiasm by EU members. The Treaties of Rome make no mention of such plans.

None the less, there has been a considerable policy harmonization.[4] The Common and Foreign Security Policy (CFSP) was established as the second pillar of the European Union in the 1993 Treaty on European Union signed at Maastricht. Its core objective, which has remained more or less unchanged, is to safeguard the common values, fundamental interests, independence and integrity of the Union in conformity with the principles of the United Nations Charter. A number of important changes were introduced in the Amsterdam Treaty which came into force in 1999, and since then there have been numerous developments in CFSP. There has been agreement to embark on a common security and defence policy (CESDP) within the overall framework of the CFSP.

In 2001, the European Council at Laeken adopted a declaration on the operational capability of the common security and defence policy, officially recognizing that the Union is now capable of conducting some crisis management operations. Interim structures established after the Amsterdam Treaty have become permanent. With the Nice Treaty, certain amendments to the CFSP provisions of the treaty were agreed. The Amsterdam Treaty also introduced the new office of a High Representative (HR) for CFSP. The office is fused with that of Council Secretary General. The HR's role is to assist the Council in matters coming within the scope of the CFSP, in particular through contributing to the formulation, preparation and implementation of policy decisions, and, when appropriate and acting on behalf of the Council at the request of the Presidency, through conducting political dialogue with non-EU countries.

In the 2007 brochure *The European Union: Furthering Human Rights and Democracy Across the Globe* we get a general overview of EU tools and policies in the field of human rights and democratization.[5] First, the EU intends to mainstream human rights and democratization, that is, incorporate concerns on the two issues into all policies, programmes and projects. Work is guided by the human rights guidelines that the EU has issued on the death penalty, torture, dialogues with third countries, children affected by armed conflict and human rights defenders, as well as by the international human rights conventions, which translate into the founding Treaties of the European Union. Through the European Neighbourhood Policy (ENP) the Union has set up forums to discuss human rights and democracy issues with Jordan, Morocco, Lebanon and Tunisia.

With China and Iran, the EU has engaged in so-called 'structured human rights dialogues'. In China's case since 1995 (with few exceptions), these have taken place every six months, alternately in China and in Europe. The formal dialogue has been complemented by EU-China human rights legal seminars bringing together officials, academics and representatives of the NGO community. Since 2002, the EU has also held four sessions of human rights dialogue with Iran, with the last occurring in 2004. In spite of an agreement between the EU and Iran on revised modalities for the dialogue, in December 2006 Iran withdrew its participation, as it had done before, following the EU's co-sponsoring of the Iran country resolution in the UN General Assembly. Such a withdrawal is deplorable, although the EU remains committed to the dialogue, provided that Iran confirms its willingness to engage seriously in the process.

Second, the EU is financing specific projects to promote and protect human rights. Through the European Instrument for Democracy and Human Rights (EIDHR), which currently has an average annual budget of some €140 million, the EIDHR has in accordance with the first approach focused on promoting human rights issues of particular importance to the European Union. Examples of such are the fight against the death penalty, the prevention of torture and the rehabilitation of torture victims, and work towards an effective system of global justice for human rights violators through support to the ad hoc international criminal tribunals in Rwanda and Sierra Leone and the International Criminal Court (ICC). On 1 January 2007, a new Regulation for the EIDHR entered into force. Now called the European Instrument for Democracy and Human Rights, it provides continuity with its predecessor while introducing a range of changes, including a strong focus on democracy promotion and support to human rights defenders.

One example is the support for the free trade union of Burundi. This EIDHR project, implemented by the Italian NGO ISCOS-Cisl, aimed at strengthening the political role and the effectiveness of the Burundi Trade Union, COSYBU (Union Confederation of Burundi), in order to increase the level of respect for fundamental labour rights and to support the overall democratic process in the country. This two-year project foresaw a series of training courses for specific trade union activists, as well as training for trainers. Areas covered by the training included organizational processes, labour legislation, social dialogue, international cooperation, debt and globalization and communication methodologies. About 50 trade union activists from different categories participated (50 per cent of the beneficiaries are women). Once the training was concluded, they continued the training for other workers. As one of the concrete results of this project, the beneficiaries created, at the end of the activities, their own Trade Union Education Association (AFoSy).[6]

Of course there are disparities in how truly influential these aspects of a common foreign policy are. The lack of policy focus and consistent leadership positions (if I want to speak to Europe, who do I call?) was to some degree eased in 1999 when four external portfolios in the Commission were replaced with one, and a High Representative was appointed to be the first point of contact on foreign and security policy matters.[7] On some areas, like global trade negotiations, third parties must deal with the EU as a whole. But on defence and security policy, states still mainly go their own way (with some notable exceptions, like Frontex).[8] This creates a dilemma; on the one hand, it is obvious that the EU would have more power and influence in the world if the Member States managed to act in concert. The thoughts of such coordination leading to interference in national matters and the freedom to outline their own opinions, on the other hand, encourage those who fear loss of national sovereignty. Either way, we approach the main question: where does culture fit in?

Why culture in foreign policy?
Culture has been a vital part of foreign relations among Member States for quite some time. Promoting languages, cultural exchange and cultivating a sense of cultural identity across national borders have for long been a task for several large European states. Quasi-governmental organizations like the French Alliance Française,[9] the German Goethe-Institut,[10] or the Spanish Instituto Cervantes[11] are but a few examples. The last was established in 1991, and has grown to include offices in 42 countries. Anyone interested in the culture of Spain and the score of Latin American countries where Spanish is spoken will encounter unceasing activity: every day in the academic year an average of 22 cultural events take place. It has even established interactive links through the online game *Second Life*: the virtual Head Office of

Cervantes recreates the building which houses the institution, with exhibition rooms, events room, video screens and virtual classrooms for learning Spanish, at the service of internet users interested in virtual reality and three-dimensional interaction.[12]

But these initiatives are all nation-based, with historical connections which are not always seen with cordial eyes, hence limiting the span of culture as a European Union foreign relations tool. One argument favouring the inclusion of cultural aspects in the EU's external relations is the possibility it brings of helping to rebalance asymmetrical trade patterns, by providing access to both European and other markets, for cultural goods and services from developing countries. Another argument is that European colonialism has left members of the European Union with a heritage of economic, political and cultural ties to countries in Latin America, South Asia and Africa. France and Belgium still had large colonies when the Treaty of Rome was signed, and when Britain joined in 1973 it brought several new countries into the equation. Predominantly, these ties have been manifested through economic arrangements. Beginning with the so-called Yaoundé Conventions in 1963 and 1969, which gave 18 former colonies preferential access to Community markets in return for limited duty-free or quota-free access by the EC to their markets, they have expanded to include commercial ties and developmental projects.[13]

Artistically, widespread debates are less visible. A reflection group coordinated by the European Cultural Foundation (ECF), which in the period of 2002–04 explored the cultural dimension to European integration, concludes that culture 'is today a security consideration *par excellence* and cultural ties can nurture trust and dialogue where, at the moment, hatred and prejudice reign'.[14] Furthermore, the reflection group states that 'if the EU is determined to shape its own foreign and security policy, its specific quality should be a prominent cultural component and it should draw inspiration from the high articulation of cultural policies in Europe in order to determine its cultural approach.'[15] As an example they suggest the establishment of European Houses of Culture in some key cities outside the EU – they mention Istanbul and Cairo – spreading the intellectual debate away from Brussels, run by locals. In this way, the notion of European culture would be constructed from the outside, experimentally and in a non-elitist way, with houses staffed by cultural operators rather than diplomats.[16] An example related to this is the Union's setting up, in Alexandria, of the Anna Lindh Euro-Mediterranean Foundation for the Dialogue between Cultures.[17]

Also bearing this in mind, the EU wishes to follow what it calls a 'twin-track' cultural approach to countries outside the Union, consisting of support for specific cultural actions and events on the one hand, and on the other, seeking systematic integration of the cultural dimension and different components of culture in all external and development policies, projects and programmes. This twin-track approach then itself divides in two: first, the EU's cultural actions seek to help other countries preserve and restore heritage sites, produce and circulate works of art, promote the mobility of artists, create or restore museums, support the development of cultural industries, especially the cinema and audiovisual sector, build the capacity of cultural operators and artists and organize major cultural events.

The Culture Programme is for instance open to cooperation with non-EU countries that have concluded association or cooperation agreements with the Community, provided that they contain cultural clauses. In 2007 projects were aimed at India and China. Reading the list of 13 selected projects[18] instantly prompts optimism: one example is 'Spice', a joint venture coordinated by the inexhaustible British arts organization Brouhaha,[19] co-organized by Spanish Ballet Entradas, and with an associated partner in Attakalari Centre for Movement Arts in Bangalore, India. In 2008 the focus is on Brazil[20] and for the special action in 2009, the eligible 'third countries' are Armenia, Belarus, Egypt, Georgia, Jordan, Moldova, the occupied Palestinian Territory and Tunisia.[21]

Second, the EU aims to further develop political dialogue with all countries and regions, and to promote both cultural exchange and access between EU and non-EU countries. It also seeks to include culture in the enlargement process, to pursue its efforts through the UN's Alliance of Civilizations[22] and to be a committed party to the UNESCO Convention on the Protection and the Promotion of the

Diversity of Cultural Expressions from 2005. Herein comes, for instance, the education and training links set forth by the Bologna Declaration of 1999,[23] where European education ministers stated that 'we need to ensure that the European higher education system acquires a worldwide degree of attraction equal to our extraordinary cultural and scientific traditions.' Two examples of this are the ALFA and Alßan programmes for Latin America.[24] In 2008, the European Commission also invited proposals from Japanese universities to establish three new EU centres in Japan. The EU Centres initiative is aimed at encouraging greater awareness and knowledge of the EU through support for EU-focused curriculum development and research, outreach activities and academic links.[25]

Both these approaches were affirmed by the EU Education, Youth and Culture Council which, in November 2008, called on the Member States and the Commission to pursue the promotion of cultural diversity and intercultural dialogue in the external relations of the Union and its Member States.[26] It was the first ever high-level – and comprehensive – document on this topic to combine policy objectives, consistent approaches, concise aims, and methods and instruments. Among a lot of ideas embedded in the document, it seeks to draw up a European strategy for incorporating culture consistently and systematically in the external relations of the Union. These specific strategies could be defined, it was suggested, in accordance with the distribution of powers established in the Treaty, at the end of processes involving expertise and consultation with the regions and countries concerned. Consequently, involving culture in external relations is not a one-way process. It demands a channel of communication – a certain kind of dialogue.

The rise of soft power

For many, the recognition of culture in foreign policy could be described as a form of sophisticated diplomacy.[27] 'Though a politically accepted and conceptually defined EU foreign cultural policy does not yet exist and the topic will remain controversial in the foreseeable future,' two academics wrote in 2004, 'there is already a cultural dialogue with non-EU countries on European questions and aspects.'[28] The EU echoes this argument in its new agenda for culture: 'the Union has increasingly focused on promoting support for human rights, including the protection and promotion of cultural rights, the rights of indigenous peoples as well as the rights of persons belonging to minorities and socially marginalized people. Intercultural dialogue as one of the main instruments of peace and conflict prevention is obviously among the basic objectives of such actions.' Additional explanations can be found elsewhere in the Communication: 'The EU is, and must aspire to become even more, an example of a "soft power" founded on norms and values such as human dignity, solidarity, tolerance, freedom of expression, respect for diversity and intercultural dialogue.'[29]

Mark the term soft power. Tzvetan Todorov, the Bulgarian sociologist and author, once wrote that the strength of Europe lies not in military force or imperial fantasies from the old days, but in the foursome of European modernity: democracy, human rights, the rule of law and freedom of speech.[30] At a time when there is an ongoing war on terror, such policies are routinely bashed, particularly by American political 'hawks'. Different strategies for chasing al-Qaida and the invasion of Iraq, following the carnage on 11 September 2001, exposed some rifts, which signalled that transatlantic ties could end up being 'no longer the central relationship of the world order'.[31] None the less, even though European countries disagreed internally about whether the war in Iraq was justified, soft power is probably the EU's most constructive contribution to settling global unease. A Pew Research Survey from 2007, covering more than 45,000 respondents from 47 countries and comparing findings with a similar survey done in 2002, shows that while the US image continues to be extremely popular throughout much of Sub-Saharan Africa, it remains abysmal in most Muslim countries in the Middle East and Asia, and continues to decline among the publics of many of America's oldest allies.[32]

In other words, it seems like there is a free chair for a different kind of foreign policy from the browbeating US way that has dominated the Bush administrations. As far as rift warnings between Europe and the US go, the term 'soft power' was in fact first coined by an American: Harvard University Professor Joseph Nye, who remains its most prominent proponent, in a 1990 book, *Bound to Lead: The Changing Nature of American Power*. He further developed the concept in his 2004 book, *Soft Power: The Means to Success in World Politics*. In essence, soft power is the ability to get what you want by attracting and persuading others to adopt your goals. It differs from hard power, the ability to use the carrots and sticks of economic and military might to make others follow your will.[33] Attraction depends on credibility, and it is therefore not the case, as some have assumed, that American ideas of soft power are all about the influence of Coca-Cola and blue jeans. It is also wrong to argue that soft power excludes the use of hard power. Soft power is merely a belief that it is possible to develop legitimate means and common ground for changing the international war climate and people's minds in other ways than using tanks and bombs. Culture serves as a vehicle for generating goodwill and understanding for the goals and interests of one's own society.[34]

One of those who know a thing or two about the advantages of taking a comprehensive view of soft power, culture and the EU's foreign relations is Gijs de Vries, former coordinator of anti-terrorism issues in the office of Javier Solana, the EU's High Representative in foreign policy. To de Vries, introducing culture as a part of foreign relations is central to modern diplomacy, and soft power – his overarching concept – should be a synergy between the tools of cultural diplomacy (the protection of heritage and stimulation of exchange, for example translation of European books and films into Arabic) and the promotion of human rights. Rooted in values like tolerance, human rights and liberty, such cultural relations must then be adapted to the classical ideal of diplomacy – long-lasting and mutually beneficial relationships.[35] Only this way, by using cultural activities and attitudes to expose a community's idea of itself, can the EU promote soft power as a solution to *questions de société*. As de Vries writes unsentimentally, 'the effectiveness of the Union's Common Foreign and Security Policy partly depends on the image of the Union in third countries.'[36]

If one is to utilize soft power, trust is thus a keyword. One basic ingredient of trust is reputation. On this point, the EU seems to have a good view of itself, even though the legacy of years of colonialism and imperialism still influences public opinion about Europe around the world. The book *The EU Through the Eyes of Asia*, for instance, contains some disturbing findings. Based on media representations and interviews, the researchers found good and positive coverage of Europeans when it came to celebrities, fashion and sports. Sadly, they also found a negative image when it came to racial tensions in Europe and the connections which some European politicians make between ordinary Muslims and terrorism. Most symbolic for the EU was not democracy, but the euro (even though only 12 out of 25 countries had adopted the currency by the time of the research).[37] This is to a certain extent expected. Even though the cultural 'products' of the EU Member States, according to Jozef Batora and Monica Mokre, represent a combined soft power asset ('as various aspects of the national cultures of EU Member States continue to generate by and large positive perceptions of "Europe" in the world'),[38] soft power also risks, as Ying Fan of Brunel University rightly observes,[39] creating an ethnocentric worldview and contains an assumption that there is a link between attractiveness and the ability to influence others in international relations.

Fan also makes us aware of the fact that developing external policies which include culture at state level is far more complicated than doing this at the personal level. As Nye himself points out: 'Iranian officials excoriate America as a "great satan" while teenagers secretly watch smuggled Hollywood videos.'[40] Besides that, Batora and Mokre point out that irrespective of the political aims of cultural policies – be they nationally or supra-nationally defined – the question arises of whether it is legitimate and effective to use culture and the arts in order to promote political goals or if culture and the arts should be seen as values in their own right. As history shows, exemplified by Richard I Cohen's *Jewish Icons: Art and Society in Modern Europe*, art and society have been in constant tension.[41] Finally, being aware of the role of culture as paramount to the construction of a collective identity, defining us also implies identifying them – and, as explored in previous chapters, that's easier said than done.

To improve the situation, de Vries wants the EU to operate pragmatically on different levels. Most urgently, owing to the fact that 'the external dimension of the Union's cultural relations is characterized by conceptual confusion', de Vries desires the EU and its Member States to jointly prepare a European Strategy of Cultural Diplomacy. Concretely, on the local level, he proposes that all schools in the EU should be linked to a partner school abroad, either in another EU Member State or elsewhere in the world. On a community level, de Vries wants a strengthening of the rule of law in non-EU countries and within the EU, especially when it comes to freedom of expression and expanding cultural choice for citizens. To do this, he suggests that the EU systematically urges its partners to ratify and implement all six main UNESCO conventions in the field of culture. None of the 16 partners of the EU under the European Neighbourhood Policy has done this: Moldova has adopted only one, Israel only two. Changes need to come *now*, de Vries argues, since all too often the EU's voice in addressing violations of the right to freedom of expression is weak.

Religious resurgence and the freedom of expression

Because freedom of expression is meant to be a core element of the EU's foreign policies and soft power, which I will come back to in a moment, it is peculiar to observe the double standards sometimes shown by European politicians. Commission President Barroso said this in a speech on 15 February 2006, in connection with the reactions to the Muhammad caricatures:

> 'Freedom of speech is part of Europe's values and traditions. Let me be clear. Freedom of speech is not negotiable. Like all freedoms, its preservation depends on responsible use by individuals. Governments or other public authorities do not prescribe or authorize the opinions expressed by individuals. Conversely, the opinions expressed by individuals engage these individuals, and only them. They do not engage a country, a people, a religion. And we should not allow others to pretend that they do.'[42]

Three years later, European politicians have demonstrated that freedom of speech is negotiable. What I have in mind is the decision by the British government to ban Freedom Party MP Geert Wilders from the UK. Wilders had been invited by the UK Independence Party's Lord Pearson to show his controversial film *Fitna* – which links the Islamic holy book to terrorism – in the UK's House of Lords. Before he went, however, the British ambassador in The Hague told Wilders that he was denied entry because he was a threat to public security and public harmony as a result of the controversy created by *Fitna*. Arguing along similar lines as the ambassador was Cabinet Office minister Liam Byrne, who on BBC One's *Question Time* said: 'This guy wasn't coming here to exercise his right of free speech. This guy was trying to come here in order to sow division between us in this country. Everything I've heard about this guy tells me he's a bigot and the right place for him is to stay at home.'[43]

Wilders' motives may well be questionable, but this is not a sufficient argument to ban him from British soil. If everybody who tried to sow division between people were to be denied access to other countries, then customs would have a hard time keeping up. What's more, as several bloggers and commentators across Europe remarked, the banning of Wilders and the following media frenzy ensured that people watched a film which otherwise they would never have bothered to see. I've seen *Fitna* and it is undoubtedly a horrible film, for many reasons. Tragedies of terror are displayed uncensored. Shock and provocation are the preferred dramaturgic elements. None the less, *Fitna* could be useful in terms of realizing the full extent of the current situation.

Sadly, this is a striking example of freedom of expression, no matter how lame or stupid it may be, being sacrificed on the altar of religious indignation. There are of course cases where expressions are simply hurtful and nothing else, or where media broadcasting is misused to legitimize criminal actions (like the mass killings in Rwanda). Those events should be investigated and sanctioned. But in Wilders' case the context actually favoured those inclined to serious debate and respectful dialogue more than sensationalist allegations of an Islamization of Europe. The House of Lords event was to be hosted by Lord Malcolm Pearson of Rannoch, a UKIP peer with a special interest in the European Union, Islamism and education. It was to be chaired by

Baroness Caroline Cox of Queensbury, a crossbench peer and a human rights campaigner with a strong commitment to humanitarian aid and education. She is also the founder of the International Islamic Christian Organisation for Reconciliation and Reconstruction.[44]

On a European level, this, and several other cases in latter years, proves that advocates of the secularization thesis, according to which the old religious past has been defeated by modern enlightenment values, have been wrong all along. As a matter of fact, as Professor Shmul N Eisenstadt wrote in 2008, 'a far-reaching resurgence or reconstruction of religions is taking place in the contemporary world'. Eisenstadt continues by saying that this resurgence is manifest in many ways: the rise of new religious communities, the crystallization of new diasporas with strong religious identities, the growing importance of religious components in public arenas, and the constitution of collective identities.[45] Eisenstadt mentions not only Muslims but also Catholic, Jewish and Buddhist communities as examples of groups making, in various ways, extensive claims to redefine citizenship and the rights and entitlements connected with it.[46]

Does this development create conflicting liberties – religious vs expressive? There can be no doubt, for reasons explored in chapter 1, that we live in societies that are both diversified and globalized in more ways than ever before. For the debate on religious rights and free speech this implies an underlying assumption of a more nuanced form of rhetorical sensibility. In an essay, British-Indian writer Kenan Malik says there is an argument that for such societies to function and to be fair, 'we need to show respect for other peoples, cultures and viewpoints. And we can only do so by being intolerant of people whose views give offence or who transgress firmly entrenched moral boundaries.'[47] However, Malik strongly disagrees. 'Part of the problem in this debate,' he continues, 'is that there is a continuous blurring of the distinctions between giving offence, fomenting hatred, and inciting violence. Fomenting hatred may well create political and social problems; but these are not problems that can be solved by legislation restricting free speech.'[48]

Liberal principles and the real world don't always coincide, and in the real world clashes are unavoidable. In Malik's view, we should deal with those conflicts head-on rather than suppressing them. That's why I think the banning of Wilders was wrong. Never mind his inconsistency in wanting to ban the Koran while simultaneously chanting on about civic liberties and freedom of speech; this is about something else. In the long term, Malik finishes, giving offence might even be necessary because 'it is the freedom to blaspheme, to transgress, to move beyond the pale that is at the heart of all intellectual, artistic and political endeavours.' Galileo's vision of the universe, Darwin's theory of evolution, women's suffrage, every social advance worth having – they all began, according to Malik, by outraging the conventions of their time.[49]

Prior to the recent development in the Wilders' case, the EU seemingly could not make up its mind about it. In 2008 the Slovenian Presidency issued a statement in connection to *Fitna* that emphasized the importance of freedom of speech while at the same time introducing some preconditions: 'The European Union and its Member States apply the principle of the freedom of speech which is part of our values and traditions.' However, the Presidency emphasizes that it should be exercised in a spirit of respect for religious and other beliefs and convictions: 'Mutual tolerance and respect are universal values we should uphold. We believe that acts, such as the above-mentioned film, serve no other purpose than inflaming hatred.'[50] In other words, a clumsy way of saying that being able to show the film is part of your democratic liberties, but we think you undermine democratic values by actually doing so. Later that year, in December 2008, the EU parliament itself prevented the showing of *Fitna* in the Strasbourg building. A spokeswoman for the parliament's presidency said the decision not to allow the film to be shown had been taken by parliamentary president Hans-Gert Poettering and party leaders back in March, after it caused 'problems' when shown in the Netherlands. British MEP Gerard Batten, who had organized the event, was highly critical of the decision, pointing out that at the same time as the parliament in Strasbourg was awarding its Sakharov Prize in absentia to jailed Chinese dissident Hu

European party leaders were denying free speech to one of their own members.[51]

What this adds up to is that the EU cannot expect to successfully export the principles of soft power to either China or Iran, least of all freedom of speech, when it does not have a cohesive idea of its ramifications on home turf. In its 2007 Communication, as already quoted, the EU writes that 'the EU is, and must aspire to become even more, an example of a "soft power" founded on norms and values such as human dignity, solidarity, tolerance, freedom of expression, respect for diversity and intercultural dialogue, values which, provided they are upheld and promoted, can be of inspiration for the world of tomorrow.'[52] If this is to be fulfilled there can be no more situations like the banning of Wilders, and the hypocrisy in debates about freedom of expression must evaporate.

Questioning the UNESCO way

In sync with UNESCO's 2005 Convention on the Protection and Promotion of Diversity, the EU sees specific regulation of cultural expressions and their markets as key to protecting and developing diversity, and henceforth developing strong cultural ties with non-European countries. The real danger, from its point of view, is the demand within the WTO framework for 'the unconditional opening of all markets, including markets for cultural property, and in the WTO's practices, which are generally identified with the negative effects of globalization'.[53] Initially these ideas seem appealing to those of us who value cultural expression over and above any financial value. But they have some flaws when put into practice. Is a strong EU, capable of holding its ground internationally, 'more a guarantor for, than a danger to, the preservation of European national and regional cultures?'[54]

I am not so sure. From the outset, UNESCO's intentions are straightforward and uncontroversial.[55] In article 1, paragraphs a, b and c, we can read that the objectives of the Convention are 'to protect and promote the diversity of cultural expressions, and to create the conditions for cultures to flourish and to freely interact in a mutually beneficial manner, and to encourage dialogue among cultures with a view to ensuring wider and balanced cultural exchanges in the world in favour of intercultural respect and a culture of peace.' In order to make this more than elegant words, we discover in article 18 that the Convention also implies the establishing of an International Fund for Cultural Diversity. Its financial base is grounded in voluntary contributions made by states, by organizations and programmes of the United Nations system, by other regional or international organizations and by public or private bodies or individuals.

Looking behind the generalizations of the UNESCO Convention, where the EU was a key player, loopholes are revealed. Professor of Social Anthropology Odd Are Berkaak, who was invited by the Norwegian UNESCO commission to make an analytical comment on the Convention, forms some interesting conclusions. First and foremost, he argues, the text is plagued by conceptual haze. Diversity is a diagnosis, a goal and a means. It is unclear whether the principles of respect, equal access, sustainable development and solidarity are goals or values. 'Implicitly,' he writes, 'it may seem like they envision attributing these values and principles to a specific part of mankind, whereas others are left out. One could ask why this Convention is necessary if these are universal principles anyway. Seen this way, the Convention becomes a tool used by particular societies in order to make their values universal.'[56]

This exemplifies a well-known concern with global institutions: rather than developing a *global* cultural policy and becoming a QUANGO (quasi-autonomous non-governmental organization), UNESCO – like the EU – is sometimes too much a tool in the hands of states for handling their (inter)national interests. Consequently, the UNESCO Convention – and the EU's contributions to it – is only as strong and global in reach as its members want it to be. This is the Janus face of the Convention: protecting diversity is in the hands of nation-states, even though many of the very same nation-states have throughout their history proved themselves poor backers for cultural diversity.[57]

Discussions leading up to the 2005 UNESCO Convention were too extensive to reproduce in full here. But I believe a closer look at some of the basics could be useful.[58] From its emergence in the 1940s as one of several new international trading protocols, the General Agreement on Tariffs and Trade (GATT) has embodied a series of policies helping to restructure capitalism after the Second World War. Originally an economic instrument, it soon became part of the nuptials between culture and economy, especially the film industry. The 1948 Beirut Agreement eliminated duty and licensing costs for educational audiovisual imports, but not for texts designated as cultural or popular. Film quotas were permitted because Europeans maintained, against the US, that films were services, not commodities. And so the story goes. The US argued against public subsidies for television and film during the Agreement's Tokyo Round of negotiations between 1973 and 1979, to no effect.

In the late 1980s, the US tried to thwart the EU's plans for import quotas on audiovisual texts, better known as the Television without Frontiers directive, including an annual limit on texts imported by Member States of 49 per cent of broadcast time. While the US argued for free markets and claimed that government intrusion in the media industry equated to interference with freedom of speech and hampering of consumers' rights (to make their own choices), the EU and more or less every other country in the world opposed these arguments in the name of cultural sovereignty. In 1995 WTO replaced GATT, making it easier for the Hollywood industry because of its greater power and legal secretariat, and because the relationship between culture and economy had never been closer. Commodities previously excluded from GATT are now included in WTO's remit. In 1995, UNESCO's *Our Creative Diversity* was also published, aiming to draw the line between defending diversity while promoting worldwide values, and giving culture a higher place on the globalization agenda.

What seems to receive less attention here is that the ultimate discussion on global arenas for culture policies is not really whether culture is a commodity or a service, but how to deal with the fact that the world is globalized. After reviewing the literature on GATT and WTO, Toby Miller et al write that 'each party trades off concessions in other areas via a diplomacy that is rarely unveiled in anything approximating to democratic openness. Does this make for a transformation of the world system, away from state-centrism?'[59] I'm sceptical. While the relationship between culture and territoriality has shifted, it remains governed by interstate bodies, albeit dominated by the G8 countries. This has made its mark on the debates about the globalization of culture. Again we come across different opinions on human rights and freedom of expression. The Bangkok Declaration from 1993, for instance, states that 'while human rights are universal in nature, they must be considered in the context of a dynamic and evolving process of international norm-setting, bearing in mind the significance of national and regional particularities and various historical, cultural and religious backgrounds.'[60]

In March 2008, top UN rights body the Human Rights Council (UNHRC) passed two resolutions that, according to protesting rights groups, including 21 organizations from Islamic states, change the focus from protecting freedom of expression to limiting it. The first resolution, proposed by the Organisation of the Islamic Conference (OIC), was passed by 32 council members with 15 abstentions. It requires the UN Special Rapporteur on Freedom of Expression to report on abuses of the right to freedom of expression when they constitute an act of racial or religious discrimination. The freedom of expression organization Article 19 and the Cairo Institute for Human Rights Studies 'condemn the repeated misuse of the Human Rights Council process to push for an agenda that has nothing to do with strengthening human rights and everything to do with protecting autocracies and political point scoring'. The second resolution passed by the UNHRC was proposed by Islamic countries saying it was deeply concerned about the defamation of religions and urging governments to prohibit it. Canada and Europe opposed the resolution, which was adopted 21–10, with 14 abstentions. Although the text refers frequently to protecting all religions, the only religion specified as being attacked is Islam, making specific reference to the increased 'ethnic and religious profiling of Muslim minorities in the aftermath' of 11 September 2001.[61]

Even if the European Union has been an ally of developing countries against the US, the UNESCO discussions in the 1970s show a similarly ambiguous picture. Third world countries, as they were called, lobbied in UNESCO (it was run at the time by Frenchman Jean Maheu and the Senegalese Amadou Mahtar M'Bow) for a 'New International Information and Communication Order' (NIWCO). Mirroring calls from the MacBride Commission, reporting in 1980 on the need for equal distribution of the electronic spectrum among many things, it didn't, however, succeed. In addition to internal disagreements, it got caught in the line of fire between Europe and the US. According to Toby Miller et al, the NIWCO position was vulnerable from all sides. Inadequacies in dealing with internal and international class relations, the role of the state, the mediating power of indigenous culture and its own internal struggles – a pluralism that insisted on the relativistic equivalence of all cultures, which came into conflict with distinctively powerful national identities of members – all made a joint stand difficult.[62] Unfortunately, it seems, UNESCO, even though it has done a tremendous amount of work in other areas, didn't manage to fill these voids.

Everyday cosmopolitics

With the discussion above in mind, I think cultural actions on a global scale must include *cosmopolitan* reflections on a more philosophical level. Brilliantly described by Ghanaian-American philosopher and Princeton Professor Kwame Anthony Appiah, we learn that cosmopolitanism is one of humanity's oldest ideas and simply implies that all human beings are fellow citizens of the world. This creed has underwritten some of the great moral achievements of the Enlightenment, including the 1789 'Declaration of the Rights of Man' and Immanuel Kant's idea of a league of nations. It means that we have obligations and ties that stretch beyond those to whom we are related, and that since humanity consists of individuals, the cosmopolitan neither expect nor desire that every person or every society should converge on a single mode of life.[63]

It is in simple terms, as Joseph Rotblat, the 1995 Nobel Peace Laureate says, a matter of pleading an 'allegiance to humanity'.[64] Many, unfortunately, tend to see cosmopolitanism as opposed to nationalism, or as elitist mumbo-jumbo. The English conservative political thinker

Roger Scruton said that the cosmopolite 'is often seen as a kind of parasite, who depends upon the quotidian lives of others to create the various local flavours and identities in which he dabbles.'[65] And to some degree, sadly, Scruton is right. But he's also completely wrong. Appiah illustrates the point when he says that 'cosmopolitanism isn't hard work, repudiating it is.'[66] If cosmopolitanism is to succeed, it must be true to its inner core – a global (not merely European) idea of cultural action. Ulrich Beck expresses it well: 'The concept of a cosmopolitan Europe makes possible a critique of EU reality which is neither nostalgic nor national but radically European.'[67]

Reading the 2007 Eurobarometer survey *Intercultural Dialogue in Europe*, we find some interesting attitudes to cosmopolitanism in Europe.[68] Overall, 55 per cent of EU citizens surveyed expressed an attitude of being open to other cultures, but preserving their own as well ('pro diversity and keep roots'), while 25 per cent believed that cultural openness does not go hand-in-hand with the need to consciously maintain one's own traditions (that is, a 'cosmopolitan' attitude to diversity). To be honest, I don't see the difference between these two categories. There is nothing in cosmopolitanism that excludes the possibility of maintaining one's own traditions. Anyway, sticking to Eurobarometer's methodological conceptualization, the segment that was not open to intercultural dialogue – referred to as those 'not in favour of diversity' – comprised 13 per cent of all EU citizens. Favouring cultural diversity (considering intercultural dialogue as beneficial, but wanting to preserve their cultural heritage in parallel) was the most widely held attitude. Certainly that is the case among the elderly (over the age of 55, 59 per cent), but even among the youngest respondents (15–24 years of age, 51 per cent) this was the case.

Cosmopolitan attitudes increase with the level of educational attainment, mostly at the expense of isolationist attitudes. On the other hand, the younger the respondent, the more likely he or she (there are no gender differences in this regard) is to have a 'cosmopolitan' view, mostly at the expense of the 'pro diversity, and keep roots' attitude. Across all EU Member States, the survey found that the cosmopolitan mindset is more typical of the EU 15 (and especially in Denmark 56 per cent; Sweden 48 per cent and the Netherlands 47 per cent). On the other hand, citizens of the new Member States tend to be less cosmopolitan and more pro diversity in their attitudes, this being most characteristic of the Polish (76 per cent) and Cypriot (74 per cent) respondents. Those who do not see a value in having young people interacting with their peers of differing cultural background are very high in Belgium (22 per cent), Austria (19 per cent) and the Netherlands (18 per cent) among the old Member States. Similar levels can be found in a number of new Member States as well, where Bulgaria has the highest levels (27 per cent) followed by Romania (22 per cent) and Malta (20 per cent).

If we return to the UNESCO Convention and its implementation of culture in global politics, the case might be that it is not global enough. Rightly, the Convention challenges neoliberalism, arguing that market forces alone cannot guarantee the preservation and promotion of cultural diversity. But it also invokes certain aspects of citizenship that have tended to subordinate cultural diversity under the guise of fostering cultural unity. Toby Miller and associates write that the 'EU's cultural policies that promote a pan-European common culture based on a white colonial Christian heritage are examples of heritage in need of redefinition, not preservation.'[69] Moreover, Miller et al make a reference to sociologist Tony Bennett who, in a report commissioned and endorsed by the then 44 members of the Council of Europe, presents a methodological approach to cultural citizenship including 'the right to maintain and develop specific cultural practices that will function as the organising foci for cultural lives that are not centred on the notional mainstream of a nationally defined society'.[70]

Embracing a slightly relativistic outlook like Bennett's, we overlook the danger of societal incoherence which to some degree is conditioned by what kind of diversity societies are able to manage. Yet, he's right – like Ugrešić in chapter 1 – when he points out the need for a cultural policy that also includes those outside the national mainstream. 'Rather than focus cultural diversity principles on preserving cultural heritage or sovereignty, modern notions do not account for the accelerating international circulation of people and cultures,' Miller et al write in similar vein. 'Diversity principles might take the form of rights to participate fully and fairly in the production of culture.'[71] On a European level, this does not necessarily mean imagining Europe as something post-national, philosopher Jürgen Habermas, among others, halfway argues in *The Postnational Constellation*.[72] Acting cosmopolitan does not imply the abolition of nations – but it does imply a different view of the world from the one dominant today.

Professor David Held, who is an expert on cosmopolitanism, acutely says that from a cultural point of view, 'states can be conceived as vehicles to aid the delivery of effective public regulation and equal justice and rights, but they should not be thought of as ontologically privileged.'[73] We don't have to abandon the idea of nation-states, or envision Europe as the United States of EU. To Held, cultural cosmopolitanism should simply be understood as a frame of mind, 'the capacity to mediate between national cultures, communities of fate and alternative styles of life. It encompasses the possibility of dialogue with the traditions and discourses of others with the aim of expanding the horizons of one's own framework of meaning and prejudice.' Political agents who can 'reason from the point of view of others' are better equipped to resolve, and resolve fairly, the challenging transboundary issues that create overlapping communities of fate.[74]

Elements of an analogous attitude can be found in the Slovenian Presidency Declaration based on the recommendations of the May 2008 conference 'New Paradigms, New Models – Culture in EU's External Relations'. In the conference's recommendations related to governance, it states that the development of the new strategy on external policy should build on a reinforced dialogue between public authorities and civil society.[75] As examples, the recommendations cite potential cooperation between cultural environments in non-EU countries and EU delegations, EUNIC centres, European foundations and the networks of civil society. Advice on how to ground this outlook surfaced during the Sixteenth Conference of Culture Action Europe/the European Forum for the Arts and Heritage which was held in Marseilles from 23 to 25 October 2008.[76] Besides the usual pleas for, and debates concerning, intercultural dialogue, some really ingenious ideas appear in the conference report, written by Simon Mundy, the former president of Culture Action Europe.

Based on the discussions from the weekend, he points out that there is a considerable problem emerging because of the different aims pursued by national governments and by other cultural players: an 'opposition between cultural diplomacy and cultural exchange,' as Fabien Janelle from the ONDA said. Philippe Le Moine, from the Avignon Festival, backed up this point by asserting that the purpose of cultural collaboration was not national affirmation, but creating the space for encounters, and exploring the confrontation between the artist's work and the audience's response.[77] That's cosmopolitics in a nutshell.

[1] http://ec.europa.eu/culture/our-policy-development/doc1567_en.htm

[2] European Commission, 2007a.

[3] McCormick, 2008: 193.

[4] http://ec.europa.eu/external_relations/cfsp/intro

[5] European Commission, 2007e.

[6] European Commission, 2007e.

[7] McCormick, 2008: 189–90.

[8] Frontex, the EU agency based in Warsaw, was created in 2004 as a specialized and independent body to coordinate the operational cooperation between Member States in the field of border security. Frontex promotes a pan-European model of Integrated Border Security. For more information, see www.frontex.europa.eu

[9] www.alliancefr.org/

[10] www.goethe.de/enindex.htm

[11] www.cervantes.es

[12] http://secondlife.cervantes.es

[13] McCormick, 2008: 206–8.

[14] ECF, 2005: 5.

[15] ECF, 2005: 25.

[16] ECF, 2005: 25–6.

[17] This foundation brings together the 27 Members of the European Union and 12 Southern Mediterranean states, the latter including Libya, Morocco and Algeria. See www.euromedalex.org

[18] http://eacea.ec.europa.eu/culture/calls2007/results/documents/eacea_21_2007_results_en.pdf

[19] www.brouhaha.uk.com

[20] http://ec.europa.eu/culture/our-programmes-and-actions/doc587_en.htm

[21] http://eacea.ec.europa.eu/culture/guide/strand_1_3/funding_en.htm

[22] www.unaoc.org

[23] http://ec.europa.eu/education/policies/educ/bologna/bologna.pdf

[24] http://ec.europa.eu/education/policies/cooperation/cooperation_en.html

[25] http://ec.europa.eu/external_relations/japan/grants/2008/index_en.htm

[26] www.consilium.europa.eu/ueDocs/cms_Data/docs/pressData/en/educ/104189.pdf

[27] http://ec.europa.eu/external_relations/policies/index_en.htm

[28] Weringh and Schürmann, 2004: 12.

[29] European Commission, 2007a.

[30] Todorov, 2003.

[31] Gardels, 2007: 233.

[32] Pew, 2007.

[33] Nye, 2003.

[34] Batora and Mokre, 2008: 79.

[35] De Vries, 2008: 40.

[36] De Vries, 2008: 16.

[37] Holland et al, 2007.

[38] Batora and Mokre, 2008: 76.

[39] Fan, 2008.

[40] Nye, 2003.

[41] Cohen, 1998.

[42] www.europa-eu-un.org/articles/en/ article_5696_en.htm

[43] *BBC News*, 2009.

[44] Landen, 2009.

[45] Eisenstadt, 2008: 21. See also Motzkin and Fischer, 2008.

[46] Eisenstadt, 2008: 23–24.

[47] Malik, 2006.

[48] Malik, 2006.

[49] Malik, 2006.

[50] www.eu2008.si/en/News_and_Documents/ CFSP_Statements/March/0328MZZ_Fitna. html

[51] www.eubusiness.com/news-eu/ 1229524321.57

[52] European Commission, 2007a: 3.

[53] Weringh and Schürmann, 2004: 6.

[54] Weringh and Schürmann, 2004: 6.

[55] UNESCO, 2005.

[56] Berkaak, 2007.

[57] O'Brien, 1993.

[58] Miller et al, 2005: 85–91.

[59] Miller et al, 2005: 90.

[60] www.unhchr.ch/html/menu5/wcbangk.htm

[61] IFEX, 2008.

[62] Miller et al, 2005: 76.

[63] Appiah, 2006: xv.

[64] Rotblat, 1997.

[65] Cited by Waldron, 2000: 227.

[66] Appiah, 2006: xx.

[67] Beck, 2006: 166.

[68] Eurobarometer, 2007b.

[69] Miller et al, 2005: 339.

[70] Bennett, 2001: 25.

[71] Miller et al, 2005: 340.

[72] Habermas, 2001.

[73] Held, 2002: 12.

[74] Held, 2002: 12.

[75] www.eu2008.si/en/News_and_Documents/ download_docs/May/0513_MZZ/Declaration. pdf

[76] http://marseille2008.cultureactioneurope. org/home_en.html

[77] Mundy's report is available at http:// marseille2008.cultureactioneurope.org/ conference-report-en.pdf

7 EU goes culture ... and then what?

When all is said and done, Thomas Hylland Eriksen writes appositely, the EU has many similarities to the philosophy of Jürgen Habermas: 'It is an extremely thorough and slowly grinding machine, it can be deadly boring, but it is honest in its own way and important to those whom it concerns.'[1] This is also my overall impression after trying to explore the European Union's new agenda for culture. To explain why my conclusion mirrors Eriksen's I will wrap up the discussion in this chapter. My main attention is given to a group which is particularly important to follow if we are to increase our understanding of the European: youth, and why the future of the EU's role in European culture may lie in establishing an 'Erasmus Cultura' – an Erasmus programme for cultural workers.

After having discussed the European Union's new strategy for culture through the previous chapters, and although I have touched upon a wide range of matters by merely scratching the surface (leaving out sport and tourism, for instance), I think it is no understatement to say that the EU shows considerably more interest in European culture than before. By relating the new strategy to neighbouring policies the EU has managed to bring cultural activities closer to the centre of contemporary political visions. That doesn't change the fact that parts of the strategy are almost free of sharp edges. Particularly significant in this context is the enduring debate on cultural policy motivation where traditional enhancement of national identities battles with objectives in which cultural diversity is the organizing principle.

Disappointingly – or luckily, depending on how you feel about it – the new policy will not have any thorough impact on national cultural policies unless the politicians want it to. Spending something equivalent to annual subsidies of a German opera house[2] – but intended for 450 million to 500 million citizens – disparages the worth of culture. The conclusion from The Rainbow Paper is epigrammatic: 'No investment, no visible results.' Sure, Union membership requires alignment with the common objectives, but as long as they are as wide-ranging as they are now, politicians fearing loss of national sovereignty should definitely keep their hair. Having said that, by allying with the EU's objectives and culture initiatives, national governments do in fact have the opportunity to help build a cultural consciousness on a European scale – answering questions such as what is Europe, whose Europe is it, and how can we use the cultural impressions of Europe to improve our relations with the rest of the world? These are real questions, relating both to EU expansion eastwards and to globalization issues from McDonald's in every city to the French ban on hijabs in public schools.

One apparent danger is the rather functionalist attitude which can be found in central EU documents on cultural policy. A passage from the 2001 Ruffolo report summarizes the EU's view well:

'Such a [cultural] policy would serve three principal functions. It would be a factor of cohesion making the most of diversities as richness, not as grounds for division. It would be a factor of identity in the world, and identity that is not self-centered and over-protected but open to the world. And, it would be a factor empowering all European citizens to take democratic part in their common destiny. It would be a way, in short, to instill [sic] a "feeling" of union.'[3]

One who sees problems with this 'neofunctionalist' view on European unification is Cris Shore. Not only does he feel the assumption that culture can be harnessed as a tool for advancing the EU's project for European construction to be false; the idea that European identity needs to be 'rebranded' also represents to him 'a project of social engineering uncomfortably reminiscent of other failed modernist ideologies of the twentieth century'.[4] Furthermore, the risk that the project could easily backfire is apparent, since it assumes consensus for a 'European model' of society that 'does not exist and which, even if it did exist, would be of questionable value to democracy in a modern transnational and multicultural context'.[5]

Although I agree for the most part with Shore, especially when it comes to culture as part of the EU's external relations, reasons for the neofunctionalist attitude are not just present among the EU's institutions; they can also be found in Member States, which differ greatly in their response to the EU's pledge to intercultural dialogue. In Sweden, for instance, the government proclaimed 2006 the Year of Cultural Diversity, and in 2007, in the 477-page SOU report *Mångfald är framtiden* (*Diversity is the future*), Yvonne Rock, the Coordinator of the initiative, recommends that a provision of SEK10 million of the appropriation item *Cultural policy development activities* be distributed in the form of organizational support to cultural policy actors working with cultural diversity, intercultural dialogue and intercultural exchange.[6]

Poland declares that, as a response to EYID 2008, there has been a Common Commission of the Government and National and Ethnic Minorities operating in Poland since 2005. Its tasks are, among other things, to take actions aimed at protecting and developing cultural diversity. Some of these actions are gathered in the report as a schedule (see p170).

Schedule of EYID activities in Poland

No	Activity	Dates for implementation
1	Developing the EYID strategy in Poland	January 2007 – February 2007
2	Disseminating information on the EYID	March 2007 – June 2007
3	National call for proposals for the EYID	April 2007 – May 2007
4	Appointment of the EYID Council in Poland	April 2007 – June 2007
5	Selection of national projects to be co-financed	June 2007
6	Preparation of the application for the EYID in Poland	July 2007 – August 2007
7	Submission of the application for the EYID in Poland to the European Commission	14 September 2007
8	Constructing the website of the EYID in Poland	June 2007 – October 2007
9	Promotion of the EYID idea (debates, information in press)	October 2007 – March 2009
10	Updating the website of the EYID in Poland	November 2007 – March 2009
11	Creating the catalogue of 'good practice'	November 2007 – March 2008
12	Implementation of activities indicated in the national project of the EYID	1 January 2008 – 31 January 2009
13	Promotion of 'good practice'	April 2008 – March 2009
14	Selection of activities implemented under the auspices of the EYID in Poland (activities under the common logo)	January 2008 – March 2008
15	Final financial report for EU grant	June 2009
16	Activities of the EYID Team in the NCC	January 2007 – March 2009

Source www.interculturaldialogue2008.eu/fileadmin/downloads/
documents/133-nationalcampaigns/national_strategy/strategy_poland.pdf

As the schedule shows, the mechanisms the Polish government is adopting to guide cultural development imply a no less functionalistic approach than the EU is being criticized for. Form and content are, moreover, not the same. It is perfectly feasible to have a functionalistic cultural policy without controlling the content. In my view this is, with the exception of intercultural dialogue, what the EU tries to accomplish with their new agenda for culture. Yes, of course they get to decide what kind of cultural expressions are granted funds, but they have no guarantee whatsoever that the applications fall in line with whatever views they might have on European culture. As I have argued in chapter 5, I even see the possibility for increased functionalism, that is, a spearheaded programme for supporting the development of video games.

The bottom line is that we have no real reason to give up the thought of a European cultural policy that enables European citizens to be free to explore their cultural visions, dreams and fears. As Shore indirectly reminds us, given the transnational realities of European countries, we have still a lot to gain from cooperating culturally within Europe, and with countries and milieus outside of Europe, and debating the European in a more up-to-date way. Taking into account the global context, with a new sense of cultural complexity and looming financial crisis, as elaborated in chapter 1, a down-to-earth policy may be useful in an environment already filled with unrest and movement. As I have argued in chapters 2–6, this requires a lot from the EU and its Member States. More than anything else, I think it's about listening to the 'Eurogeneration'.

Voices of the Eurogeneration

A general necessity for coming to grips with the things I have discussed in this book – diversity issues, the video game industry, or using culture as a diplomatic tool – is to allow people to define European culture on their own. During his talk at The Network Effect conference in Budapest, March 2008, Tommi Laitio said that we 'need to fiercely defend the right to self-definition and redefinition. We have to try to see through and look past these constructs to challenge the inherent prejudices that are hampering social cohesion and the development of a more humane society.'[7] Sociologically, and as European demographics progresses, this requires the availability and recognition of certain instruments and modes of action that people – especially youth – can utilize. In the years until 2020, the number of Europeans between 15 and 29 years of age will diminish from 90 million to 81 million, a reduction of 9 million or 10 per cent. This will have a profound impact on education, the economy, society and European culture.

It is thus interesting to note that the High-Level Expert Forum on Mobility explicitly states in its 2008 report that the European Union 'should forge a new European generation fully equipped to cope with the new global challenges, with a deepened sense of European identity, openness and cooperation'.[8] On the one hand, we should be careful not to overstate the synergy effects of European integration through the younger cohorts. Just as globalization does not automatically create 'global people', Europeanization does not necessarily produce Europeans. Karen Hauff points to the novel *Plush* by young Slovakian writer Michael Hvorecky, where a rather bleak image of young Europeans is painted. The protagonist lives in the capital city of 'Supereurope' where the meaning of distance is relative, everything is networked, and brand names and consumption have replaced more existential reasons to live.[9] On the other hand, a Eurogeneration already exists, says French sociologist Michel Fize, who specializes in youth research and has written several books about young Europeans. In an interview with *cafebabel.com* he points out that it is related to student status, low-budget airlines and growing up in a culture which in his view has been the property of young people since the 1960s.[10]

Such sentiments are apparent if we talk to young Europeans themselves. Tamás Baranyay, 26, lives in Budapest and was a student of the EU's Erasmus programme in the small town of Ancona, Italy, in 2004. When I ask him what the best thing about Erasmus is, he simply replies 'freedom'. He approves of Fize's sanguinity, saying that 'this is the very best way of connecting different people and cultures: through common experience, living together, getting to know nations, not from books but by yourself. The EU should pump even more money into it, not just because it makes Europe mixed, but because it has many long-term effects, too: people will have fewer stereotypes, and will be more open. Personally positive emotions towards people from different nations can stop the formation of hostile attitudes, even war.' He thinks, though, the integration of foreign students into the local people or with native-born students could be improved, for instance, by having more common programmes and common tasks, or deliberately creating mixed groups at seminars. But overall his memories from Erasmus are nothing but positive, and when asked about what he thought was the cultural experience of his residence as an Erasmus student, he answered: 'Young people are young people, regardless of where they come from.'

A barometer of social change

Hence, my emphasis on popular culture throughout this book. Its relation to youth is pivotal to any strategy concerning creative industries, and it is essential to strengthening the idea of the European and should be part of whatever cultural aspects the EU wants to implement in its external relations. Professor Anthony D Everitt writes that Shakespeare 'is as much a part of an Italian's cultural heritage as Dante is of a Spaniard's', whereas 'popular culture has largely failed to bring together distinctive national traditions into a coherent European "field"'.[11] I find good reasons to disagree. It depends what you mean by coherent field. Historian Peter Burke shows in his *Popular Culture in Early Modern Europe* that in pre-industrial Europe, there was a world of professional entertainers – minstrels, fools, jugglers – and he documents a cross-national plethora of popular songs, stories and plays.[12] Tommi Laitio even claims that today's European youth culture, emblemized by pop cultural expressions such as hip-hop, contains 'the germ of the European ideal'.[13]

Laitio also states that in the absence of official appreciation, the commercial actors swoop in. Apple has gone beyond selling hardware when commercials ask us to decide whether we want to be the boring PC person in a brown suit or the relaxed Mac guy in a hoodie and jeans.[14] Contemporary Europe is in fact a hotbed of various pop cultural icons, especially in food, fashion and sports. From those keeping score, we know that there are about twice as many reasonably authentic Italian restaurants *outside* of Italy as there are McDonald's restaurants in the entire world, including the US.[15] Every year, the consulting firm Interbrand checks out the Billboard Top 100 to see what it's popular to mention in hit songs. Not surprisingly, honourable brands like Mercedes-Benz, Bvlgari and Courvoisier regularly attain the top spots.

Even the more artistic fields can claim belonging to a European pop culture. An obvious example is the French film *Le Fabuleux Destin d'Amélie Poulain* from 2001. Starring French superstar Audrey Tautou and renowned director Mathieu Kassovitz, the romantic comedy about sweet Amélie was loved by everybody, nominated for five Oscars (it also won 51 other awards and was nominated for a further 46)[16] and got a massive 81 per cent share of its total lifetime grosses from foreign markets.[17] Musical examples are bands like the Gypsy Kings, Rammstein or Ricchi e Poveri. The latter have been active since the late 1960s, singing in Italian, and have sold over 20 million records. In 1981, they had a huge hit with *Sarà perche ti amo*. A crossover version for Latin American countries was later recorded with Spanish lyrics. The song, now titled *Será porque te amo*, also became a huge hit in Mexico, the Caribbean, Central and South America. As of 2008 the song is still being covered and it has achieved something of a cult/nostalgia status in several Spanish-speaking countries as a symbol of a generation, while the band still has an active fan club online consisting of members from nine countries.[18]

Perhaps more than anything, pop culture is a barometer of social change, cultural creativity and expressive means for individualism. Tommi Laitio highlights how 'youth phenomena with an American origin can even function as tools for voicing European concerns in ways impossible through national, elite-driven culture.' Hip-hop – one of the biggest youth cultures of today – is a good example of this. In Poland hip-hop is a powerful tool for the *blockers*, unemployed white youth from the suburbs. Meanwhile, in France hip-hop is *the* genre to employ for immigrant youths. Alan Riding, a *New York Times* journalist who lives in Paris, wrote in the aftermath of the suburban riots in 2005 that 'art, in the form of movies and rap music, has long been warning that French-born Arab and black youths felt increasingly alienated from French society and that their communities were ripe for explosion.'[19]

Donald Morrison, in his infamous article in *Time Magazine* called 'The Death of French Culture', sees its escape from the Grim Reaper as being in the hands of its immigrant population:

'France has become a multiethnic bazaar of art, music and writing from the banlieues and disparate corners of the non-white world. African, Asian and Latin American music get more retail space in France than perhaps any other country. (. . .) Thus will the world discover the eternal youth of France, a nation whose long quest for glory has honed a fine appreciation for the art of borrowing. And when the more conventional minds of the French cultural establishment – along with their self-occupied counterparts abroad – stop fretting about decline and start applauding the ferment on the fringes, France will reclaim its reputation as a cultural power, a land where every new season brings a harvest of genius.'[20]

An example mentioned by Morrison is Diam's, one of France's most popular female rappers (her album *Ma Bulle* was the best-selling one in 2006), who according to Katrin Bennhold 'has galvanized young people in this country'.[21] Born in Cyprus as Mélanie Georgiades, raised in a Paris suburb since the age of three, Diam's incarnates a new generation of French artists with immigrant roots who are claiming France as their own. Musically fusing reggae, North African Zouk and Rai rhythms, she has become a model for identity construction, not only among disaffected kids in the suburbs but for French youth in general. However, it is not a matter for Diam's of rejecting France all in all, for instance its democratic values and secular constitution, but only of being herself without being harassed for being 'un-French'. Metaphorically speaking, she has merely swapped celebration of the Beaujolais Festival in favour of urban street poetry. 'The France of the baguette and the beret is not my France,' 26-year-old Diam's said in an interview. 'I don't relate to that France. It doesn't mean anything to me. I like to eat kebabs. I wear hoods.'[22]

Beware: I'm not suggesting that hip-hop alone is the future of European culture – I don't even listen to it. My point is just that assisting cultural dynamics is not necessarily so much about content as it is about facilitating creative possibilities. If we consider pop culture as a sociological mode of expression – not a list of icons – for revitalizing or crafting new ideas, we see that it possesses quite a few important properties: it is commercial, easily available to a great number of people, less intellectually demanding than for example most contemporary art and linked to recreation and entertainment. Most importantly, it is also popular in the very strict sense of the word – it acts upon, and responds to, what a lot of people want: it tickles their emotional nerves, and thus satisfies different cultural needs and desires.[23]

The emergence of a Video Republic

The Treaty of Maastricht in 1993 was the first time that the scope of EU policies was extended to include the youth 'field', the Treaty stating that the EU should 'encourage the development of youth exchanges and of exchanges of socio-educational instructors'. But with time, things have changed. On 15 November 2006, the European Parliament and the Council established the Youth in Action Programme for the period 2007–13, the EU Programme for young people aged between 15 and 28 (in some cases between 13 and 30). It aims to inspire a sense of active citizenship, solidarity and tolerance among young Europeans and to involve them in shaping the Union's future. With a total budget of €885 million for seven years (2007–13), the Programme supports a large variety of activities for young people and youth workers through five 'Actions'.[24]

This is decent facilitation of an age group's fears and dreams that has a range of identity-voicing tools custom-made for their generation. Parallels are striking with the Canadian English Professor Marshall McLuhan (1931–80) who, in the 1960s, wrote visionary books about how new technologies (like alphabets, printing presses and even speech itself) exert a gravitational effect on cognition, which in turn affects social organization. Connected to his famous slogan about 'the global village', first coined in *The Gutenberg Galaxy*,[25] McLuhan saw the emergence of a new borderless culture of communication based upon 'electronic interdependence'. While the global village in McLuhan's eyes was a term with predominantly negative connotations, Tommi Laitio encompasses a different view: millions of young people upload their videos on online platforms. YouTube, Facebook and MySpace function as megaphones for radical Islamists and for the next coming of punk as well as a forum for teenage girls who are into 18th century British poetry.[26]

A study by DEMOS, in the wake of StrangerFestival 2008, confirms that a 'Video Republic' – incredibly akin to McLuhan's global village – is under way among European youth. New tools change political participation, create a new public space for deliberation, and twist cultural identity like a Rubik's cube. The researchers state that 'the ability to act as reporters, distributors, artists and commentators allows some young people to assume positions of power in the Video Republic. Their voices, ideas and emotions can travel further and are more likely to influence others.'[27] To Laitio, this development is lead vocal in the European music. 'It should not come as a shock to anyone that most active videomakers are between 15 and 25 years of age,' he says. 'Having your first boyfriend, moving to your own home, having sex for the first time and selecting a field of studies are life-changing experiences, which cause both anxiety and excitement. At this time of personal turmoil, video functions as a tool for public deliberation on who you are, to what groups you belong and what you feel passionate about.'[28]

Laitio's reflections resonate with the findings from the 2007 Eurobarometer survey mentioned in chapter 1. Cultural participation is highest among the youngest, educated and urbanized respondents. A table may clarify the findings.

Participation rates for selected activities: analysis by age (%)

	15–24	25–39	40–54	55+	Difference youngest/oldest
Cinema	82	66	53	24	+58
Sport	61	47	45	22	+39
Public library	55	38	33	24	+31
Concert	52	43	37	27	+25
Books	82	72	74	63	+19
Historical monuments	61	59	59	45	+16
Museums/ galleries	48	42	45	34	+14
Theatres	35	32	33	27	+8

Source Adapted from Eurobarometer, 2007a: 17

As the table shows, age is a key factor in participation rates, with these declining as respondents get older. Such an effect is most pronounced for visiting the cinema – 82 per cent of those in the 15–24 age bracket had done this in the past year compared to 24 per cent of those aged 55 and over, a difference of 58 percentage points.

We must not forget that inequalities in media access are still generally a problem. When people were asked which barriers, if any, they faced in accessing culture or taking part in cultural activities, 42 per cent cited lack of time. After this, issues of expense are given by almost three out of ten (29 per cent) with lack of interest mentioned by a similar figure (27 per cent). Other reasons register much lower as barriers to access: 17 per cent say lack of information is a problem, 16 per cent that the choice and quality of activities in their area is poor and just 13 per cent that a lack of cultural knowledge and background prevents access.[29] Laitio endorses these findings, saying that even if the cost of equipment and internet access has dramatically dropped over the last years, 12–25 year old white men still produce a vast majority of the YouTube content uploaded on the site.

Statistics on internet access offer another part of the explanation. Currently, only 22 per cent of the world's population has access to the internet. Even within Europe the differences are gigantic with Moldova at 16 per cent and the Netherlands at 90 per cent.[30] Related to this are also the darker sides of an emergent 'Video Republic': bullying, harassment, abuse of visual imagery, or making use of the internet simply to spread hate must not be forgotten. A Facebook picture taken at a party, in all its juvenile innocence, may be the reason why you fail to get the promotion 15 years later. In the worst of all cases, sites like YouTube become a window for advertising and showcasing murderous acts like school shootings – tragically illustrated by the Finnish killing sprees in 2007 and 2008.

Enable civil society

What's the best way for the EU to deal with all we have discussed in the previous chapters? Throughout this book, I have consulted a variety of sources and cited several experts on culture – Xavier Troussard, Violeta Simjanovska, Gottfried Wagner, Tommi Laitio and the people behind The Rainbow Paper – who all seem to concur with the notion that civil society is essential for enabling a European cultural policy. Reinforcing their arguments is the notion that communities work as an effective counterweight to tendencies to isolation and alienation. Providing opportunities to solve social problems efficiently by offering participation in the public sphere, they cater to the fundamental human psychological need for belonging.[31] One interesting book shedding light upon this is the Tocqueville-inspired book *De la Culture en Amérique* by French sociologist Frederic Martel, who spent five years in Boston as the cultural attaché to the French Consulate.[32] Having criss-crossed the country, visiting 110 cities in 35 states and conducting 700 interviews, his findings, according to one reviewer, go far beyond the common stereotype: the US is not a land of mass commercial culture and doubtful taste.[33]

Much of this image owes its debt to a specific form of cultural policy. Whereas in Europe the common view, for many reasons, is that the state should handle cultural politics, the Americans don't even have a Ministry of Culture. Instead, they have a large number of charities, countless indirect public subsidies, thousands of foundations, active Black and Latino communities and an undeniable cultural diversity. A sociological explanation for why this works is a more self-defined and individual sense of belonging. This could lead to an increase in direct participation, because there are fewer 'gatekeepers' and less direction from above, in addition to a more tangible ownership of cultural development since people contribute with time, talent and money themselves. But the most important thing is how it stimulates the creation of interest communities.

As Xavier Troussard is quoted as saying in chapter 4, in order to come closer to civil society, the EU needs more mediators. 'If you really want to develop a policy,' Troussard says, 'you must have stronger capacity in the sector you intend to serve. And the reality in the cultural sector is that it is a very scattered sector, with little organization at European level, with different slices of subsectors which have been used to fighting each other for small slices of small pies. What we're inviting them to do with the Civil Society Platform is to work across the board and to say "if you are interested in culture you also have common

objectives that you can serve together; you can still have bilateral or
sectoral discussions with the Commission. But you have to work on
what is the common claim of the cultural sector, on the way the cultural
sector can show itself as an asset to the European project." This is also a
big shift for the sector itself, because, in a way, it puts a lot of pressure on
it to come up with new representational structures and a new innovation.'

In the light of this, foundations and NGOs have the potential to
help manage 'cultural Europe' in ways national initiatives alone cannot
do. First, they act as invaluable nodes in the network of cultural workers,
providing information and services about EU funding opportunities.
Second, they are themselves active participants in the cultural
sector, offering meeting places and arrangements which stimulate
the bloodstream of any cultural life. Third, they are able to spearhead
some concretizations of the general aims written in, for instance, EU
documents. Fourth, as pointed out by Erik Rudeng, Director of the
Freedom of Expression Foundation Oslo, they potentially combine the
best aspects of both state and market, engage in long-term thinking
irrespective of market forces and are able to respond unbureaucratically
to new ideas and foster informal networking.[34] One example is the King
Baudouin Foundation's 'SmartVisa initiative'. A recent study shows
that students from the western Balkans experience limited knowledge
of possibilities to study abroad; a key scholarship scheme such as the
EU's Erasmus Mundus was only known to 2.4 per cent. To counter this,
the SmartVisa Initiative focuses on increasing knowledge about student
exchange programmes and working for visa liberalization.[35]

It is therefore tempting to suggest a closer, and more long-term,
alliance between foundations with a particularly European outlook
and the EU in order to maintain and enhance the work being done
in the civil sector when it comes to bringing people together. A joint
venture between the European Foundation Centre (an association of
foundations and corporate funders)[36] and the Network of European
Foundations (NEF)[37] could for instance act as a point of departure.
According to Diana Leat and Helmut Anheier, both distinguished policy
experts within the foundation community, foundations could take on
'a new concept of their role which plays to their distinctive strengths

and is adapted to today's environment'.[38] This implies a different role for governments. A declaration published by Kulturpolitische Gesellschaft, in reply to the EU's new agenda for culture (after more than 500 participants from 36 European and non-European countries had their say at the Fourth Federal Congress on Cultural Policy), states that 'a new division of labour must be established between the political sector and civil stakeholders (arm's length principle). Such cooperation serves the heterogeneity of the cultural sector, in both conceptual and operative terms, more effectively than a centralised project management structure.'[39]

This is especially relevant in light of mobility. In chapter 2, I discussed the conditions for a European public sphere, with particular emphasis on media. My conclusions were that they convey too little, and through too narrow lenses, about European topics. But such a sphere, embracing the cultural sector, is not only media-driven, it is also created by people-to-people meetings. Mobility is a requirement for artists, as French Liberal Member of the European Parliament and orchestra director Claire Gibault said at the second of the so-called Brussels debates (see chapter 4), but not everybody can afford to spend the weekend in London or Barcelona. Travel in Europe is both expensive and bureaucratic.[40] It's a pity, therefore, that, as Astrid Bjerke, the Norwegian Cultural Contact Point, once told me, all other EU programmes apart from Culture offer individual mobility schemes.

Some options in this area do exist, however. Res Artis is a worldwide network of residential arts centres and programmes which provide artists with facilities and conditions conducive to creative work. STEP *beyond* is an ECF mobility scheme which encourages cross-border cultural cooperation and exchange between all European countries, especially aimed at strengthening cultural ties between EU members and non-members. The European 'Pepinières' Programme for Young Artists supports talented young artists in developing projects during a residency abroad. I would in particular highlight Gulliver Connect, the longest-established and most flexible mobility and work placement programme in Europe. Thanks to a large network of cultural organizations throughout Europe, not least in Eastern Europe, Gulliver

Connect offers hands-on work experience for young professionals who have two or three years working experience in the field of performing and visual arts, new media, project coordination and arts development or management. Bursaries of approximately €1,500 each are available to cover the costs of the work placement, travel, accommodation and daily allowance for a period of three to six weeks, if feasible within the budget. Application guidelines and forms are easily accessible on their webpage.[41]

To some extent, the EU is also on the case. Judith Staines, General Editor of www.onthemove.org, a website dedicated to international mobility opportunities in theatre, dance, music and other contemporary performing arts disciplines, has gathered recent developments in the Union's work for promoting cultural mobility.[42] Mobility of people working in the cultural sector is one of the three objectives of the EU Culture Programme (2007–2013), and is on the agenda of 2009 EU Presidencies (Czech Republic and Sweden). The policy framework for the current and upcoming EU Presidencies has been published and includes this statement: 'The presidencies will also address the issue of improving the internal market for cultural goods and services as well as creating better conditions for professionals within the cultural and creative sectors, and improving the mobility of artists and of art collections.'[43] Promoting the mobility of young people in Europe is also the subject of a Culture Ministers' pledge to boost artists' mobility as a wider set of recommendations for a 'Work Plan for Culture 2008–2010', adopted by a ministers' meeting in the Education, Youth and Culture Council in Brussels on 21 and 22 May 2008.[44]

A High-Level Expert Forum on Mobility was set up in December 2007 by the European Commissioner for Education, Training, Culture and Youth, Ján Figel, to strengthen and promote the mobility of young people. Their report *Making Learning Mobility an Opportunity for All* was released on 10 July 2008. Expectations and motivations are high: the Forum's aim is that, by 2020, 50 per cent of all young people between 16 and 29 should 'be offered the opportunity to engage in some form of cross-border mobility at some point'. This target should be reached by having 6 per cent of all university students study in another country,

3.5 per cent of trainees in vocational education and training, and 0.5 per cent of secondary school students engaging in a mobility-based voluntary action. The group also focuses on the importance of mainstreaming mobility into all relevant EU policies, increasing focus on language training in preparation for mobility periods and strengthening the present EU mobility programmes.[45]

A pilot scheme for artist mobility was also voted by the European Parliament in the 2008 budget and has an allocation of €1.5 million. This programme is funding a Call for Networking of Structures Supporting Mobility and a Feasibility Study for a comprehensive scheme designed to provide a European-wide system of information on the different aspects of mobility in the cultural sector. Projects are due to start in December 2008 and can last up to three years. The aim of this call for proposals is to support, on an experimental basis, the mobility of workers in the cultural sector through networks of existing structures supporting mobility, with a view to exploring ways of improving the overall environment for mobility at EU level. The total budget earmarked for co-financing these projects amounts to €1,250,000. The size of the grants will range between €150,000 and €350,000.[46] Related to this is the Culture Programme selection of projects by objective in 2008, where transnational mobility of people working in the cultural sector accounted for 87 of the 246 selected proposals.[47]

Establish an Erasmus Cultura
While there are a good many EU initiatives for the mobility of cultural workers, they are also hard to find and spread across too many fields. An exploratory opinion paper issued in May 2008 by the European Economic and Social Committee (EESC) is symptomatic: 'The EESC believes that the main problem faced by the EU in terms of young people's cross-border mobility is the clear lack of solutions to the problems that have already been described on numerous occasions.'[48] Therefore, I believe that one solution could be to establish an Erasmus Cultura, an overarching programme for cultural workers and artists[49] organized in the same manner as the Erasmus programme.[50] If the intellectual and artistic hegemonies of nations are to be challenged and something

similar to a European public sphere surface, a facilitating role of
bringing artists and cultural workers together should be at the core of
the EU's cultural policies.

By any lights, the Erasmus programme is a success. Named after
the humanist and theologian Desiderius Erasmus of Rotterdam (1465–
1536), the programme seeks to enhance the quality and reinforce the
European dimension of higher education by encouraging transnational
cooperation between universities and boosting European mobility.
Around 90 per cent of European universities take part in Erasmus and
1.9 million students have participated since it started in 1987. The annual
budget is in excess of €400 million, more than 3,100 higher education
institutions in 31 countries participate, and even more are waiting to join.
With its sister programmes Erasmus Mundus[51] and Tempus[52] reaching
outside the EU, they epitomize European integration far more than the
euro. Organizationally, in establishing an Erasmus Cultura, differences
don't need to be drastic. As things are now, the European Commission
is responsible for the Erasmus programme's overall implementation
and its Directorate-General for Education and Culture coordinates its
different actions. So-called 'decentralized actions' regarding individual
mobility are run by national agencies in the 31 participating countries.

Hywel Ceri Jones, one of the true veterans of European cultural
policy and founder of the Erasmus programme, recalls that he 'had a
clear policy vision for Erasmus that was not simply about mobility. I
conceived of Erasmus as embedding a European teaching and learning
perspective in the curricula of universities for which mobility and
exchange were instruments.'[53] I think the very same idea is valid for
increasing mobility for cultural workers. Samuel Jones at DEMOS
said at the 2008 Festival of Politics in Edinburgh that 'in policy-making,
culture is too often thought of in its functional forms, be they films, art,
music, museums, theatres and so on, or the professionals who work in
them. But these are the touch points of wider behaviour and attitudes.
What connects these as a culture is our capacity and will to read
meaning and identity in them.'[54] As a sociologist, I find the best way to do
this is through face-to-face interactions.

Much infrastructural groundwork in this respect is already done. Felix Meritis ('Happy through Merit') is one of the most profiled actors in this area. It is an independent European centre for art, culture and science and a national and international meeting place in Amsterdam. It works with partners such as the Caucasus Foundation (Tbilisi), Cultural Front (Beograd), Kuhnya (Novosibirsk), KulturKontakt (Vienna), Red House (Sofia), the Berlin Conference for European Cultural Policy (through 'A Soul for Europe'), European House for Cultures (Brussels), SICA, the Month of Philosophy Foundation and the Globalisation Lecture Foundation.[55] Another significant actor is the International Debate Education Association (IDEA). Established in 1999 to coordinate pilot debate programmes initiated by the Open Society Institute, IDEA acts as an independent membership organization of national debate clubs, associations, programmes and individuals that share a common purpose: to promote mutual understanding and democracy globally by supporting discussion and active citizenship locally. IDEA's debates take place in over 60 languages in over 50 countries throughout the world.[56]

Given the success of the traditional Erasmus programme I therefore have, with the words of my friend Baranyay in mind, a hard time seeing why an Erasmus Cultura would not contribute in new ways to every objective the European Union has set in its new agenda for culture. On a broad level, it bears the potential for improving intercultural dialogue in other ways than through political talk: it could utilize culture as a catalyst for creativity in 'edgy' ways fundamental to the cultural economy; and it could establish cultural collaboration as part of foreign policy while easing the political connotations. On an everyday level, Erasmus Cultura grants would probably make a world of difference to people living in the poorer regions of Europe, who can't afford to use a month's salary to travel to a cultural event in Paris or Copenhagen. Sometimes it's just about bringing people together. They will work out the rest.

[1] Eriksen, 1995: 250.

[2] Everitt, 2008: 32.

[3] Ruffolo, 2001, quoted in Obuljen, 2005: 31.

[4] Shore, 2006: 21.

[5] Shore, 2006: 21.

[6] SOU, 2007.

[7] Laitio, 2008b.

[8] The High-Level Expert Forum on Mobility, 2008: 7.

[9] Hauff, 2008: 152.

[10] Bordet, 2008.

[11] Everitt, 2008: 18–19.

[12] Burke, 1994.

[13] Laitio, 2007.

[14] Laitio, 2007.

[15] Veseth, 2005: 125.

[16] A complete list can be found at www.imdb.com/title/tt0211915/awards [Read October 9, 2008]

[17] Numbers are derived from www.boxofficemojo.com/movies/?id=amelie.htm [Read October 9, 2008]

[18] www.vivaricchiepoveri.it/menu.htm

[19] Riding, 2005.

[20] Morrison, 2007.

[21] Bennhold, 2007.

[22] Citations are from Bennhold, 2007.

[23] Lindgren, 2005.

[24] http://ec.europa.eu/youth/youth-in-action-programme/doc74_en.htm

[25] McLuhan, 1962.

[26] Laitio, 2008b.

[27] Hannon, Bradwell and Tims, 2008: 42.

[28] Laitio, 2008c.

[29] Eurobarometer, 2007a.

[30] www.internetworldstats.com/stats4.htm#europe. Numbers date from 30 June 2008.

[31] Jovchelovitch, 2007: 73–4.

[32] Martel, 2006.

[33] *Clemenceau, 2007.*

[34] Cited in Watkiss, 2008: 112.

[35] Lundström, 2009.

[36] www.efc.be

[37] www.nefic.org

[38] Leat and Anheier, 2008: 20.

[39] Culture powers Europe, 2007.

[40] Şuteu, 2006.

[41] www.gulliverconnect.org/en

[42] www.on-the-move.org/EN/index.lasso. See also Şuteu, 2006.

[43] www.eu2008.fr/webdav/site/PFUE/shared/ProgrammePFUE/Trio_EN.pdf

[44] www.euractiv.com/en/culture/ministers-pledge-boost-artists-mobility/article-172618

[45] The High-Level Expert Forum on Mobility, 2008.

[46] http://ec.europa.eu/culture/archive/culture_program/word/mobility/EAC-2008-00285-01-00-EN-TRA-00_13-06.DOC

[47] http://eacea.ec.europa.eu/culture/infoday/documents08/pres/statistics.pdf

[48] http://eescopinions.eesc.europa.eu/EESCopinionDocument.aspx?identifier=ces\soc\soc296\ces996-2008_ac.doc&language=EN

[49] This idea, in a slightly different version, has also been proposed by Gijs de Vries (2008).

[50] http://ec.europa.eu/education/lifelong-learning-programme/doc80_en.htm

[51] http://ec.europa.eu/education/external-relation-programmes/doc72_en.htm

[52] http://ec.europa.eu/education/external-relation-programmes/doc70_en.htm

[53] ECF Newsletter, 2007 (www.eurocult.org/uploads/docs/598.pdf)

[54] Jones, 2008.

[55] www.felix.meritis.nl/en

[56] http://idebate.org

Essential websites

General information
The European Union's pages about culture – information about objectives and how to apply for money.
http://ec.europa.eu/culture

Cultural policies
Cultural policies and trends in Europe
www.culturalpolicies.net

Cultural policy resources in South-east Europe
www.policiesforculture.org

European Institute for Comparative Cultural Research (ERICarts)
www.ericarts.org

Meeting places and funding information channels
Anna Lindh Euro-Mediterranean Foundation for the Dialogue between Cultures
www.euromedalex.org

Culture Action Europe
www.cultureactioneurope.org

EUNIC – European Union National Institutes for Culture
www.eunic-europe.eu

European Cultural Foundation
www.eurocult.org

Felix Meritis
www.felix.meritis.nl/en/

Lab for Culture
www.labforculture.org

Think Europe
www.culturefund.eu

Media
Café Babel
www.cafebabel.com

EurActiv – The official information site for Union activities
www.euractiv.com

Europocket Television
www.europocket.tv

Eurotopics
www.eurotopics.net

Sign and Sight
www.signandsight.com

Literature

All internet URLs were active on 22 January 2009.

Ahnström, Leif (1996), 'Europa: Kulturområde – Geoideologisk konstruksjon – Lokale', in Kate Hansen Bundt and Lars Martin Fosse (eds), Kulturmark. Perspektiver på Europeisk Historie og Tankeliv. Oslo: Europaprogrammet

Anderson, Benedict (1991), Imagined Communities. Second Edition. London: Verso

Anheier, Helmut (2009), 'How can the Cultural Sector Survive the Financial Crisis?' labforculture,org, January. Available at www. labforculture.org/en/content/view/full/39830

Anheier, Helmut and Yudhishthir Raj Isar (eds) (2007), Conflicts and Tension (The Culture and Globalization Series). London: Sage

Anheier, Helmut and Yudhishthir Raj Isar (eds) (2008), The Cultural Economy (The Culture and Globalization Series). London: Sage

Antoine, Prune (2007), 'Ukraine's New Rock 'n roll Literature', available at www.eurocult.org/ uploads/docs/958.pdf

Appiah, Kwame Anthony (2006), Cosmopolitanism: Ethics in a World of Strangers. New York: W W Norton & Co

Arsiwala, Sakina (2007), 'YouTube in 9 More Domains', The Official Google Blog, 19 June. Available at http://googleblog.blogspot. com/2007/06/youtube-in-9-more-domains. html

Arts & Business (2008), What now for Arts Sponsorship in the Economic Downturn? Report available at www.aandb.org.uk/Asp/ uploadedFiles/Image/artssponsorship_ findings.pdf

Arts Council Norway (2007), CCP Norway Activity Report 2007. Oslo: Arts Council Norway

Ash, Timothy Garton (2007), 'Europe Needs a Bold New Story – and to invent new ways to tell it', The Guardian, 22 March. Available at www.guardian.co.uk/commentisfree/2007/ mar/22/comment.eu

Banús, Enrique (2007), 'Key element or Ornament?' in Foreign Cultural Policy in Europe. Edited by the Institut für Auslandsbeziehungen and the Robert Bosch Stiftung in cooperation with the British Council, the Swiss Art Council Pro Helvetia and the Foundation for German-Polish Cooperation. Stuttgart: IFA. Available at www.ifa.de/fileadmin/content/publikationen/ kulturreport/kulturreport_en.pdf

Barroso, José Manuel (2004), 'Europe and Culture', draft opening address at the conference 'A Soul for Europe', Berlin, 26–27 November. Available at www. berlinerkonferenz.net/uploads/media/ Jose_Manuel_Barroso_President_of_the_EU_ Commission_Portugal.pdf

Batora, Jozef and Monica Mokre (2008), 'International Cultural Relations in and of the European Union. Perspectives of EUNIC', background paper for the conference on 'New Paradigms, New Models – Culture in EU External Relations', Ljubljana, Slovenia, 13–14 May. Available at www.mzz.gov.si/fileadmin/

pageuploads/Kulturno_sodelovanje/New_ Paradigms__BACK_GROUND_PAPERS.pdf

Bauman, Zygmunt (1991), *Modernity and Ambivalence*. Ithaca, NY: Cornell University Press

Bauman, Zygmunt (2007), *Liquid Times: Living in an Age of Uncertainty*. London: Polity

BBC News (2009). 'Dutch MP Refused Entry into Britain', 12 February. Available at http://news.bbc.co.uk/2/hi/uk_news/politics/7885918.stm

Beck, Ulrich (2002), 'The Cosmopolitan Society and its Enemies', *Theory, Culture and Society*, Vol 19, 1–2: 17–44

Beck, Ulrich (2006), *Cosmopolitan Vision*. London: Polity

Bedell, Geraldine (2006), 'To face the Facts beyond the Veil', *The Observer*, 29 October

Bennett, Tony (2001), 'Differing Diversities: Transversal Study on the Theme of Cultural Policy and Cultural Diversity', in Tony Bennett (ed), *Differing Diversities*. Strasbourg: CoE Publishing

Bennhold, Katrin (2007), 'Rapper with Attitude updates "Frenchness"', *International Herald Tribune Europe*, 5 June

Bentley, Tom (2004), Foreword, in Richard Florida and Irene Tinagli, *Europe in the Creative Age*. London: Demos

Berkaak, Odd Are (2007), *Kulturpolitikk i den Globale Offentlighet. En analyse av UNESCOs Konvensjon av 20 oktober 2005 om å verne og fremme et mangfold av kulturuttrykk*. Available at www.unesco.no/nyheter/arkiv/2007/oddaressrapport.html

Beunderman, Mark (2005), 'Blow to Kiev as Brussels closes door to further Enlargement', *euobserver.com*, 9 November. Available at http://euobserver.com/9/20289

Bjerke, Astrid (ed) (2007), *EUs Kulturprogram. Norsk Deltagelse i EUs Rammeprogram for Kultur 2000–2006*. Oslo: Norsk kulturråd. Available at www.kulturrad.no/eus_kulturprogram/nyheter/brosjyre-om-norsk-deltakelse-i/

Boe, Carolina and Peter Hervik (2008), 'Integration through Insult?' in Elisabeth Eide, Risto Kunelius and Angela Phillips (eds), *Transnational Media Events: The Mohammed Cartoons and the Imagined Clash of Civilizations*. Nordicom: Gothenborg

Bognar, Srebina (2007), 'Chalga Folkpop: "Forget yourself in the rhythm"', *CaféBabel.com*, 9 February. Available at www.cafebabel.com/eng/article/19977/chalga-folkpop-forget-yourself-in-our-rhythm.html

Bordet, Aurélien (2008), 'Eurogeneration or the Erasmus effect?' *CaféBabel.com*, 8 May. Available at www.cafebabel.com/eng/article/24649/eurogeneration-or-the-erasmus-effect.html

Bromark, Stian and Dag Herbjørnsrud (2004), 'Cultural Revolution! Now!' *00TAL – Journal of Literature and Fine Arts*, #17/18. Available at www.00tal.com/eng/revolution.html

Bryne, Snorre (2008), 'Noe av det Største innen Underholdning', *Dagbladet*, 27 April

Buck, Naomi (2006), 'The Medium is English', *signandsight.com*, 15 May. Available at www.signandsight.com/features/752.html

Bundt, Kate Hansen and Lars Martin Fosse (1996), 'Forord', in Kate Hansen Bundt and Lars Martin Fosse (eds), *Kulturmark. Perspektiver på europeisk historie og tankeliv*. Oslo: Europaprogrammet

Burke, Peter (1994), *Popular Culture in Early Modern Europe*. London: Ashagate

Buruma, Ian (2006), *Murder in Amsterdam: The Death of Theo van Gogh and the Limits of Tolerance*. New York: Penguin

Campbell, Joseph (1972), *The Hero with a Thousand Faces*, Princeton, NJ: Princeton University Press

Castells, Manuel (2000), *The Network Society. 2nd Edition*. Oxford: Blackwell

Chanda, Nayan (2007), *Bound Together: How Traders, Preachers, Adventurers and Warriors Shaped Globalization*. Boston, MA: Yale University Press

Chervel, Thierry (2005), 'Let's talk European', *signandsight.com*, 1 March. Available at www.signandsight.com/service/28.html

Chrisafis, Angelique (2008), 'Sarkozy Voodoo Doll remains on Sale', *Guardian*, 29 October. Available at www.guardian.co.uk/world/2008/oct/29/sarkozy-voodoo-france

Clemenceau, François (2007), 'A Constructive Take on the US-French "Culture Wars"', *European Affairs*, Vol 23, Summer/Fall. Available at http://europeanaffairs.org/current_issue/2007_summer_fall/2007_summer_fall_23.php4

Cohen, Richard I (1998), *Jewish Icons: Art and Society in Modern Europe*. London: University of California Press

Cooper, Robert (2005), 'Europe: Why Europe Will Run the 21st Century', *TimesOnline*, 27 February. Available at http://entertainment.timesonline.co.uk/tol/arts_and_entertainment/books/article517916.ece

Cowen, Tyler (2004), *Creative Destruction: How Globalization is Changing the World's Cultures*. Princeton, NJ: Princeton University Press

Crienglish (2009), 'Culture Industry Sees Chances amid Global Financial Crisis', 10 January. Available at http://english.cri.cn/6826/2009/01/10/168s442342_4.htm

Culture Powers Europe (2007), *Appeal for an Activating Cultural Policy for Europe*. Declaration – Fourth Federal Congress on Cultural Policy: culture.powers.europe – europe.powers.culture, 7–8 June. Available at www.kupoge.de/presse/2007-06-07_kultur-macht-europa_engl.pdf

Cunningham, Stuart, John Banks and Jason Potts (2008), 'Globalization and the Cultural Economy: The Shape of the Field', in Helmut Anheier and Yudhishthir Raj Isar (eds), *The Cultural Economy*. (The Culture and Globalization Series). London: Sage

Danan, Martine (1995), 'Marketing the Hollywood Blockbuster in France', Journal of Popular Film and Television, Autumn, 23 (3), 131–41.

Davies, Norman (1996), *Europe: A History*. Oxford: Oxford University Press

de Rougemont, Denis (1961), *Vingt-huit Siècle d'Europe*. Paris: Gallimard

de Vries, Gijs (2008), 'Proposals for a European Strategy of Cultural Diplomacy'. Paper prepared in connection with the conference on 'New Paradigms, New Models – Culture in EU External Relations', Ljubljana, Slovenia, 13–14 May. Available at www.mzz.gov.si/fileadmin/pageuploads/Kulturno_sodelovanje/New_Paradigms__BACK_GROUND_PAPERS.pdf

Delanty, Gerard (1995), *Inventing Europe*. Basingstoke: Macmillan

Delanty, Gerard and Paul R Jones (2003), 'Europe, Post-national Identities and Architecture', in J Peter Burgess (ed), *Museum Europa. The European Cultural Heritage between Economics and Politics*. Kristiansand: Norwegian Academic Press

Delanty, Gerard and Chris Rumford (2005), *Rethinking Europe. Social Theory and the Implications of Europeanization*. London: Routledge

Der Spiegel (2008), 'Moderate Islam is a Contradiction', 31 March. Available at www.spiegel.de/international/europe/0,1518,544347,00.html

Deutsche Welle (2008), 'Cultural Sponsoring Untouched By Financial Crisis Woes', 20 October. Available at www.dw-world.de/dw/article/0,2144,3724693,00.html

Duelund, Peter (2008a), 'Nordic Cultural Policies: A critical view', *International Journal of Cultural Policy*, Volume 14, Issue 1: 7–24. Available at www.informaworld.com/smpp/title~content=t713639985~db=all~tab=issueslist~branches=14 - v14

Duelund, Peter (2008b), 'Reflections on the National Dimension of European Cultural Policy'. Paper to the International Conference on Cultural Policy Research, Yeditepe University, Istanbul, 20–24 August. Available at http://iccpr2008.yeditepe.edu.tr/papers/Duelund_Peter.doc

Dussel, Enrique (1993), 'Eurocentrism and Modernity', *Boundary 2*, 20, 3: 65–76

ECF (European Cultural Foundation) (2005), *Europe as a Cultural Project*. ECF: Amsterdam

ECF (European Cultural Foundation) (2007a), *Background paper on the Stranger Festival*. Available at www.eurocult.org/uploads/docs/780.pdf

ECF (European Cultural Foundation) (2007b), *Civil Society Platform for Intercultural Dialogue. Mobilizing civil society across Europe*. Available at www.interculturaldialogue2008.eu/fileadmin/downloads/documents/400-showcase/440-ecf/Platform_Communique_Sept07.pdf

The Economist (1998), 'Culture Wars', 12 September

The Economist (2001), 'The Bridget Jones Economy', 20 December. Available at www.the economist.com/diversions/displaystory.cfm?story_id=883664

The Economist (2008), 'Just Bury It', 19 June. Available at www.the economist.com/opinion/displayStory.

cfm?source=hptextfeature&story_
id=11580732

Eisenstadt, Shmul N (2008), 'The
Transformations of the Religious Dimension
and the Crystallization of New Civilizational
Visions and Relations', in Gabriel Motzkin and
Yochi Fisher (eds), *Religion and Democracy
in Contemporary Europe*. London: Alliance
Publishing Trust

Elmer, Greg and Mike Gasher (2005),
'Introduction: Catching up to Runaway
Productions', in Greg Elmer and Mike Gasher
(eds), *Contracting Out Hollywood: Runaway
Productions and Foreign Location Shooting*,
Lanham, MD: Rowman & Littlefield, 1–21

Eriksen, Erik Oddvar (2004), 'Religion eller
toleranse?', *Dagbladet*, 1 July

Eriksen, Thomas Hylland (1995), 'In Search of
Brussels', in J Peter Burgess (ed), *Cultural
Politics and Political Culture in Postmodern
Europe*. Amsterdam: Rodopi

Eriksen, Thomas Hylland (2002), *Ethnicity
and Nationalism (2nd Edition)*. London: Pluto
Press

Eriksen, Thomas Hylland (2006), 'Diversity
versus Difference: Neoliberalism in the
minority debate', in Richard Rottenburg,
Burkhard Schnepel, and Shingo Shimada
(eds), *The Making and Unmaking of Difference*.
Bielefeld: Transaction

Eriksen, Thomas Hylland (2007), *Globalization:
The Key Concepts*. London: Pluto Press

Eriksen, Jens-Martin and Frederik
Stjernfelt (2009), 'Culturalism: Culture
as Political Ideology', *Eurozine*, 9
February. Available at www.eurozine.com/
articles/2009-01-09-eriksenstjernfelt-en.html

Espeland, Tordis Marie (2008), 'Historie på
Tvers av Grenser', *Itinera*, nr 1, 20–21

EU ICT Task Force (2006), *Fostering the
Competitiveness of Europe's ICT Industry*.
Available at http://ec.europa.eu/enterprise/
ict/policy/doc/icttf_report.pdf

Eurobarometer (2006a), *Public Opinion in the
European Union*. (Standard Eurobarometer
66). Available at http://ec.europa.eu/public_
opinion/archives/eb/eb66/eb66_en.pdf

Eurobarometer (2006b), *EU Communication
and the Citizens*. (Flash Eurobarometer 189a).
Available at http://ec.europa.eu/public_
opinion/flash/fl_189a_en.pdf

Eurobarometer (2007a), *European Cultural
Values* (Special report 278). EU: Brussels

Eurobarometer (2007b), *Intercultural Dialogue
in Europe* (Flash Eurobarometer 217). EU:
Brussels

Eurimages (2008), *Guide 2008. Support for the
Co-production of Full-length Feature Films,
Animation and Documentaries*. EU: Brussels.
Available at www.coe.int/t/dg4/eurimages/
Source/Regulations/CE_Eurimages%20-%20
Guide%20coproduction%20GB%20_%202008.
pdf

European Commission (1977), *Community
Activities in the Cultural Sector*. Commission
Communication to the Council sent on 22
November 1977. Available at http://aei.pitt.
edu/5321/01/001743_1.pdf

European Commission (2005), *Working
Together for Growth and Jobs. A New Start for
the Lisbon Strategy*. EC: Brussels

European Commission (2007a), *A European
Agenda for Culture in a Globalizing World*.
Communication from the Commission
to the European Parliament, the Council,
the European Economic and Social
Committee and the Committee of the
Regions, 10 May. Available at http://
eur-lex.europa.eu/LexUriServ/LexUriServ.
do?uri=COM:2007:0242:FIN:EN:PDF

European Commission (2007b), *Programme
Guide Culture Programme (2007–2013)*.
Education, Audiovisual and Culture Executive
Agency: Brussels. Available at http://eacea.
ec.europa.eu/culture/guide/documents/
culture_programme_guide_en.pdf

European Commission (2007c), *Media
2007 (2007–2013) – A Big Push for
Europe's Audiovisual Industry*, Brussels:
Directorate-General for Press and
Communication. Available at http://ec.europa.
eu/information_society/media/docs/
overview/media-en.pdf

European Commission (2007d), 'Migration
and Asylum: New actions to cooperate
with third countries', press release, 25
June. Available at http://europa.eu/rapid/
pressReleasesAction.do?reference=IP/07/87
2&format=HTML&aged=0&language=EN&gu
iLanguage=en

European Commission (2007e), *The
European Union: Furthering Human Rights
and Democracy Across the Globe*. EU:
Brussels. Available at http://ec.europa.eu/

external_relations/human_rights/doc/
brochure07_en.pdf

European Council (1973), *Communiqué of European Community 'Summit' Meeting and Annexes*. Washington, DC: European Community Information Service. Available at aei.pitt.edu/1439/01/copenhagen_1973.pdf

European Council (2008), *Press release 2868 Council meeting: Education, Youth and Culture, 21–22 May*. EU: Brussels. Available at www.consilium.europa.eu/cms3_applications/Applications/newsRoom/LoadDocument.asp?directory=en/educ/&filename=100577.pdf

EuroStat (2007), *Cultural Statistics*. EuroStat: Luxembourg

Everitt, Anthony D (2008): *Europe: United or Divided by Culture?* Cardiff: Institute of Welsh Affairs/European Cultural Foundation

Fan, Ying (2008), 'Soft power: Power of attraction or confusion?' *Place Branding and Public Diplomacy*, Vol 4, (2): 147–58

Figel, Ján (2005), 'The Role of Culture in an Inclusive Europe', speech at the Horizon 2020 Conference 'The Inclusive Europe?', Budapest, 17–19 November. Available at www.inclusiveeurope.hu/index.php?page=figelspeech

Florida, Richard (2004), *The Rise of the Creative Class*. New York: Basic Books

Florida, Richard and Irene Tinagli (2004), *Europe in the Creative Age*. London: Demos

Fossum, John Erik (2001), 'Identity Politics in the European Union', ARENA working paper no 17. Available at www.arena.uio.no/publications/working-papers2001/papers/wp01_17.htm

Fossum, John Erik and Phillip Schlesinger (eds) (2007), *The European Union and the Public Sphere*. London: Routledge

Forbes (2008): 'Financial Crisis Cools Down Art Market', 31 October. Available at www.forbes.com/2008/10/31/christies-sothebys-frieze-pf-art-in_se_1031artmarket_inl.html

Fukuyama, Francis (2007), 'Identity and Migration', *Prospect Magazine*, issue 131, February. Available at www.prospect-magazine.co.uk/article_details.php?id=8239

Furedi, Frank (2003), 'The Children won't Grow Up", *Spiked*, 29 July. Available at www.spiked-online.com/Articles/00000006DE8D.htm

Gabler, Neal (1988), *An Empire of Their Own: How the Jews Invented Hollywood*. New York: Anchor Press

Gardels, Nathan (2007), 'Europe versus America: A Growing Clash within the West?' in Helmut Anheier and Yudhishthir Raj Isar (eds) (2007), *Conflicts and Tension (The Culture and Globalization Series)*. London: Sage

Gellner, Ernest (1983), *Nations and Nationalism*. London: Verso

Giddens, Anthony (2002), *Runaway World: How Globalisation is Reshaping our Lives*. London: Routledge

Glenny, Mischa (2008), *McMafia: Crimes without Borders*. London: Jonathan Cape

Goldblatt, David (2007), 'Cosmopolitan Chronicler', *The Independent*, 30 March

Grindheim, Jan Erik (2007), 'Kjønn og religion splitter Europa', *Minerva*, 26 October. Available at www.minerva.as/?vis=artikkel&fid=3018&id=260320080959083935&magasin=ja

Gripsrud, Jostein (ed) (2002), *Populærmusikken i Kulturpolitikken*. Oslo: Norsk kulturråd

Grund, Jan (2008), *Kulturpolitikk er Kunst*. Oslo: Universitetsforlaget

Gyory, Michel (2000), *Making and Distributing Movies in Europe: The Problem of Nationality*. Strasbourg: European Audiovisual Observatory. Available at www.obs.coe

Haas, Stefan (2002), 'History and Computer Games. Narrative Structures in the Age of Electronic Media and their Implications for Historical Consciousness and the Theory of History', in Attila Pók, Jörn Rüsen and Jutta Scherrer (eds), *European History: Challenge for a Common Future*. Hamburg: Körber-Stiftung

Habermas, Jürgen (2001), *The Postnational Constellation. Political Essays*. Boston: MIT Press

Hall, Peter (1998), *Cities in Civilization: Culture, Technology and Urban Order*. London: Weidenfeld & Nicolson

Hall, Stuart (2000), 'Conclusion: The Multi-cultural Question', in Barnor Hesse (ed), *Un/settled Multiculturalisms: Diasporas, Entanglements, Transruptions*. London: Zed

Hannerz, Ulf (2004), *Foreign News: Exploring the World of Foreign Correspondents*. Chicago: University of Chicago Press

Hannon, Celia, Peter Bradwell and Charlie Tims (2008), *Video Republic*. London: DEMOS

Hauff, Karen (2008), 'Generation Erasmus', in *Europe in the Media – Media in Europe*. edited by the Institut für Auslandsbeziehungen and the Robert Bosch Stiftung in cooperation with the British Council and the Foundation for German-Polish Cooperation, Stuttgart: ifa, 2008. Available at www.ifa.de/fileadmin/content/publikationen/kulturreport2008/hauff_en.pdf

Hauss, Charlie (2003), 'Civil Society', in Guy Burgess and Heidi Burgess (eds), *Beyond Intractability*. Conflict Research Consortium. Boulder: University of Colorado. Available at www.beyondintractability.org/essay/civil_society

Held, David (2002), 'Globalization and Cosmopolitanism', *Logos: Journal of Modern Society & Culture*, vol 1, 3: 1–18

Hendry, Joy (2000), 'Constructions of Europe in Japanese Theme Parks: Power or Parody?' in Attila Pók, Jörn Rüsen and Jutta Scherrer (eds), *European History: Challenge for a Common Future*. Hamburg: Körber-Stiftung

High-Level Expert Forum on Mobility (2008), *Making Learning Mobility an Opportunity for All*. Available at http://ec.europa.eu/education/doc/2008/mobilityreport_en.pdf

Higson, Andrew (1989), 'The Concept of National Cinema', *Screen*, 30 (4): 36–46

Hillauer, Rebecca (2005), 'Neither Whores nor Submissive', *signandsight.com*, 3 August. Available at www.signandsight.com/features/288.html

Holland, Martin, Peter Ryan, Alojzy Nowak, and Natalia Chaban (eds) (2007), *The EU through the Eyes of Asia: Media, Public and Elite Perceptions in China, Japan, Korea, Singapore and Thailand*. Singapore-Warsaw: University of Warsaw

Honneth, Axel (1996), *The Struggle for Recognition: The Moral Grammar of Social Conflict*. London: Polity

Hughes, Kirsty (2001), 'The "Open Method" of Coordination: Innovation or Talking-Shop?' *Centre for European Reform Bulletin*, Issue 15. Available at www.cer.org.uk/articles/issue15_hughes.html

IFEX (International Freedom of Expression eXchange) (2008), 'IFEX Members Condemn UN Resolutions Supporting Limits on Free Speech', *IFEX Communiqué*, vol 17, issue 13. Available at www.ifex.org/280fr/content/view/full/92151

Isaksen, Runo (2008), 'Kunsten å Håndtere en Kompleks Virkelighet', *Itinera*, nr 1, 22–24

ISFE (Interactive Software Federation of Europe) (2008), *Video Gamers in Europe*. Available at www.isfe-eu.org/index.php?oidit=T001:662b16536388a7260921599321365911

ITA (International Trade Association, US Department of Commerce) (2001), *The Migration of US Film and Television Production: Impact of Runaways on Workers and Small Business in the US Film Industry*. Available at www.ita.doc.gov/media/migration11901.pdf

Jones, Samuel (2008), 'Overcoming Cultural Inertia', speech at The Festival of Politics, Edinburgh, 26 August. Available at www.demos.co.uk/projects/theculturalage/blog/overcomingculturalinertia

Jordan, Terry G (2002), *The European Culture Area*. New York: Harper & Row

Jovchelovitch, Sandra (2007), *Knowledge in Context: Representations, Community and Culture*. London & New York: Routledge

KEA European Affairs (2006), *The Economy of Culture*. KEA: Brussels. Available at www.keanet.eu/ecoculturepage.html

Kelemen, R Daniel (2007), 'Build to Last? The Durability of EU Federalism', in *European Union Studies Association Biennial Conference*, 17–19 May, 2007, Montreal, Canada. Available at http://aei.pitt.edu/7932

Keulemans, Chris (2005), 'Reaching the heart of the matter', in Chris Keulemans and David Cameron (eds), *The Heart of the Matter. The Role of the Arts and Culture in the Balkans' European Integration*. Amsterdam: ECF

Klamer, Arjo, Lyudmilla Petrova, and Anna Mignosa (2006), *Financing the Arts and Culture in the European Union*. Brussels: The European Parliament. Available at www.helgatruepel.de/fileadmin/user_upload/PDF-Datein/Financing_the_arts_and_culture_in_the_European_Union.pdf

Klein, Christina (2003), 'The Asia Factor in Global Hollywood', *YaleGlobal Online*, 25 March. Available at http://yaleglobal.yale.edu/display.article?id=1242

Kloc-Konkolowicz, Jakub (2008), 'Waking a Polish Demon', *signandsight.com*, 21 January. Available at www.signandsight.com/features/1642.html

Kok, Wim (ed) (2004), *Facing the Challenge*. Luxembourg: Office for Official Publications of the European Communities

Kozlov, Vladimir (2008). 'Is the Financial Crisis Threatening Culture?' *The Moscow News*, 7 November. Available at http://rbth.ru/articles/2008/11/07/071108_cuture.html

Krzeminski, Adam (2007), 'From closed circuits to communication tubes', *signandsight.com*, 18 June. Available at www.signandsight.com/features/1400.html

Kunelius, Risto, Elisabeth Eide, Oliver Hahn and Roland Schroeder (eds) (2007), *Reading the Mohammed Cartoons Controversy*. Projekt Verlag: Bochum/Freiburg

Kunz, William M (2007), *Culture Conglomerates*, Lanham, MD: Rowman & Littlefield.

LabforCulture (2008), *The Rainbow Paper. Intercultural Dialogue: From Practice to Policy and Back*. Available at http://rainbowpaper. labforculture.org/signup/_media/public/rainbowpaper.pdf?id=public%3Aread&cache=cache

Laitio, Tommi (2007), 'Superlocal Identities. The European in the Youth Experience', *Eurozine*, 13 November. Available at www.eurozine.com/articles/article_2007-12-13-laitio-en.html

Laitio, Tommi (2008a), 'European Culture – Just do it', speech at the EUNIC Network Effect in Stockholm, 23–25 April 2008. Manuscript received from the author

Laitio, Tommi (2008b), 'Exclusive Culture? Representation and Prejudice', speech at The Network Effect conference in Budapest, 5–7 March 2008. Manuscript received from the author

Laitio, Tommi (2008c), 'Sharing Strangers', speech at the Kyrnéa International/Passeurs d'images Conference in Paris, December. Manuscript received from the author

Lammert, Norbert (2005), 'Auch die EU braucht ein ideelles Fundament', *Die Welt*, 13 December. Available at www.welt.de/print-welt/article183928/Auch_die_EU_braucht_ein_ideelles_Fundament.html

Landen, Thomas (2009), 'Will Geert Wilders Be Arrested at Heathrow?' *The Brussels Journal*, 10 February. Available at www.brusselsjournal.com/node/3793

Landry, Charles (2000), *The Creative City*. London: Earthscan

Landry, Charles and Phil Wood (2007), *The Intercultural City: Planning for Diversity Advantage*. London: Earthscan

Lang, Jack (2002), 'Culture and the Economy', in Jeremy Ahearne (ed), *French Cultural Policy Debates*. London: Routledge

Leadbeater, Charlie and Kate Oakley (1999), *The Independents. Britain's New Cultural Entrepreneur*. London: DEMOS. Available at www.demos.co.uk/files/theindependents.pdf

Leat, Diana and Helmut Anheier (2008), 'How can Foundations add value in the 21st Century?', *Effect*, Vol 2 (1): 20–21

Legrain, Philippe (2007), *Immigrants: Your Country Needs Them*. London: Little, Brown

Leonard, Mark (2005), *Why Europe will Run the 21st Century*. London: Fourth Estate

Lichfield, John (2004), '"French" War Film takes flak for US Funding', *The Independent*, 27 October. Available at www.independent.co.uk/news/world/europe/french-war-film-takes-flak-for-us-funding-535450.html

Lindgren, Simon (2005), *Populärkultur*. Malmö: Liber

Littger, Stephan (2006), *The Director's Cut: Picturing Hollywood in the 21st Century*. New York: Continuum Press

Loomba, Ania (2005), *Colonialism/Postcolonialism. 2nd Edition*. London & New York: Routledge

Los Angeles Times (2008), 'Financial Crisis – or Arts Opportunity?' 14 October. Available at http://latimesblogs.latimes.com/culturemonster/2008/10/financial-crisi.html

Lundström, Cecilia (2009), *Students from the Western Balkans*. Paper published in relation to a study by the King Baudouin Foundation on the visa problems of students: the SMART Visa for Students from the Western Balkans. Available at www.kbs-frb.be/otheractivity.aspx?id=228446&LangType=1033

Mach, Zdzislaw and Grzegorz Pozarlik (2008), *Collective Identity Formation in the Process of EU Enlargement*. RECON Online Working Papers 2008/14, September. Available at www.

reconproject.eu/main.php/RECON_wp_0814.
pdf?fileitem=16662557

Malik, Kenan (2006), 'Say What You Think: The Importance of Giving Offence', *Eurozine*, 9 February. Available at www.eurozine.com/articles/2006-02-09-malik-en.html

Marling, William H (2006), *How 'American' is Globalization?* Baltimore, ML: Johns Hopkins University Press

Martel, Frédéric (2006), *De la Culture en Amérique*. Paris: Gallimard

Marushiakova, Elena (ed) (2008), *Dynamics of National Identity and Transnational Identities in the Process of European Integration*. Newcastle: Cambridge Scholars Press

McCormick, John (2008), *Understanding the European Union*. Basingstoke: Palgrave Macmillan

McLuhan, Marshall (1962), *The Gutenberg Galaxy: The Making of Typographic Man* Toronto: University of Toronto Press

Medved, Michael (1993), *Hollywood vs America*. New York: Harper

Miller, Toby, Natan Govil, John McMurria, Richard Maxwell and Ting Wang (2005), *Global Hollywood 2*. Berkeley, CA: University of California Press

Mokre, Monika (2003), 'Identity Matters: On European Cultural Policy'. Paper available at European Institute for Progressive Cultural Policies: http://eipcp.net/policies/aecp/mokre/en

Mokre, Monica (2006), 'European Culture Policies and European Democracy'. Paper available at European Institute for Progressive Cultural Policies: http://eipcp.net/policies/dpie/mokre/en

Monnet, Jean (1976), *Mémoires*. Paris: Fayard

Morrison, Donald (2007), 'The Death of French Culture', *Time Magazine*, 21 November. Available at www.time.com/time/magazine/article/0,9171,1686532,00.html

Moseng, Maria (2008), 'Film på kartet', *minerva. as*, 9 October. Available at www.minerva.as/?v is=artikkel&fid=2138&id=091020080837289351 &magasin=ja&t=Film%20på%20kartet

Motzkin, Gabriel and Yochi Fisher (eds) (2008), *Religion and Democracy in Contemporary Europe*. London: Alliance Publishing Trust

Mrozek, Andrea (2000), 'Heavy on the Leitkultur', *Central Europe Review*, Vol 2, No 42, **4** December. Available at www.ce-review.org/00/42/mrozek42.html

Muukkonen, Marita (ed) (2002), *Under [De]construction. Perspectives on Cultural Diversity in Visual and Performing Arts*. Helsinki. The Nordic Institute for Contemporary Art (NIFCA)

Neumann, Iver B (2006), 'European Identity and Its Changing Others', speech to the EU summit fringe conference 'Constructing New Identities in Transforming Europe: Enlargement and Integration: Are They Compatible?', University of Helsinki, 5 October. Available at www.nupi.no/content/download/613/12217/version/8/file/710.pdf

NIC (National Intelligence Council) (2008), *Global Trends 2025: A Transformed World*. US Government Printing Office: Washington, DC. Available at www.dni.gov/nic/PDF_2025/2025_Global_Trends_Final_Report.pdf

Nowell-Smith, Geoffrey (1985), 'But Do We Need It?' in M Auty and N Roddick (eds), *British Cinema Now*, London: British Film Institute

Nye, Joseph (2003), 'Propaganda isn't the Way: Soft Power', *International Herald Tribune*, 10 January. Available at http://belfercenter.ksg.harvard.edu/publication/1240/propaganda_isnt_the_way.html

O'Brien, Conor Cruise (1993), 'The Wrath of Ages: Nationalism's Primordial Roots', *Foreign Affairs*, November/December. Available at www.foreignaffairs.org/19931201fareviewessay5225/conor-cruise-o-brien/the-wrath-of-ages-nationalism-s-primordial-roots.html

Obuljen, Nina (2004), 'Assessing the Impact of EU Enlargement on Cultural Policies in Countries in Transition', in Nada Švob-Đoki and Jirina Šmejkalova (eds), *Cultural Transitions in Southeastern Europe*. Zagreb: Institute for International Relations. E-book available at www.culturelink.org/publics/joint/cultid06/Svob-Djokic_Cultural_Transitions.pdf

Obuljen, Nina (2005), *Why we need European Cultural Policies: The Impact of EU Enlargement on Cultural Policies in Transition Countries*. Amsterdam: ECF

OECD (Organisation for Economic Cooperation and Development) (2005), *Digital Broadband Content: The Online Computer and Video Game Industry*. Paris: OECD

Olson, Scott R (1999), *Hollywood Planet: Global Media and the Competitive Advantage of Narrative Transparency*. Mahwah, NJ: Lawrence Earlbaum

Palmer, Robert R, Joel Colton and Lloyd Kramer (2002), *A History of the Modern World*. New York: Alfred A Knopf

Pells, Richard (2002), 'American Culture Goes Global, or Does It?' *The Chronicle Review*, 12 April. Available at http://chronicle.com/free/v48/i31/31b00701.htm

Pew Research Center (2007), *47-Nation Pew Global Attitudes Survey*. Washington, DC: Pew

Pew Research Center (2008), *Unfavorable Views on Jews and Muslims in Europe*. Washington, DC: Pew

Plesu, Andrei (2005), 'Nostalgia and Hope', in Dragan Klaic (ed), *Europe as a Cultural Project*. Amsterdam: ECF

Pók, Attila, Jörn Rüsen and Jutta Scherrer (2002), 'European History: Challenge for a Common Future. An Introduction', in Attila Pók, Jörn Rüsen and Jutta Scherrer (eds), *European History: Challenge for a Common Future*. Hamburg: Körber-Stiftung

Pratt, Andy C (2008), 'Locating the Cultural Economy', in Helmut Anheier and Yudhishthir Raj Isar (eds), *The Cultural Economy* (The Culture and Globalization Series). London: Sage

Prodi, Romano (2000), *Europe as I See It*. Cambridge: Polity Press

Putnam, Robert D (2000), *Bowling Alone*. New York: Simon & Schuster

Queiroz, Mario (2008), 'Hitting 40 Languages', *The Official Google Blog*, 18 July. Available at http://googleblog.blogspot.com/2008/07/hitting-40-languages.html

Riding, Alan (2005), 'In France, Artists Have Sounded the Warning Bells for Years', *New York Times*, 24 November

Rifkin, Jeremy (2004), *The European Dream*. New York: Tarcher/Penguin

Robins, Kevin (2006), *The Challenge of Transcultural Diversities – Cultural Policy and Cultural Diversity*. Report prepared for the Council of Europe. Strasbourg, Council of Europe Publishing

Rotblat, Joseph (1997), *World Citizenship: Allegiance to Humanity*. London: Palgrave Macmillan

Rouse, Richard (2004), *Game Design. Theory and Practice*. Plano, TX: Wordware

Roy, Olivier (2004). *Globalized Islam. The Search for a New Ummah*. New York: Columbia University Press

RSF (Reporters sans frontiers) (2007), 'Charlie Hebdo Editor's Acquittal in Mohammed Cartoon Case hailed as positive for French Society', 22 March. Available at www.rsf.org/article.php3?id_article=21408

Ruffolo, Giorgio (ed) (2001), *Report on Cultural Cooperation in the European Union*. Strasbourg: European Parliament

Rushdie, Salman (2003), *Step Across this Line*. London: Virgin

Ruth, Arne (2007), 'The Press and Europe's Public Sphere', *signandsight.com*, 9 May. Available at www.signandsight.com/features/1337.html

Said, Edward (1994), *Culture and Imperialism*. New York: Vintage

Sardar, Ziauddin and Merryl Wyn Davies (2004), *American Dream, Global Nightmare*. London: Icon Books.

Saxenian, Annalee (1999), *Silicon Valley's New Immigrant Entrepreneurs*. San Francisco: Public Policy Institute of California

Scott, Allen J (2004), *On Hollywood: The Place, The Industry*. Princeton, NJ: Princeton University Press

Screen Digest (2006), *Interactive Content and Convergence: Implications for the Information Society*. A Study for the European Commission (DG Information Society and Media). London: Screen Digest

Shohat, Ella and Robert Stam (1994), *Unthinking Eurocentrism*. New York/London: Routledge

Shore, Cris (2000), *Building Europe: The Cultural Politics of the European Union*. London: Routledge

Shore, Cris (2001), 'The Cultural Policies of the European Union and Cultural Diversity', in Tony Bennett (ed), *Differing Diversities*. Strasbourg: CoE

Shore, Cris (2006), '"In Uno Plures?" EU Cultural Policy and the Governance of Europe', *Cultural Analysis*, 5: 7–26

Simjanovska, Violeta (2002), 'Transition and Cultural Policy in the Republic of Macedonia', 1 November, *policiesforculture.org*. Available

at www.policiesforculture.org/resources.
php?id=75&idc=29&t=h

Smith, A D (2003), *Nationalism and Modernism*. New York: Routledge

SOU (2007), *Mångfald är Framtiden*. SOU: 2007: 50, June. Available at www.regeringen.se/sb/d/8299/a/85168

Spini, Debora (2003), 'Europe, Memory, History', in J Peter Burgess (ed), *Museum Europa. The European Cultural Heritage between Economics and Politics*. Kristiansand: Norwegian Academic Press

Stradling, Robert (2001), 'A Council of Europe Handbook on Teaching 20th Century History', in Joke van der Leeuw-Roord (ed), *History for Today and Tomorrow. What Does Europe Mean for School History?* Hamburg: Körber-Stiftung

Stråth, Bo (2002), 'A European identity: To the Historical Limits of a Concept', *European Journal of Social Theory*, Vol 5, No 4: 387–401

Sucha, Vladimir (2008), Speech at the European Heritage Awards Ceremony. Available at www.europanostra.org/downloads/speeches/vladimir_sucha_durham_ceremony_030812.pdf

Şuteu, Corina (ed) (2006), *Mobility and Cultural Cooperation in the Age of Digital Spaces*. Bucharest/Helsinki: On the Move. Available at www.on-the-move.org/documents/Reader_training_Oct2006.pdf

Švob-Đokić, Nada (2004), Introduction, in Nada Švob-Đokić and Jirina Šmejkalova (eds): *Cultural Transitions in Southeastern Europe*. Zagreb: Institute for International Relations. E-book available at www.culturelink.org/publics/joint/cultid06/Svob-Djokic_Cultural_Transitions.pdf

Švob-Đokić, Nada and Jirina Šmejkalova (eds) (2004), *Cultural Transitions in Southeastern Europe*. Zagreb: Institute for International Relations. E-book available at www.culturelink.org/publics/joint/cultid06/Svob-Djokic_Cultural_Transitions.pdf

Theiler, Tobias (1999), 'Viewers into Europeans? How the European Union Tried to Europeanize the Audiovisual Sector, and Why it Failed', *Canadian Journal of Communication*, Vol 24, No 4. Available at www.cjc-online.ca/index.php/journal/article/view/1126/1035

Theiler, Tobias (2005), *Political Symbolism and European Integration*. Manchester: Manchester University Press

Tibi, Bassam (2000), *Europa ohne Identität: Die Krise der multikulturellen Gesellschaft*. Berlin: Siedler Verlag

Tibi, Bassam (2001), 'Leitkultur als Wertekonsens – Bilanz einer missglückten deutschen Debatte', in *Aus Politik und Zeitgeschehen (Das Parlament)*: 23–6

Tilly, Charles (1990), *Big Structures, Large Processes, Huge Comparisons*, New York: Russell Sage

Timmermans, Frans (2008), 'No Danger in Cultural Difference', speech at the European Cultural Foundation, 22 May. Available at www.minbuza.nl/nl/actueel/speeches,2008/05/No-danger-in-cultural-difference.html

Todorov, Tzvetan (2003), *Die verhinderte Weltmach – Reflexionen eines Europäers*. Berlin: Wilhelm Goldmann

Trenz, Hans-Jörg (2008), *In Search of the European Public Sphere. Between Normative Overstretch and Empirical Disenchantment*. RECON Working papers 2008/07. Available at www.reconproject.eu/main.php/RECON_wp_0807.pdf?fileitem=16662548

Ugrešić, Dubravka (2005), 'Why Europe needs a Cultural Policy', in David Cameron (ed), *On the Road to a Cultural Policy for Europe*. Amsterdam: ECF

UNESCO (2005), *Convention on the Protection and Promotion of the Diversity of Cultural Expressions*. Paris: UNESCO. Available at http://unesdoc.unesco.org/images/0014/001429/142919e.pdf

Veseth, Michael (2005), *Globaloney: Unraveling the Myths of Globalization*. Lanham, MD: Rowman & Littlefield

Vogue (2008), 'Allegra's Hitch', 3 September. Available at www.vogue.co.uk/news/daily/080903-allegra-hicks-pulls-out-of-lfw.aspx

Wagner, Gottfried (2007), 'Does Europe need a Cultural Policy?' in Hannes Swoboda and Christophe Solioz (eds), *Conflict and Renewal: Europe Transformed. Essays in Honour of Wolfgang Petritsch*. Baden-Baden: Nomos Verlagsgesellschaft

Wagner, Richard (2008), 'War Joseph Roth vielleicht Ruthene?', *Neue Zürcher Zeitung*, 3 June. Available at www.nzz.ch/nachrichten/kultur/aktuell/war_joseph_roth_vielleicht_ruthene_1.749156.html

Waldron, Jeremy (2000), 'What is Cosmopolitan?' *Journal of Political Philosophy*, Vol 8, No 2: 227–43

Watkiss, David (2008), 'Protecting and Promoting Freedom of Expression in Norway and Beyond', in Norine MacDonald and Luc Tayart de Borms (eds), *Philanthropy in Europe*. London: Alliance Publishing Trust

Wenders, Wim (2006), 'Giving Europe a Soul?' speech at the conference 'A Soul For Europe' in Berlin, 18 November. Available at www.signandsight.com/features/1098.html

Weringh, Kathinka Dittrich van and Ernst Schürmann (2004), 'Does Europe Need a Foreign Cultural Policy?' Available at www.labforculture.org/en/content/download/13095/147612/file/Does%20Europe%20need%20a%20Foreign%20Cultural%20Policy.pdf

Wischenbart, Rüdiger (2007), 'Cultural Diversity? A Pipe Dream', *signandsight.com*, 22 March. Available at www.signandsight.com/features/1261.html

Ye'or, Bat (2005), *Eurabia: The Euro-Arab Axis*. London: Fairleigh Dickinson University Press

Zizek, Slavoj (2008), 'Tolerance as an Ideological Category', *Critical Inquiry* 34: 660–82

Østergård, Uffe (1999), 'Hvad er det særlige ved Europa?' in Hans-Åke Persson and Fredrik Lindström (eds) (1999), *Europa – en Svårfångad Historia*. Malmö: Studentlitteratur, Lund

ISBN 978-0-9558804-3-8

Alliance Publishing Trust
1st Floor, 25 Corsham Street
London N1 6DR
UK

publishing@alliancemagazine.org
www.alliancemagazine.org

Registered charity number: 1116744
Company registration number: 5935154

A catalogue record for this book is available from the British Library.

Typeset in Grotesque MT

Design by Benedict Richards

Printed and bound by Hobbs the Printers, Totton, Hampshire, UK

This book is printed on FSC approved paper.